SMART
English Grammar
for Speaking & Writing

1권

SMART English Grammar
for Speaking & Writing 1권

2025년 01월 02일 인쇄
2025년 01월 10일 발행

지 은 이 E & C
발 행 인 Chris Suh
발 행 처 MENTORS
경기도 성남시 분당구 황새울로 335번길 10 598
TEL 031-604-0025 FAX 031-696-5221
mentors.co.kr
blog.naver.com/mentorsbook
* Play 스토어 및 App 스토어에서 '멘토스북' 검색해 어플다운받기!
등록일자 2005년 7월 27일
등록번호 제 2009-000027호
I S B N 979-11-94467-25-0
979-11-94467-24-3
가 격 18,000원(정답 및 해설 PDF 무료다운로드)

SMART English Grammar
for Speaking & Writing

1권

머리말

▸ 문법이란?

문법이란 문장을 만들어 말을 하고(speaking) 또한 문장을 만드는(writing) 것을 말한다. 모국어를 하는데는 그리 많은 문법이 필요하지 않는다. 어머니 뱃속에서부터 히어링을 하면서 모국어를 익히기 때문에 저절로 알게 되며 나중에 문법의 체계화를 위해 후천적으로 문법을 약간 학습할 뿐이다. 그러나 모국어가 아닌 외국어로 영어를 배우는 과정은 모국어 습득과 정반대가 된다.

▸ 외국어로 영어배우기는…

우리는 영어듣기와 영어말하기에 먼저 노출될 수 없기에 역으로 영문법을 통해서 영어를 말하고 쓰게 되는 과정을 밟아간다. 즉 한 언어, 즉 여기서는 영어를 문법을 통해서 이해하고 이를 발판으로 해서 영어회화, 영어작문 그리고 영어듣기 등에 많은 시간을 쏟고 주구장창 몰두하게 된다. 모국어로 영어를 배우는 네이티브와는 비교될 수 없는 싸움을 하는 것이다. 미국이나 영국에서 네이티브들과 소통하면서 몇년 살면 저절로 배워지는 영어지만 다 그럴 수 없기 때문에 우리는 어쩔 수 없이 비효율적인 방법으로 영어로 익힐 수밖에 없다. 여기에 문법의 중요성이 생기게 된다.

▸ 문법에만 흠뻑 빠지면 안돼…

여기서 한가지 범하기 쉬운 오류가 있다. 문법이 외국어를 배우는 최초의 단계임에는 분명하지만 너무 문법에 사로잡혀서 그래서 완벽한 문장 아니면 말을 하지 못하는 어리석음에 놓일 수가 있다. 언어는 시대에 따라 시시각각 변하고 이를 밑받침하는 문법 역시 계속 변화가 된다. 역으로 생각을 해보자. 우리가 특히 일상생활에서 우리말을 할 때 얼마나 국문법 규칙을 지키면서 말하는지 말이다. 이 말은 문법을 꼭 알아야 하지만 너무 문법에 얽매이면 안된다는 얘기이다.

▸ 이거 알면 남들보다 앞서가…

이 책 <BASIC English Grammar 1권, 2권>과 <SMART English Grammar 1권, 2권>은 지금 시대에 가장 잘 맞는 그리고 꼭 알아야 하는 문법규칙들을 무겁지 않게 정리하여 문법을 공부하는 사람들이 부담스럽지 않게 학습할 수 있도록 꾸며져 있다. 또한 이를 각종 Test들로 확인하게 되어 이를 다 풀고 나면 남들보다는 한두단계 영어에서 앞서 갈 수 있을 것이라 확신한다.

New Grammar is About

1 실용영어를 위한 문법

문법도 실용영어를 하는데 필요한 최소한의 도구이다. 따라서 문법을 위한 문법이 아닌 '실용영어를 위한 문법' 이란 캐치프레이즈를 내걸고 실제로 영어를 읽고 말하는 데 필요한 영어문법 사항들만을 정리하였다. 가장 실용적인 영어회화문(Dialogue)을 통해 우리가 학습해야 할 문법사항을 언급하는 것 또한 '지금,' '현재' 쓰이고 있는 문법을 지향하기 위함이다.

2 영어회화를 위한 문법

실용영어의 목적은 영어로 하는 의사소통이다. '영어말하기' 란 목표를 달성하기 위해 문법에 영어회화를 접목해본다. 문법을 단순한 지식으로 책상에서만 필요한 것이 아니라 실제 영어로 말하는데 활용할 수 있도록 매 Unit별로 학습한 문법지식을 바탕으로 다양한 문장을 영어로 옮겨보는 훈련을 해보며 간접적인 영어회화훈련을 시도해본다. 이는 또한 점점 실용화되고 있는 영어시험자격증인 TOEFL, TOEIC, IELT 등에서 고득점을 취할 수 있는 기본 베이스가 될 수 있을 것이다.

3 다양한 테스트

학습한 문법사항은 연습을 통해 훈련하지 않으면 다 날아가버린다. 이런 과오를 범하지 않기 위해 각 Unit마다 다양한 연습문제를 그리고 각 Chapter가 끝날 때마다 Review Test를 통해 이중으로 테스트를 해보며 머리 속에 오래도록 각인해본다. '영어말하기' 뿐만 아니라 각종 시험에서도 높은 점수를 받을 수 있을 것이다.

Level 2-A

New Grammar is Organized

1 Chapter

기본개념인 단어, 구, 절 그리고 문장 등의 성격과 종류를 일목요연하게 정리한 Pre-Study를 시작으로 문장만들기의 핵심으로 시제, 동사, 명사 그리고 형용사, 부사 등의 수식어 등 총 4개의 Chapter에 중급 실용영문법의 엑기스만을 집중 정리하였다. Chapter 1 시제에서는 자주 쓰이는 현재, 과거, 미래 등의 기본시제를 중심으로 진행형 시제와 현재완료 시제를 아울러 정리한다. Chapter 2 동사에서는 동작/상태동사, 사역/감각/지각 동사 그리고 다양한 의미를 띄며 동사의 의미에 새로운 의미를 부여하는 조동사들을 상세히 살펴본다. 다음 Chapter 3 명사에서는 명사의 종류와 명사 앞에 오는 관사 그리고 대명사의 기본에 대해 알아본다. 끝으로 Chapter 4 수식어에서는 문장에서 명사와 동사 등을 꾸며주며 문장을 윤택하게 해주는 형용사와 부사 그리고 그 비교급과 최상급에 대해 기술해 본다.

1개의 Pre-Study와 총 4개의 Chapters

Pre-Study | 단어 · 구 · 절 · 문장
Chapter 01 | 시제
Chapter 02 | 동사류
Chapter 03 | 명사류
Chapter 04 | 수식어류

2 Unit

Chapter는 다시 세분되어 각 Chapter별로 6~10개의 Unit로 정리된다. 따라서 총 4개의 Chapter는 총 62개의 Unit로 구성되어 있으며 각 Unit는 다시 Grammar in Practice, Grammar in Use, Unit Test, Writing Pattern Practice 등으로 나누어 진다.

각 Unit의 구성

Grammar in Practice
Grammar in Use
Unit Test
Writing Pattern Practice

3 Review

각 Chapter가 끝날 때마다 Chapter에서 학습한 내용을 다시 복습할 공간을 마련하였다. Review 1, 2에서 종합적으로 문제를 풀어보면서 자신이 학습한 내용을 얼마나 습득하였는지를 확인해볼 수 있다.

4 정답 및 해설

각 Unit의 테스트와 Review의 문제에 대한 정답을 별도의 부록으로 처리하여 문제를 풀 때 정답에 접근하는 것을 어렵게 하여 가급적 스스로 풀어보도록 꾸며졌다.

How to Use this Book

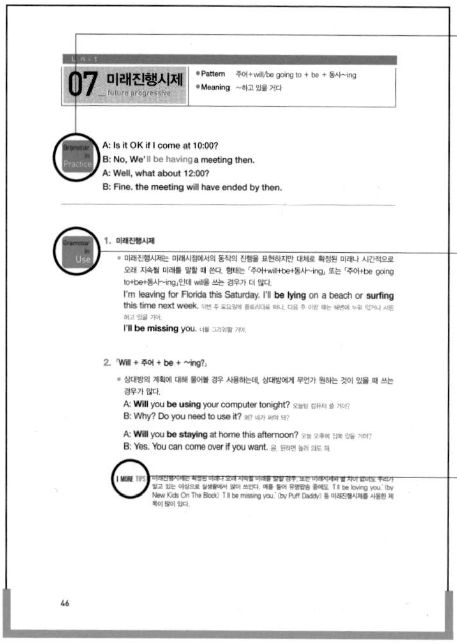

Unit
07 미래진행시제
future progressive
•Pattern 주어+will/be going to + be + 동사~ing
•Meaning ~하고 있을 거다

Grammar in Practice
A: Is it OK if I come at 10:00?
B: No, We'll be having a meeting then.
A: Well, what about 12:00?
B: Fine. the meeting will have ended by then.

Grammar in Use
1. 미래진행시제
I'm leaving for Florida this Saturday. I'll be lying on a beach or surfing this time next week.
I'll be missing you.

2. 「Will + 주어 + be + ~ing?」
A: Will you be using your computer tonight?
B: Why? Do you need to use it?
A: Will you be staying at home this afternoon?
B: Yes. You can come over if you want.

MORE TIPS

46

Grammar in Practice

영어회화와 문법을 접목시키는 부분. 각 Unit에서 학습할 문법사항이 실제 영어회화에서는 어떻게 쓰이는지 보면서 문법을 왜 배워야 하는지를 느껴본다.

Grammar in Use

역시 실용성에 focus를 맞춰 불필요한 문법지식을 다 걷어내고 오직 실제로 영어를 말하고 쓰는데 필요한 문법엑기스만을 간단하지만 밀도있게 서술하고 있는 부분이다.

More Tips

Grammar in Use에서 못다한 추가정보를 그때그때마다 간략이 설명해준다.

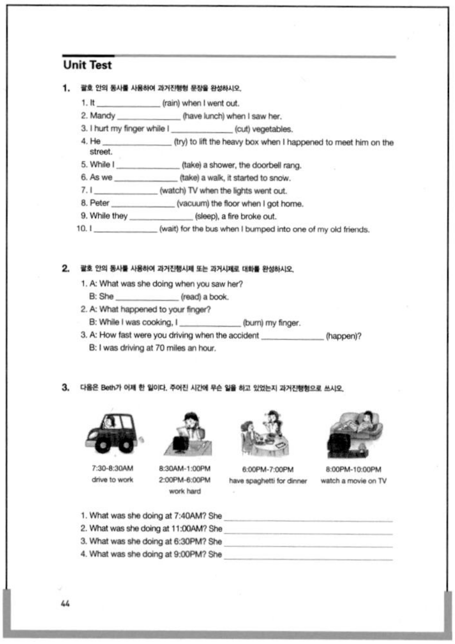

Unit Test

1. 괄호 안의 동사를 사용하여 과거진행형 문장을 완성하시오.
1. It ____________ (rain) when I went out.
2. Mandy ____________ (have lunch) when I saw her.
3. I hurt my finger while I ____________ (cut) vegetables.
4. He ____________ (try) to lift the heavy box when I happened to meet him on the street.
5. While I ____________ (take) a shower, the doorbell rang.
6. As we ____________ (take) a walk, it started to snow.
7. I ____________ (watch) TV when the lights went out.
8. Peter ____________ (vacuum) the floor when I got home.
9. While they ____________ (sleep), a fire broke out.
10. I ____________ (wait) for the bus when I bumped into one of my old friends.

2. 괄호 안의 동사를 사용하여 과거진행시제 또는 과거시제로 대화를 완성하시오.
1. A: What was she doing when you saw her?
B: She ____________ (read) a book.
2. A: What happened to your finger?
B: While I was cooking, I ____________ (burn) my finger.
3. A: How fast were you driving when the accident ____________ (happen)?
B: I was driving at 70 miles an hour.

3. 다음은 Beth가 어제 한 일이다. 주어진 시간에 무슨 일을 하고 있었는지 과거진행형으로 쓰시오.

7:30-8:30AM drive to work
8:30AM-1:00PM 2:00PM-6:00PM work hard
6:00PM-7:00PM have spaghetti for dinner
8:00PM-10:00PM watch a movie on TV

1. What was she doing at 7:40AM? She ____________
2. What was she doing at 11:00AM? She ____________
3. What was she doing at 6:30PM? She ____________
4. What was she doing at 9:00PM? She ____________

44

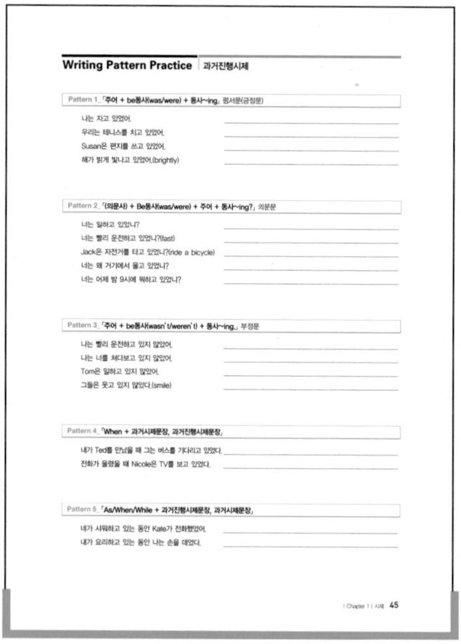

Writing Pattern Practice 과거진행시제

Pattern 1 「주어 + be동사(was/were) + 동사~ing」 평서문(긍정문)
나는 자고 있었어.
우리는 테니스를 치고 있었어.
Susan은 편지를 쓰고 있었어.
해가 밝게 빛나고 있었어.(brightly)

Pattern 2 「(의문사) + Be동사(was/were) + 주어 + 동사~ing?」 의문문
너는 일하고 있었니?
너는 빨리 운전하고 있었니?(fast)
Jack은 자전거를 타고 있었니?(ride a bicycle)
너는 왜 거기에서 울고 있었니?
너는 어제 밤 9시에 뭐하고 있었니?

Pattern 3 「주어 + be동사(wasn't/weren't) + 동사~ing」 부정문
나는 빨리 운전하고 있지 않았어.
나는 너를 쳐다보고 있지 않았어.
Tom은 일하고 있지 않았어.
그들은 웃고 있지 않았다.(smile)

Pattern 4 「When + 과거시제문장, 과거진행시제문장」
내가 Ted를 만났을 때 그는 버스를 기다리고 있었다.
전화가 울렸을 때 Nicole은 TV를 보고 있었다.

Pattern 5 「As/When/While + 과거진행시제문장, 과거시제문장」
내가 샤워하고 있는 동안 Kate가 전화했었어.
내가 요리하고 있는 동안 나는 손을 데었다.

Chapter 1 | 시제 45

Unit Test

각 Unit마다 학습한 문법사항을 바로 확인해보는 자리이다. 다양한 형태의 테스트를 통해 학습한 문법지식을 머리 속에 차곡차곡 잊지 않고 기억해둘 수 있다.

Writing Pattern Practice

이번에는 좀 더 적극적으로 문법과 영어회화를 접목시키는 공간이다. 학습한 문법사항을 실제로 영어말하는데 활용해 볼 수 있는 공간으로 문법이 살아있음을 느낄 수 있다.

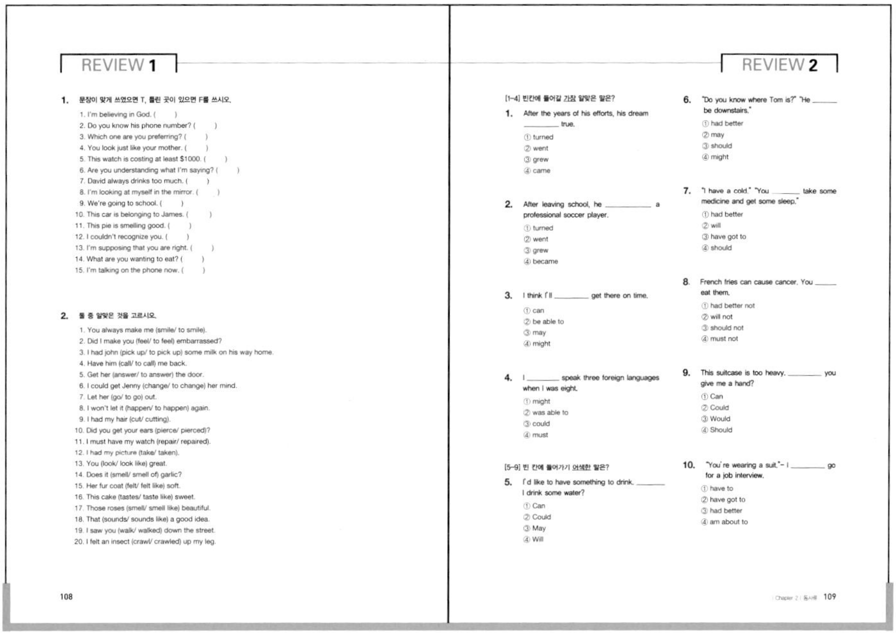

REVIEW 1

1. 문장이 맞게 쓰였으면 T, 틀린 곳이 있으면 F를 쓰시오.

1. I'm believing in God. ( )
2. Do you know his phone number? ( )
3. Which one are you preferring? ( )
4. You look just like your mother. ( )
5. This watch is costing at least $1000. ( )
6. Are you understanding what I'm saying? ( )
7. David always drinks too much. ( )
8. I'm looking at myself in the mirror. ( )
9. We're going to school. ( )
10. This car is belonging to James. ( )
11. This pie is smelling good. ( )
12. I couldn't recognize you. ( )
13. I'm supposing that you are right. ( )
14. What are you wanting to eat? ( )
15. I'm talking on the phone now. ( )

2. 둘 중 알맞은 것을 고르시오.

1. You always make me (smile/ to smile).
2. Did I make you (feel/ to feel) embarrassed?
3. I had john (pick up/ to pick up) some milk on his way home.
4. Have him (call/ to call) me back.
5. Get her (answer/ to answer) the door.
6. I could get Jenny (change/ to change) her mind.
7. Let her (go/ to go) out.
8. I won't let it (happen/ to happen) again.
9. I had my hair (cut/ cutting).
10. Did you get your ears (pierce/ pierced)?
11. I must have my watch (repair/ repaired).
12. I had my picture (take/ taken).
13. You (look/ look like) great.
14. Does it (smell/ smell of) garlic?
15. Her fur coat (felt/ felt like) soft.
16. This cake (tastes/ taste like) sweet.
17. Those roses (smell/ smell like) beautiful.
18. That (sounds/ sounds like) a good idea.
19. I saw you (walk/ walked) down the street.
20. I felt an insect (crawl/ crawled) up my leg.

108

REVIEW 2

[1~4] 빈칸에 들어갈 가장 알맞은 말은?

1. After the years of his efforts, his dream ________ true.
① turned
② went
③ grew
④ came

2. After leaving school, he ________ a professional soccer player.
① turned
② went
③ grew
④ became

3. I think I'll ________ get there on time.
① can
② be able to
③ may
④ might

4. I ________ speak three foreign languages when I was eight.
① might
② was able to
③ could
④ must

[5~9] 빈 칸에 들어가기 어색한 말은?

5. I'd like to have something to drink. ________ I drink some water?
① Can
② Could
③ May
④ Will

6. "Do you know where Tom is?" "He ________ be downstairs."
① had better
② may
③ should
④ might

7. "I have a cold." "You ________ take some medicine and get some sleep."
① had better
② will
③ have got to
④ should

8. French fries can cause cancer. You ________ eat them.
① had better not
② will not
③ should not
④ must not

9. This suitcase is too heavy. ________ you give me a hand?
① Can
② Could
③ Would
④ Should

10. "You're wearing a suit."- I ________ go for a job interview.
① have to
② have got to
③ had better
④ am about to

Chapter 2 | 동사류 109

▍Review

각 Chapter별로 제공되는 테스트시간으로 일종의 종합문제이다. 이미 Unit Test로 한번 확인한 문법을 다시 한번 꼼꼼 기억할 수 있는 공간이다.

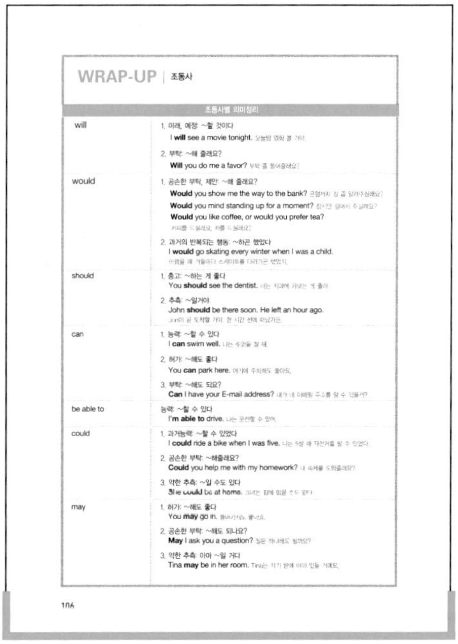

WRAP-UP | 조동사

조동사별 의미정리	
will	1. 미래, 예정: ~할 것이다 I **will** see a movie tonight. 2. 부탁: ~해 줄래요? **Will** you do me a favor?
would	1. 공손한 부탁, 제안: ~해 줄래요? **Would** you show me the way to the bank? **Would** you mind standing up for a moment? **Would** you like coffee, or would you prefer tea? 2. 과거의 반복되는 행동: ~하곤 했었다 I **would** go skating every winter when I was a child.
should	1. 충고: ~하는 게 좋다 You **should** see the dentist. 2. 추측: ~일거야 John **should** be there soon. He left an hour ago.
can	1. 능력: ~할 수 있다 I **can** swim well. 2. 허가: ~해도 좋다 You **can** park here. 3. 부탁: ~해도 되요? **Can** I have your E-mail address?
be able to	능력: ~할 수 있다 I'm **able to** drive.
could	1. 과거능력: ~할 수 있었다 I **could** ride a bike when I was five. 2. 공손한 부탁: ~해줄래요? **Could** you help me with my homework? 3. 약한 추측: ~일 수도 있다 She **could** be at home.
may	1. 허가: ~해도 좋다 You **may** go in. 2. 공손한 부탁: ~해도 되나요? **May** I ask you a question? 3. 약한 추측: 아마 ~일 거다 Tina **may** be in her room.

106

▍Wrap UP

군데군데 혼란스럽거나 복잡해보일 때마다 일목요연하게 1페이지로 학습내용을 깔끔하게 정리하였다.

Contents

Chapter 03 | 명사류

Chapter 04 | 수식어류

정답 및 해설(별책)

* Pre-Study | 단어 · 구 · 절 · 문장

- 단어 – 총 8가지의 종류 (명사, 대명사, 동사, 형용사, 부사, 전치사, 접속사, 감탄사)가 있다.
- 구 – 두 개 이상의 단어가 모여 하나의 품사와 같은 역할을 한다.
- 절 – 절은 '주어와 술어'를 포함한 완전한 문장이다. 독립적으로 쓰지 않고 더 큰 문장 안에서 일부의 역할을 한다.
- 문장 – 문장은 크게 긍정문, 부정문으로 구분되고 내용이나 형식에 따라 평서문, 의문문, 부정의문문, 부가의문문, 간접의문문, 명령문, 감탄문 등으로 나뉜다.

1. 단어(Word)

단어란 낱말 하나하나를 가리킨다. 그 단어들은 역할에 따라 8가지 품사로 나눌 수 있다.

1. 명사(noun), 대명사(pronoun)

명사는 사람이나 사물의 이름 또는 개념을 나타내는 말이다. 대명사는 명사를 대신해서 쓰는 말로 명사처럼 문장에서 주어, 보어, 목적어, 전치사의 목적어 역할을 한다.

명사	book, computer, Katie, David, New York, love, friendship 등
대명사	I, you, they, this, that, one, another, all, who, what 등

- 주어역할

  You always look happy. (대명사) 너는 항상 행복해 보인다.

- 보어역할

  Dogs are **animals**. (명사) 개는 동물이다.

- 목적어역할

  Susan is a writer. She writes **books**. (명사) Susan은 작가다. 그녀는 책을 쓴다.

2. 동사(verb)

동사는 주어의 행동이나 상태를 나타내는 말로, 문장의 의미와 시제를 결정하는 중요한 역할을 한다. 동사는 크게 동작과 상태를 나타내는 동사로 구분된다.

동사	동작동사	go, come, eat, drink, drive 등
	상태동사	be, understand, like, hate 등

- Paul **drives** to school. (동작동사) Paul은 학교에 차를 몰고 다닌다.
- You **are** so lazy. (상태동사) 너는 정말 게으르다.

3. 형용사(adjective), 부사(adverb)

형용사는 사람이나 사물의 상태나 성질을 나타내며 명사나 대명사를 꾸미거나 설명한다. 부사는 시간, 장소, 정도, 빈도 등을 나타내며 동사, 형용사, 또는 다른 부사를 꾸미는 역할을 한다.

형용사	pretty, hard, easy, difficult, terrific, terrible, tired, embarrassing 등
부사	yesterday, often, sometimes, quickly, late 등

- David is a **good-looking** man. (형용사) David은 잘 생긴 남자다.
- Those answers are **probably** wrong. (부사) 그 답들은 아마도 틀렸을 것이다.

4. 전치사(preposition)

전치사는 명사, 대명사, 동명사 앞에 와서 도와주는 말이다. 동사나 형용사와 함께 결합하여 쓰이기도 한다.

전치사	at, in, about, for, of, to, on, over, by, with 등

- Thank you **for** helping me. 나를 도와줘서 고마워.
- I'm looking forward **to** seeing you. 당신을 뵙기를 손꼽아 기다리고 있어요.
- Take a look **at** this. 이것을 봐.
- Sorry **about** that. 그것에 대해 미안해.

5. 접속사(conjunction)

접속사는 단어, 구, 절, 그리고 문장들을 연결해 주는 말이다. 대등하게 연결해주는 등위접속사, 주절에 종속절을 연결해 주는 종속 접속사, 두 개 이상의 단어가 관계를 맺어 말을 이어주는 상관 접속사가 있다.

등위접속사	and, but, or, so 등
종속접속사	because, although, when, if only 등
상관접속사(짝 접속사)	both~and…, (n)either~(n)or…, not only~but also… 등

- We drank, talked **and** danced. 우리는 마시고 이야기하고 춤 췄다.
- The place was **not only** cold, **but also** damp. 그 곳은 추울 뿐 아니라 축축했다.

6. 감탄사(exclamation)

기쁨, 놀람, 감탄 등을 나타내는 말로, 독립적으로 쓴다.

감탄사	wow, oh, ouch, oops 등

- **Ouch**, it really hurts! 아야, 정말 아프다!
- **Oops**, I made a mistake again! 저런, 또 실수했군!

2. 구 (Phrase)

두 개 이상의 단어가 하나의 품사와 같은 역할을 할 때 이를 '구' 라고 한다.

1. 명사구 _주어, 목적어, 보어 역할을 한다.

• 주어역할

Getting up early everyday isn't easy. 매일 일찍 일어나는 것은 쉽지 않다.

• 목적어역할

I'd like **to talk to you** for a minute. 잠깐 너와 이야기하고 싶다.

• 보어역할

My dream is **to be a singer**. 내 꿈은 가수가 되는 것이다.

2. 형용사구 _명사, 대명사를 수식하거나 설명한다.

• 명사, 대명사 수식

The book **on the desk** is mine. 책상 위에 있는 책은 내 것이다.

• 명사, 대명사 설명(보어역할)

That vending machine is **out of order**. 저 자판기는 고장 났다.

3. 부사구 _동사, 형용사, 다른 부사, 또는 문장 전체를 수식한다.

• 동사 수식

Can you finish your report **by tomorrow morning?** 내일아침까지 보고서 끝낼 수 있니?

• 형용사 또는 다른 부사 수식

I'm happy **to hear from Daniel**. Daniel로부터 소식을 들어서 기쁘다.

• 문장 전체 수식

To tell the truth, I don't feel like going out with him. 사실을 말하자면 그와 데이트할 기분 아니야.

3. 절 (Clause)

절은 「주어와 술어」를 포함한 완전한 문장으로 독립적으로 쓰이지 않고 더 큰 문장 안에서 문장의 일부로 사용된다.

1. 명사절

• 주어역할

It's obvious **that you need money.** 네가 돈이 필요하다는 것은 명백하다.

• 목적어역할

I don't think **that she has feelings for you.** 그녀가 너를 좋아하는 것 같지는 않다.

• 보어역할

The problem is **that I can't afford it.** 문제는 내가 그것을 살 여유가 없다는 것이다.

2. 형용사절

• 명사, 대명사 수식

She's <u>Heather</u> **who I'm working with.** 그녀는 내가 함께 일하는 Heather야.

Who's <u>the one</u> **that won the game**? 게임에서 이긴 사람이 누구야?

3. 부사절

• 시간, 양보, 이유 등의 의미

I'm glad **that you like it.** 마음에 든다니 기뻐.

Since we have some time, let's have a cup of tea. 시간이 좀 있으니까 차 한 잔 마시자.

Take your umbrella **in case it rains.** 비가 올 경우를 대비해서 우산을 가져가.

4. 문장 (Sentence)

문장은 크게 긍정문, 부정문으로 구분되고 내용이나 형식에 따라 평서문, 의문문, 부정의문문, 부가의문문, 간접의문문, 명령문, 감탄문 등으로 나뉜다.

1. 평서문

• 긍정문 – 어떤 내용을 단정적으로 서술하는 것이다. 시제와 인칭에 따라 동사의 형태가 변하는 것에 주의한다.

• 부정문 – not, no, never 등을 이용하여 내용을 부정하는 문장이다. 일반적으로 문장에 be동사나 조동사가 쓰인 경우는 바로 다음에 not을, 일반동사가 쓰인 경우는 인칭이나 시제에 따라 동사원형 앞에 do not(don't)/ does not(doesn't)/ did not (didn't)을 쓴다.

2. 의문문

● **Yes/No questions (의문사가 없는 의문문)**

1. be동사가 있는 문장의 의문문은 「Be동사+주어~?」 형태이다.

Are you looking for a job? 직장을 찾고 있니?

Is Jim a hard worker? Jim은 열심히 일하니?

2. 조동사가 있는 문장의 의문문은 「조동사+주어~?」 형태이다.

Would you be quiet? 조용히 해 줄래요?

Can I get you a cup of coffee? 내가 커피 한 잔 갖다 줄까?

3. 일반동사가 있는 문장의 의문문은 「Do/Does/Did+주어+동사원형?」 형태이다.

Do you walk to school? 학교에 걸어 다니니?

Does Henry go out much? Henry는 자주 외출하니?

Did I wake you up? 내가 너를 깨웠니?

● wh-questions (의문사가 있는 의문문)

1. be동사가 있는 문장의 의문문은 「의문사+be동사+주어~?」 형태이다.

How are you doing? 너는 어떻게 지내니?

Where are you from? 너는 어디 출신이니?

2. 조동사가 있는 문장의 의문문은 「의문사+조동사+주어~?」 형태이다.

What can I do for you? 무엇을 해 드릴까요?

How can I get to Beverly Hills? 비벌리 힐즈에 어떻게 가야하죠?

3. 일반동사가 있는 문장의 의문문은 「의문사+do/does/did+주어+동사원형?」 형태이다.

What do you do for a living? 직업이 뭐예요?

Who do you want to speak to? 너는 누구와 얘기하고 싶니?, 누구를 바꿔 드릴까요?

4. 의문사가 문장의 주어인 의문문은 「의문사+동사~?」 형태이다.

What happened? 무슨 일이 있었어?

Who wants something to eat? 누가 먹을 것을 원하니?

What is your favorite sport? 좋아하는 스포츠가 뭐야?

Which is your cell phone? 어느 것이 네 핸드폰이니?

3. 부정의문문

부정의문문은 '~하지 않니?' 라는 뜻으로 be동사나 조동사 다음에 'n't' 를 붙인 의문문이다.

• 확인/의심/불평

Aren't you ashamed of yourself? 너는 창피하지도 않니?

Can't you stay a little longer? 조금 더 머무를 수 없니?

Didn't you go and see Ann yesterday? 어제 Ann 보러가지 않았니?

• 정중한 권유

Won't you come in? 들어오지 않을래요?

Wouldn't you like something to eat? 뭐 드시지 않을래요?

4. 부가의문문

부가의문문이란 평서문으로 말하다가 상대방의 동의를 얻기 위해 뒤에 질문을 덧붙이는 형태를 말한다. 이때 덧붙여주는 문장은 앞의 문장이 긍정이면 부정, 부정이면 긍정으로 쓴다.

• 앞 문장에 be동사나 조동사를 쓴 경우 「be동사/조동사(n't)+주어?」를 덧붙인다.

We've met somewhere before, **haven't we?** 전에 어디서 만난적 있죠, 그렇지 않아요?

Jack wasn't very nice to you, **was he?** Jack은 네게 잘 대해주지 않았어, 그랬지?

• 앞 문장에 일반동사를 쓴 경우 「do/does/did(n't)+주어?」를 덧붙인다.

Tom has a great sense of humor, **doesn't he?** Tom은 유머감각이 아주 많아, 그렇지 않아?

You don't know where Sue is, **do you?** 너는 Sue가 어디 있는지 모르지, 그지?

| MORE TIPS | Let's~ 문장의 부가의문문 만들기

• 명령문은 「will you?」를 덧붙인다.
Get me some water, will you? 물 좀 가져다줄래?

• Let's~ 는 「shall we?」를 덧붙인다.
Let's go for a walk, shall we? 산책가자, 응?

5. 간접의문문

간접의문문은 의문문이 독립적으로 쓰이지 않고 전체 문장 속의 일부가 되는 경우를 말한다. 평서문의 어순을 쓴다는 점과 의문문이 없는 의문문일 경우 간접의문문 앞에 if나 whether를 쓴다는 점을 유의한다.

• 의문사가 있는 일반의문문 What time is it?	+	Tell me~ Can you tell me~ Do you know~ I don't know~	→	• 의문사가 있는 간접의문문 **Tell me** what time it is. **Can you tell me** what time it is? **Do you know** what time it is? **I don't know** what time it is.
• 의문사가 없는 일반의문문 Is Cindy married?	+	Tell me~ Can you tell me~ Do you know~ I don't know~	→	• 의문사가 없는 간접의문문 **Tell me** if Cindy is married. **Can you tell me** if Cindy is married? **Do you know** if Cindy is married? **I don't know** if Cindy is married.

| MORE TIPS | 'do you think(suppose/believe/consider/guess/imagine 등)' 는 의문사가 있는 의문문과 결합할 경우 「의문사+do you think~?」의 형태를 취한다.

What did she do? + Do you think~
= What do you think she did?(○) Do you think what she did?(X)

Who does he love? + Do you suppose~
= Who do you suppose he loves?(○) Do you suppose who he loves?(X)

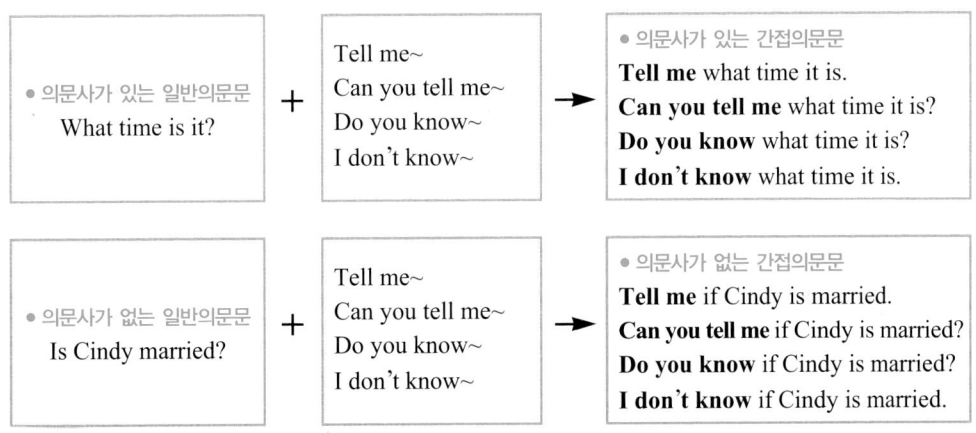

6. 명령문

명령문은 상대방에게 지시할 때나 일상생활에서 '~을 하세요' 정도의 느낌으로 쓴다. 동사 원형으로 시작하고 공손하게 말하기 위해서는 앞에 Please 또는 뒤에 ~, please를 붙인다. 부정명령문은 「Don't+동사원형~」 형태를 쓴다.

• 긍정/부정명령문 「(Don't+) 동사원형~」

Enjoy your holiday. 휴가를 잘 보내라.

Don't do that again or you'll be in a big trouble. 다시는 그러지 마라 그렇지 않으면 큰일날 거야.

• 명령문강조 1 「Do+긍정명령문」

Do be careful. 정말 조심해라.

Do keep that in mind. 그것을 꼭 명심해라.

• 명령문강조 2 「Always/Never+명령문」

Always remember that I love you. 항상 내가 너를 사랑한다는 것을 기억해.

Never be late again. 절대 다시는 늦지 마라.

• 수동 명령문 「get+과거분사」

Get vaccinated. 예방접종 받아라.

• 주어가 있는 명령문 「주어+명령문」

명령문은 보통 주어가 생략된 형태로 쓰지만 주어를 꼭 밝혀주어야 할 때나 강조할 경우 명령문 앞에 쓸 수 있다.

You be quiet. 너 조용히 해.

Somebody answer the phone. 누구 전화 받아라.

• 명령문의 부가의문문 「, will you/ would you/ can you?」

Give me a ride, **will you?** 차 좀 태워주라, 그래 줄래?

Wait for me to finish this, **would you?** 이거 끝낼 때까지 기다려줘요, 그래 줄래요?

Get me something to write with, **can you?** 필기도구 좀 주세요, 그래 줄 수 있어요?

| MORE TIPS | 앞문장이 부정명령문일 경우의 부가의문문도 긍정명령문의 부가의문문 만드는 방법과 동일하다. 다만 부가되는 문장이 can't you?, won't you?처럼 부정으로 쓰기도 하는데 이때는 자신이 말하는 '명령'을 강조하는 경우이다.

• Don't be late to school, **will you**? 학교에 늦지마, 알았지?

• 1/3인칭 명령문 「Let+목적어+동사원형」

'나' 또는 '그녀/그' 에게 '~해라' 라고 하는 명령문 표현은 없으므로 '너' 를 제외한 인칭일 경우 let 동사를 사용할 수 있다.

Let me think. 생각 좀 해볼게.

Let him go home. 그를 집에 가게 해.

7. 감탄문

놀라움이나 감정을 강조하고 싶을 때 감탄문을 쓴다.

- How로 시작하는 감탄문

「How+형용사/부사(+주어+동사)!」

How beautiful you are! 당신은 정말 아름다워요!

How fast she ran! 그녀는 정말이지 빨리 뛰더라고요!

- What으로 시작하는 감탄문

「What+(a/an)+(형용사)+명사(+주어+동사)!」

What a beautiful smile she has! 그녀의 미소는 정말 아름다워!

What great students you are! 너희들은 정말 멋진 학생들이야!

What a coincidence! 대단한(멋진/이상한) 우연의 일치군!

What a surprise! 정말 (예상치 못하게/반갑게) 놀랍다!

* What으로 시작하는 감탄문에서 형용사 없이 사용했을 경우 억양이나 표정으로 느낌을 대신할 수 있다. 감탄문에서 주어 동사는 상황에 따라 생략가능하다.

| MORE TIPS | What으로 시작하는 감탄문에서 형용사 없이 셀 수 없는 명사나 셀 수 있는 복수명사가 올 경우 부정관사 a를 쓸 수 없음에 유의한다.

〔비교〕

「What+a/an+(형용사)+셀 수 있는 단수명사!」	「What+(형용사)+셀 수 없는 명사/ 셀 수 있는 복수 명사!」
What a long day! 정말 지루한/ 힘든 하루야!	What lovely flowers! (What a lovely flowers! - X) 정말 아름다운 꽃들이다!
What a small world! 정말 세상 좁다!	What nonsense! (What a nonsense! - X) 말도 안돼!
What a woman! 대단한/ 이상한 여자야!	What luck! (What a luck! - X) 정말 운 좋다!
What a ride! 대단한/ 힘든/ 신나는 (자동차/ 버스/ 놀이기구) 여행이야!	What fools! (What a fools! - X) 바보들 같으니!

* Chapter 1 | 시제

시제란 어떤 사건이나 동작이 일어난 시간에 대한 구분이다. 기본적으로 과거, 현재, 미래 시제가 있고 완료와 진행 등을 합하여 전체 12시제가 있다. 본 교재에서는 일상생활에서 흔히 쓰이는 현재, 현재진행, 과거, 과거진행, 현재완료, 미래시제와 미래진행, 과거완료, 현재완료진행시제를 중심으로 학습해보도록 하겠다.

Unit

01 현재시제 _ simple present

● **Pattern** 주어(I/You/We/They) + 동사
주어(She/He/It) + 동사(e)s

● **Meaning** ~이다, ~한다

Grammar in Practice

A: Guess what! I have a new apartment.
B: Really? What's it like?
A: It's just great. It has a great view, too.
B: How many rooms does it have?
A: It has three bedrooms, a bathroom, a kitchen, and a living room.

Grammar in Use

1. 현재시제

● 지속적인 상태나 성질을 나타낸다.
I **have** brown hair and brown eyes. 나는 갈색 머리와 갈색 눈을 가지고 있다.
Cindy **is** bad-tempered. She **gets** angry a lot. Cindy는 성격이 고약하다. 자주 화를 낸다.

● 반복적인 일이나 습관을 나타낸다. - always, often, never, every day 등의 부사와 함께 쓰이는 경우가 많다.
We usually **go** to church on Sundays. 우리는 보통 일요일마다 교회에 간다.
"Would you like some beer?" "No, thanks. I **don't drink.**"
맥주 좀 드릴까요?? 고맙지만 괜찮아요. 술 안 마셔요.

● 과학적이거나 일반적인 사실 등을 나타낸다.
Washington D.C. **is** the capital of the United States. 워싱턴 D.C.는 미국의 수도이다.

2. 현재시제가 미래의 의미를 가지는 경우

● 시간을 나타내는 부사절 (after, before, as soon as, until, when, while 등으로 시작), 또는 조건을 나타내는 부사절 (if로 시작)일 경우
Brush your teeth <u>before you **go** to bed.</u> 자러가기 전에 이 닦아.

● 이미 정해져있는 계획이나 일정의 경우
Heather **leaves** for Athens tomorrow morning. Heather는 내일 아침에 아테네로 떠난다.
Tomorrow **is** Tom's birthday. 내일은 Tom의 생일이다.

3. 의문문과 부정문 만드는 방법

- 의문문

Do Does	I/we/you/they he/she/it	work? exercise? drink?

- 부정문

I/We/You/They He/She/It	do not(don't) does not(doesn't)	work. exercise. drink.

4. 주어가 3인칭 단수일 때 동사원형에 -(e)s 붙이는 방법

대부분의 동사는 -s를 붙인다.	get - gets　eat - eats　drink - drinks
-s, -sh, -ch, -x로 끝나는 동사는 -es를 붙인다.	miss - misses　brush - brushes teach - teaches　mix - mixes
자음+y로 끝나는 동사는 y를 i로 바꾸고 -es를 붙인다.	cry - cries　fly - flies　try - tries
불규칙동사가 있다.	have - has　do - does　go - goes

5. 주어가 3인칭 단수일 때 동사원형에 붙는 -(e)s의 발음

무성음(k, t, p, f 등) 뒤의 s	/s/	helps　likes　wants　laughs 등
-s, -sh, -ch, -x로 끝나는 동사 뒤의 -es	/iz/	misses　brushes　teaches　mixes 등
그 밖 유성음 뒤의 s	/z/	plays　rains　snows　comes 등

Unit Test

1. **괄호안의 단어를 사용하여 현재시제 문장을 완성하시오.**

1. That store ______________ (close) at 7:00.
2. Jennifer usually ______________ (drive) to work.
3. Oranges ______________ (not grow) in cold climates.
4. Ellen ______________ (speak) German very well.
5. "What does Tom do?" "He ______________ (teach) English."
6. Sarah ______________ (not drink) coffee very often.
7. David ______________ (not seem) to have time.
8. My boss often ______________ (wear) a pink necktie.
9. You ______________ (not look) like your mother.
10. The sun ______________ (set) in the west.

2. **평서문을 의문문으로 바꾸시오.**

1. Sam starts his new job next Monday.
   → ______________________________
2. You need money.
   → ______________________________
3. This shop opens on Sundays.
   → ______________________________
4. Snakes eat frogs.
   → ______________________________
5. His father drives a bus for a living.
   → ______________________________

3. **우리말과 일치하도록 괄호 안의 단어를 알맞게 배열하시오.**

1. 당신은 어디 출신인가요? (do/ where/ come from/ you/?)
   → ______________________________
2. 이 단어는 무엇을 의미하니? (this word/ does/ what/ mean/?)
   → ______________________________
3. 올림픽 경기는 4년에 한 번씩 열린다. (take place/ every four years/ the Olympic games)
   → ______________________________
4. Jackie는 갈색머리를 가졌다. (has/ Jackie/ brown hair)
   → ______________________________
5. 너는 너의 개를 매일 산책시키니? (walk your dog/ you/ do/ everyday/ ?)
   → ______________________________

Writing Pattern Practice | 현재시제

Pattern 1_ 「주어(I/ You/ We/ They) + 동사」 평서문(긍정문)

나는 갈색 머리와 갈색 눈을 가지고 있다. ______________________

자러가기 전에 네 이를 닦아라.(Brush~) ______________________

우리는 보통 일요일마다 교회에 간다.(on Sundays)

____

Tom과 Mary는 같은 학교에 다닌다.(the same school)

____

Pattern 2_ 「주어(She/ He/ It) + 동사(e)s」 평서문(긍정문)

그녀는 자주 화를 낸다.(get, a lot) ______________________

Jack은 시애틀 출신이다.(come from) ______________________

Cindy는 바퀴벌레를 정말 싫어한다.(cockroaches) ______________________

1교시는 8시에 시작한다.(The first class~) ______________________

서울행 비행기는 오늘 8시에 도착해.(The flight to Seoul~)

____

Pattern 3_ 「Do/Does + 주어 + 동사원형?」 의문문

너는 너의 개를 매일 산책시키니? ______________________

Katie는 매일 샤워하니? ______________________

너는 뭐하니?(직업이 뭐니?) ______________________

저 상점은 언제 여니?(When~, that store) ______________________

Pattern 4_ 「주어 + don't/doesn't + 동사원형」 부정문

나는 맥주를 마시지 않는다. ______________________

저 상점에서는 신발을 팔지 않는다.(They~, at that store)

____

David은 많이 외식하지 않는다.(eat out a lot) ______________________

우리는 오늘밤 떠나지 않는다. ______________________

네 신발은 네 치마와 잘 어울리지 않는다.(go well with)

____

Unit

02 과거시제 _ simple past

- **Pattern** 주어 + 과거동사
- **Meaning** ~이었다, ~했다

Grammar in Practice

A: Where were you born?
B: I was born in Mexico.
A: When did you move here?
B: I moved here five years ago when I was in high school.
A: Did you learn English in high school?
B: Yes, I did.

Grammar in Use

1. 과거시제

- 과거의 사실이나 상태를 나타낸다.
  Mozart **was** only 35 years old when he died. 모차르트는 죽었을 때 겨우 35살이었다.
- 과거의 일어난 일이나 동작을 나타낸다.
  "When did you buy this computer?" "I **bought** it two years ago."
  너는 언제 이 컴퓨터를 샀니? 2년 전에 샀어.
- 역사적인 사실을 나타낸다.
  The Gulf War **broke out** in 1991. 걸프전쟁은 1991년에 일어났다.

2. 과거시제와 함께 쓰는 부사

yesterday 어제	the day before yesterday 그저께	last night 어젯밤에
last week 지난주에	in the 1970s 1970년대에	in 1990 1990년에

3. 의문문과 부정문 만드는 방법

- 의문문

Did	I/we/you/they he/she/it	have lunch? exercise? study?

- 부정문

I/We/You/They He/She/It	did not (didn't)	have lunch. exercise. study.

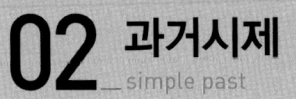

Unit Test

1. 괄호 안의 주어진 단어를 사용하여 <u>과거시제</u> 문장을 완성하시오.

1. (I, have lunch) → (평서문) ______________________________
2. (she, get up) → (평서문) ______________________________
3. (you, drive here) → (의문문) ______________________________?
4. (it, rain) → (의문문) ______________________________?
5. (we, go out last night) → (부정문) ______________________________
6. (they, know much about her) → (부정문) ______________________________

2. 보기에서 알맞은 단어를 사용하여 <u>과거시제</u> 문장을 완성하시오.

보기	invite	eat	cost	go	spend	be	sell	fall	write	put

1. Shakespeare ______________ *Hamlet*.
2. I couldn't afford to keep my car, so I ______________ it.
3. Debbie and I went shopping yesterday. We ______________ a lot of money.
4. Sharon ______________ us to her party, but we decided not to go.
5. This building ______________ $750,000 in 1999.
6. It was so cold, so I ______________ on my coat.
7. Jack ______________ down the stairs and broke his leg.
8. I ______________ in a hurry, so I couldn't stop to say hello to him.
9. We ______________ to Sally's house, but nobody was at home.
10. I was very hungry, so I ______________ three pieces of cake.

3. David은 어제 여자친구와 영화를 봤다. 괄호 안의 주어진 단어를 사용하여 David에게 묻는 질문을 완성하시오.

David

1. (see a movie?) Did you see a movie?
2. (what, see?) What did you see?
3. (have dinner?) ______________________________
4. (what, eat?) ______________________________
5. (have a good time?) ______________________________
6. (drive her home?) ______________________________
7. (when, go back home?) ______________________________

Writing Pattern Practice | 과거시제

Pattern 1_ 「주어 + 과거동사」 평서문(긍정문)

나는 일찍 일어났다. ______________________

나는 이 신발을 2년 전에 샀다. ______________________

Jack은 어제 밤 많이 마셨다.(a lot) ______________________

초인종이 울렸다.(The doorbell~) ______________________

우리는 어제 쇼핑 갔었다. ______________________

우리는 많은 돈을 썼다.(a lot of) ______________________

Pattern 2_ 「Did + 주어 + 동사원형?」 의문문

내가 너를 깨웠니?(wake) ______________________

내가 너를 방해했니?(bother) ______________________

너는 이 닦았니? ______________________

너는 샤워했니? ______________________

비가 왔니? ______________________

그들은 집에 걸어갔니?(walk home) ______________________

Pattern 3_ 「의문사 + did + 주어 + 동사원형?」 의문문

너는 어제 뭐했니? ______________________

너는 점심으로 무엇을 먹었니?(for lunch) ______________________

그것은 언제 일어났니?(happen) ______________________

너희들은 왜 싸웠니? ______________________

너는 어떻게 내 전화번호를 알았니? ______________________

너는 누구에게 전화했니?(call) ______________________

그들은 어디에서 만났니?(meet) ______________________

Pattern 4_ 「주어 + didn't + 동사원형」 부정문

나는 아무 것도 잘못하지 않았다.(anything wrong) ______________________

너 네 방을 치우지 않았구나.(clean) ______________________

David은 나를 초대하지 않았다. ______________________

비가 오지 않았다.(It~) ______________________

그들은 차로 여기에 오지 않았다.(drive here) ______________________

Unit

03 미래시제 1
simple future

● **Pattern** 주어 + will + 동사원형
주어 + be going to + 동사원형

● **Meaning** ~할 것이다/ ~할 예정이다

Grammar in Practice

A: Will you set the dining room?
B: OK, mom. Are we having guests tonight?
A: Yes. Dad's friends are going to come over for dinner.

Grammar in Use

미래의 의미를 나타내는 방법은 「will+동사원형」과 「be going to+동사원형」 등이 있다. 이 둘은 비슷한 의미로 쓰이기도 하지만 의미상 구분되는 경우도 있다.

1. 미래의 일을 예측할 경우

● will과 be going to 모두 사용할 수 있다.
There **will** be an important meeting tomorrow. 내일 중요한 회의가 있을 것이다.
= There'**s going to** be an important meeting tomorrow.

2. will

● 의지나 결심을 나타낸다.
I **won't** tell a lie again. I promise. 다시는 거짓말 안할게. 약속해.

● 사전 준비 없이 말하는 순간 결심한 일을 나타낸다.
I **will** have some orange juice. 나는 오렌지주스를 마실 거야.
"Stop watching TV." "OK. I'**ll** turn it off." TV 그만 봐. 알았어요. 끌게요.

3. be going to

● 사전에 결정한 일을 나타낸다.
We'**re going to** buy a house next year. 우리는 내년에 집을 살 예정이다.

● 상황의 결과로 예측되는 일을 나타낸디.
I'm stuck in traffic. I'**m going to** be late. 차가 막혀. 늦을거야.
Look out! We'**re going to** crash! 조심해! 충돌하겠어!

| MORE TIPS | 공식적인 일 또는 계획과 확실한 미래를 나타낼 경우 현재형과 현재진행형이 미래시제를 대신하는 경우도 있다.

• His train **arrives** at 11:45. 그가 탈 기차는 11시 45분에 도착한다.
• We**'re getting** married next month. 우리는 다음 달에 결혼한다.

4. 의문문과 부정문 만드는 방법

- will 의문문

Will	주어	exercise? study?

- 부정문

주어	will not (won't)	exercise. study.

- be going to 의문문

Am Are Is	주어	going to	exercise? study?

- 부정문

주어	am not('m not) are not(aren't) is not(isn't)	going to	exercise. study.

5. 과거의 미래 (Future in the Past)

과거에 대해 언급할 때 그 때 기준으로 미래 일을 말하는 경우가 있다. 이때는 will 대신 would를, am/are/is/ going to 대신 was/were going to를 사용한다.

I knew that Sally **would** arrive before long. Sally가 곧 올 것을 알고 있었다.
I told you that I **would** be absent. 결석할 거라고 말씀 드렸는데요.
Last time I saw Kevin, he **was going to** start a new job. 내가 지난 번 Kevin을 봤을 때 그는 새로운 일을 시작하려 하고 있었다.
Bob had no time to see me because he **was going to** have an important meeting. Bob은 중요한 회의를 할 예정이었기 때문에 나를 만날 시간이 없었다.

Unit Test

1. 괄호 안의 주어진 단어를 사용하여 미래시제(be going to 사용) 문장을 완성하시오.

1. (I, have a baby next month) → (평서문) ______________________________
2. (it, rain) → (평서문) ______________________________
3. (you, see the movie tonight) → (의문문) ______________________________?
4. (Tom, leave for Japan) → (의문문) ______________________________?
5. (we, have a meeting tomorrow morning)
   → (부정문) ______________________________
6. (they, get divorced)
   → (부정문) ______________________________

2. 괄호 안의 주어진 단어를 사용하여 미래시제(will 사용) 문장을 완성하시오.

1. (I, help you clean the house) → (평서문) ______________________________
2. (he, come on time) → (평서문) ______________________________
3. (you, go to the party) → (의문문) ______________________________?
4. (Kelly, be here in a few minutes)
   → (의문문) ______________________________?
5. (Jack, stay in Seoul)
   → (부정문) ______________________________
6. (they, lend you the money)
   → (부정문) ______________________________

3. 둘 중 문맥상 더 자연스러운 것을 골라 동그라미 하시오.

1. "The telephone is ringing." "I (will/ am going to) get it."
2. "Are you ready to order?" "Yes, I (will/ am going to) have a cheese burger."
3. "When are you going to have a party?" "I (will/ am going to) have a party this Friday.
4. "This suitcase is too heavy." "Don't worry. I (will/ am going to) help you."
5. "Do you have any plans for your holiday?" "Yes, I (will/ am going to) see my grandma in Guam."
6. "I missed the bus. What should I do?" "Don't worry. I (will/ am going to) give you a ride."
7. "When are they going to get married?" "They (will/ are going to) get married this Christmas."

Writing Pattern Practice 미래시제 1

Pattern 1_「주어 + will + 동사원형」 will 평서문(긍정문)

나는 오렌지주스를 좀 마실 거야.(have) ____________

나는 지금 집에 갈 거야. ____________

나는 점심으로 스파게티를 먹을 거야. ____________

나는 너를 그리워할 거야. ____________

곧 봄이 될 거야.(It ~) ____________

내일은 추울거야.(It ~) ____________

Pattern 2_「(의문사) + Will + 주어 + 동사원형?」 will 의문문

너 올 거니? ____________

그것 괜찮을까?(OK) ____________

너는 무엇을 할 거니? ____________

너는 언제 나갈거니? ____________

너는 밤을 어디에서 보낼거니?(spend the night) ____________

Pattern 3_「주어 + will not(won't) + 동사원형」 will 부정문

나는 다시는 거짓말 안할게.(tell a lie) ____________

Sally는 늦지 않을 거야. ____________

우리는 돌아오지 않을거야.(be) ____________

내일 비가 안 올 거야. ____________

Pattern 4_「주어 + be going to + 동사원형」 be going to 평서문(긍정문)

나는 늦게 될 거야. ____________

나는 그녀가 'yes'라고 할 때까지 계속 그녀에게 데이트 신청할거야.(keep asking her out, until she says 'yes,')

____

바람이 불 예정이야.(windy) ____________

우리는 내년에 집을 살 예정이다. ____________

Look out! 우리 충돌하겠어.(crash) ____________

Pattern 5_ 「**(의문사) + Be + 주어 + going to + 동사원형?**」 be going to 의문문

너는 머리를 자를 예정이니?(get your hair cut) ______________________

그녀는 Mark와 결혼할 예정이니?(marry) ______________________

비가 오겠니? ______________________

(날씨가) 화창할까?(sunny) ______________________

너는 무엇을 할 예정이니? ______________________

너는 언제 떠날 예정이니? ______________________

그들은 어디서 축구를 할 예정이니?(play soccer) ______________________

Pattern 6_ 「**주어 + be not going to + 동사원형**」 be going to 부정문

나는 그녀에게 데이트 신청하지 않을 거야.(ask her out)

____

Cindy는 오늘 오후에 외출하지 않을거야.(go out) ______________________

눈이 오지 않을 거야. ______________________

우리는 기차를 타지 않을 거야.(take) ______________________

Unit

04 미래시제 2
_future

● Pattern 주어 + be about to/ be supposed to/ be to + 동사원형

● Meaning 막 ~하려고 하다/ ~하기로 되어있다/ ~할 예정이다

Grammar in Practice

A: Let's go (to) see a movie after class.

B: I'm sorry, but I've got to go home early.
I'm supposed to take care of my sister this afternoon.

Grammar in Use

1. be about to

● '막 ~하려고 하다' 라는 뜻으로 매우 짧은 시간 안에 일어날 일을 말한다.

Hurry up. The movie **is about to** begin. 서둘러. 영화가 바로 시작할거야.

I'**m about to** call Jason. Jason에게 곧 전화하려고 해.

● '막 ~하려고 했었다' 라고 하려면 be동사를 과거형으로 쓴다.

We **were about to** go out. 우리 막 나가려고 했었어.

2. be supposed to

● '~하기로 되어있다' 라는 뜻으로 정해진 일이나 해야 되는 일을 말할 때 쓴다.

"What **am** I **supposed to** do?" 내가 무엇을 하기로 되어있지?/ 나 어쩌지? (=What should I do?)

You'**re supposed to** do the laundry. 너는 오늘 빨래해야지.

"What **are** you **supposed to** do?" "I'**m supposed to** meet Dr. Walf this afternoon." 뭐하기로 되어있니? 오늘 오후에 Walf 박사님을 만나기로 했어.

● '~하기로 되어 있었다' 라고 하려면 be동사를 과거형으로 쓴다.

You **were supposed to** come here an hour early. 한 시간 일찍 오기로 했잖아.

3. be to

● '~할 예정이다' 라는 뜻으로 구어체에서는 잘 안쓰이는 비교적 격식을 차린 표현(formal)이다.

The President **is to** visit Malaysia. 대통령은 말레이시아를 방문할 예정이다.

Mr. Smith **is** soon **to** be promoted. Smith 씨는 곧 승진될 것이다.

We'**re to** get a wage rise. 우리는 임금 인상을 받을 것이다.

4. 그 밖의 미래를 나타내는 표현

● 조동사 could나 might를 사용하여 확실하지 않은 미래를 말할 수 있다.

Shiela **could** be fired sooner or later. Shiela는 조만간 해고당할 수도 있어.

I **might** see a movie with my friends this weekend. 나는 이번 주말 친구들과 함께 영화 볼 지도 몰라.

Unit Test

1. **보기와 같이 be about to를 사용하여 문장을 완성하시오.**

보기 | (I, go out) → I'm about to go out.

1. (I, eat breakfast)

→ ____________________

2. (Jully, clean her room)

→ ____________________

3. (The singer, sing)

→ ____________________

4. (The movie, begin)

→ ____________________

5. (Tom and I, leave)

→ ____________________

2. **보기와 같이 be supposed to를 사용하여 문장을 완성하시오.**

보기 | (I, do my homework) → I'm supposed to do my homework.

1. (I, be at home by 11)

→ ____________________

2. (You, finish the report by noon)

→ ____________________

3. (Janet, meet Dr. Smith today)

→ ____________________

4. (David, do the laundry this afternoon)

→ ____________________

5. (Jack and I, leave tonight)

→ ____________________

3. **보기와 같이 be to를 사용하여 문장을 완성하시오.**

보기 | (Mr. Kim, be fired) → Mr. Kim is to be fired.

1. (the queen, visit next month)

→ ____________________

2. (the APEC Ministerial meeting, be held in Chile) *Ministerial meeting 각료회의

→ ____________________

3. (the *technicians, go on a strike sooner or later) *technician 정비기술자

→ ____________________

Writing Pattern Practice | 미래시제 2

Pattern 1_ 「주어 + be about to + 동사원형」

Jason에게 곧 전화하려고 해. ______

영화가 바로 시작할거야.(begin) ______

내 이가 막 빠지려고 해.(fall out) ______

우리는 막 저녁을 먹으려고 해.(eat) ______

우리 막 나가려고 했었어. ______

Pattern 2_ 「주어 + be supposed to + 동사원형」

너는 오늘 빨래해야지.(do the laundry) ______

나는 오늘 오후에 Walf 박사님을 만나기로 했어. ______

너는 한 시간 전에 여기에 도착해야 했잖아.(get here) ______

내가 무엇을 하기로 되어있지? ______

내가 너 없이 어떻게 살아야 되지?(How~) ______

Pattern 3_ 「주어 + be to + 동사원형」

대통령은 말레이시아를 방문할 예정이다. ______

Smith씨는 곧 진급될 것이다.(be soon to, promoted) ______

Pattern 4_ 「주어 + could/might + 동사원형」

Shiela는 조만간 해고당할 수도 있어.(could, sooner or later) ______

나는 이번 주말 친구들과 함께 영화 볼 지도 몰라. ______

Jane이 너를 거기에 태워줄지도 몰라.(give you a ride) ______

Unit

05 현재진행시제 _present progressive

- Pattern 주어 + be동사(am, are, is) + 동사~ing
- Meaning ~하고 있다

Grammar in Practice

A: I don't feel well. I might have to *take off early.
B: You looked just fine an hour ago. What happened?
A: I think I'm coming down with a cold or something.
My throat is getting sore and my nose is starting to run.
B: You should go home and rest then.

*take off 떠나다, 퇴근하다

Grammar in Use

1. 현재진행시제

- 현재 말하고 있는 시점의 일을 나타낼 때 쓴다.
  "What are you doing?" "I'**m vacuuming** the floor." 너 뭐하고 있니? 나는 바닥을 진공청소기로 청소하고 있어.

- 일정한 기간 동안의 일을 나타낼 때도 쓸 수 있다.
  I'**m taking** a computer class these days. 나는 요즘 컴퓨터 수업을 들어.
  Are you **going out** with Benny? 너 Benny와 사귀니?

- 주로 always와 함께 지나치게 반복되는 버릇 또는 행동을 말할 때 쓰기도 한다.
  You'**re** always **forgetting** something. 너는 늘 잘 잊어버려.
  (=You forget something too often.)

- 가깝고 확실한 미래를 나타낼 때 쓴다.
  We'**re having** a surprise party tonight. 우리는 오늘밤 깜짝파티를 연다.

2. 진행형을 쓸 수 없는 동사

- 감정동사 (like, hate, dislike 등)
- 소유동사 (belong, have, own소유하다 등)
- 지각/감각동사 (know, understand, believe, remember, look~처럼 보이다, smell냄새가~하다, taste맛이~하다 등)

MORE TIPS 동사 have가 '소유'의 뜻으로 쓰였을 경우 진행형시제를 쓸 수 없지만 '시간을 보내다' 또는 '먹다, 마시다'의 뜻으로 쓰였을 경우 진행형이 가능하다.

I **have** a lot of work to do. 나는 할 일이 많다.
We'**re having** a great time here. 우리는 여기에서 좋은 시간을 보내고 있다.
My sisters and I **are having** lunch. 언니들과 나는 점심식사를 하고 있다.

3. 의문문과 부정문 만드는 방법

● 의문문

Am Are Is	I we/you/they he/she/it	studying? drinking?

● 부정문

I We/You/They He/She/It	am not('m not) are not(aren't) is not(isn't)	studying. drinking.

| MORE TIPS | 진행형을 이용한 간접적인 표현

보다 부드럽고 간접적인 표현을 사용하기위해 현재나 과거시제를 대신해서 현재진행이나 과거진행시제를 쓰는 경우가 있다.

- When **are** you **planning** to go to Europe? (less definite and direct than When do you plan to~?) 언제 유럽에 갈 계획이에요?
- I'm afraid I must **be going.** (less definite and direct than I must go.) 미안하지만 가야해요.
- I **was wondering** if you could help me. (less definite and direct than I wondered if~.) 나를 도와줄 수 있는지 궁금했어요.
- I'm **looking forward to** seeing you. (less definite and direct than I look forward ~.) 뵙기를 손꼽아 기다립니다.

Unit Test

1. **괄호 안의 주어진 단어를 사용하여 현재진행형 문장을 완성하시오.**

1. (I, take a shower) → (평서문) ______________________________
2. (My mother and I, do the laundry)
   → (평서문) ______________________________
3. (I, talk about money) → (부정문) ______________________________
4. (you, listen to me) → (부정문) ______________________________
5. (Jack, talk on the phone) → (의문문) ______________________________?
6. (the sun, shine) → (의문문) ______________________________?

2. **둘 중 문맥상 알맞은 것을 고르시오.**

1. I (know/ am knowing) what you're talking about.
2. Janet (has/ is having) lunch now.
3. (Are you hating/ Do you hate) to see horror movies?
4. (Is David having/ Does David have) a lot of money?
5. We (believe /are believing) in God.
6. Look out the window. It (snows/ is snowing).
7. My husband and I (usually eat/ are usually eating) cereal for breakfast.
8. Something (smells/ is smelling) like pizza.
9. (Does this belong/ Is this belonging) to you?
10. (Do you understand/ Are you understanding) me?

3. **우리말과 일치하도록 괄호 안의 단어를 알맞게 배열하시오.**

1. 모두가 졸고 있다. (is/ everybody/ dozing)
   ____
2. 우리 부모님은 요즘 Seattle에 살고 계시다. (are living/ my parents/ in Seattle/ these days)
   ____
3. 너는 늘 잘 잊어버려. (always/ you/ forgetting something/ are)
   ____
4. 내가 너를 방해하고 있니? (I/ bothering/ am/ you/ ?)
   ____
5. Jack과 Mary는 오늘밤 떠나니? (Jack and Mary/ are/ leaving tonight/ ?)
   ____
6. 우리는 여기에서 좋은 시간을 보내고 있다. (having/ are/ we/ a great time here)
   ____

Writing Pattern Practice 현재진행시제

Pattern 1_「주어 + be동사 + 동사~ing」 평서문(긍정문)

나는 바닥을 진공청소기로 청소하고 있어.(vacuum) ______

나는 요즘 컴퓨터 수업을 듣는다.(take, these days) ______

너는 늘 뭔가 잊어버려.(always) ______

Janet은 늘 불평이야.(complain) ______

Jack과 나는 뉴욕에 머물고 있어. ______

Pattern 2_「Be동사 + 주어 + 동사~ing?」 의문문

내가 너를 방해하고 있니?(bother) ______

너는 샤워하고 있니? ______

Jack은 전화 통화하고 있니?(talk on the phone) ______

네 여동생은 피아노를 치고 있니? ______

비가 오고 있니? ______

Pattern 3_「의문사 + be동사 + 주어 + 동사~ing?」 의문문

내가 무엇을 하고 있는 거지?(What~) ______

너는 어디에서 마시고 있니? ______

Jessy는 언제 떠나지? ______

그들은 왜 싸우고 있니?(fight) ______

너는 어떻게 지내고 있니?(do) ______

너는 누구에 대해서 말하고 있는 거야?(talk about) ______

Pattern 4_「주어 + be동사 + not + 동사~ing」 부정문

나는 영어를 공부하고 있지 않아. ______

너는 내말을 듣고 있지 않구나.(listen to me) ______

David은 낮잠을 자고 있지 않아.(take a nap) ______

우리는 너에 대해 이야기하고 있지 않아.(talk about) ______

Unit

06 과거진행시제 _past progressive

- Pattern 주어 + be동사(was, were) + 동사~ing
- Meaning ~하고 있었다

Grammar in Practice

A: You know what? I ran into Karen.

B: Really? Where did you meet her?

A: When I was walking home, I saw her waiting for the bus.

B: Does she live near here?

A: Yes, she moved here two months ago.

Grammar in Use

1. 과거진행시제

- 과거진행시제는 과거 어떤 시점에 계속 진행되고 있던 동작을 나타내는 것이다. 형태는 「주어+be동사(was/were)+동사~ing」이며 '~하고 있었다' 라는 뜻의 동작을 강조하는 문장이다.

  "What **were** you **doing** at 8:00 yesterday?" "I **was watching** TV at home." 어제 8시에 뭐하고 있었어? 집에서 TV보고 있었어.

2. 과거시제와 과거진행시제 비교

- 과거시제는 과거 어떤 시점에 일어나서 이미 끝나버린 사실을 사건 중심으로 나타낼 때 쓰는 반면 과거진행시제는 과거 어떤 시점을 기준으로 그 전부터 진행 중이던 동작이 계속되는 것을 부각시킬 때 쓰는 표현이다.

  [비교]

  When Terry arrived, **we were having a meeting.**
  (=We had already started the meeting.) Terry가 도착했을 때 우리는 회의를 하고 있었다.
  →회의를 그 전에 시작했다는 뜻

  When Terry arrived, **we had a meeting.**
  (=Terry arrived and then we had a meeting) Terry가 도착하고 우리는 회의를 했다.
  →Terry가 도착한 후 회의를 했다는 뜻

- 과거시제와 과거진행시제가 한 문장에 쓰이는 경우, 구조는 보통 다음과 같다.

  「When + 과거시세문장, 과거진행시제문장」
  When I met Ted, he was waiting for the bus. 내가 Ted를 만났을 때 그는 버스를 기다리고 있었어.

  「As/When/While + 과기진행시제문장, 과거시제문장」
  While you were taking a shower, Kate called. 네가 샤워하고 있는 동안 Kate가 전화했었어.

Unit Test

1. 괄호 안의 동사를 사용하여 과거진행형 문장을 완성하시오.

1. It ____________________ (rain) when I went out.
2. Mandy ____________________ (have lunch) when I saw her.
3. I hurt my finger while I ____________________ (cut) vegetables.
4. He ____________________ (try) to lift the heavy box when I happened to meet him on the street.
5. While I ____________________ (take) a shower, the doorbell rang.
6. As we ____________________ (take) a walk, it started to snow.
7. I ____________________ (watch) TV when the lights went out.
8. Peter ____________________ (vacuum) the floor when I got home.
9. While they ____________________ (sleep), a fire broke out.
10. I ____________________ (wait) for the bus when I bumped into one of my old friends.

2. 괄호 안의 동사를 사용하여 과거진행시제 또는 과거시제로 대화를 완성하시오.

1. A: What was she doing when you saw her?
   B: She ______________ (read) a book.
2. A: What happened to your finger?
   B: While I was cooking, I ______________ (burn) my finger.
3. A: How fast were you driving when the accident ______________ (happen)?
   B: I was driving at 70 miles an hour.

3. 다음은 Beth가 어제 한 일이다. 주어진 시간에 무슨 일을 하고 있었는지 과거진행형으로 쓰시오.

7:30-8:30AM
drive to work

8:30AM-1:00PM
2:00PM-6:00PM
work hard

6:00PM-7:00PM
have spaghetti for dinner

8:00PM-10:00PM
watch a movie on TV

1. What was she doing at 7:40AM? She ______________________________
2. What was she doing at 11:00AM? She ______________________________
3. What was she doing at 6:30PM? She ______________________________
4. What was she doing at 9:00PM? She ______________________________

Writing Pattern Practice | 과거진행시제

Pattern 1_ 「주어 + be동사(was/were) + 동사~ing」 평서문(긍정문)

나는 자고 있었어. ______________________

우리는 테니스를 치고 있었어. ______________________

Susan은 편지를 쓰고 있었어. ______________________

해가 밝게 빛나고 있었어.(brightly) ______________________

Pattern 2_ 「(의문사) + Be동사(was/were) + 주어 + 동사~ing?」 의문문

너는 일하고 있었니? ______________________

너는 빨리 운전하고 있었니?(fast) ______________________

Jack은 자전거를 타고 있었니?(ride a bicycle) ______________________

너는 왜 거기에서 울고 있었니? ______________________

너는 어제 밤 9시에 뭐하고 있었니? ______________________

Pattern 3_ 「주어 + be동사(wasn' t/weren' t) + 동사~ing」 부정문

나는 빨리 운전하고 있지 않았어. ______________________

나는 너를 쳐다보고 있지 않았어.(look) ______________________

Tom은 일하고 있지 않았어. ______________________

그들은 웃고 있지 않았다.(smile) ______________________

Pattern 4_ 「When + 과거시제문장, 과거진행시제문장」

내가 Ted를 만났을 때 그는 버스를 기다리고 있었다. ______________________

전화가 울렸을 때 Nicole은 TV를 보고 있었다. ______________________

Pattern 5_ 「As/When/While + 과거진행시제문장, 과거시제문장」

네가 샤워하고 있는 동안 Kate가 전화했었어. ______________________

내가 요리하고 있는 동안 나는 손을 데었다. ______________________

Unit

07 미래진행시제
_future progressive

- **Pattern** 주어+will/be going to + be + 동사~ing
- **Meaning** ~하고 있을 거다

Grammar in Practice

A: Is it OK if I come at 10:00?
B: No, We'll be having a meeting then.
A: Well, what about 12:00?
B: Fine. the meeting will have ended by then.

Grammar in Use

1. 미래진행시제

- 미래진행시제는 미래시점에서의 동작의 진행을 표현하지만 대체로 확정된 미래나 시간적으로 오래 지속될 미래를 말할 때 쓴다. 형태는 「주어+will+be+동사~ing」 또는 「주어+be going to+be+동사~ing」인데 will을 쓰는 경우가 더 많다.

  I'm leaving for Florida this Saturday. I'll **be lying** on a beach or **surfing** this time next week. 이번 주 토요일에 플로리다로 떠나. 다음 주 이맘 때는 해변에 누워 있거나 서핑하고 있을 거야.

  I'**ll be missing** you. 너를 그리워할 거야.

2. 「Will + 주어 + be + ~ing?」

- 상대방의 계획에 대해 물어볼 경우 사용하는데, 상대방에게 무언가 원하는 것이 있을 때 쓰는 경우가 많다.

  A: **Will** you **be using** your computer tonight? 오늘밤 컴퓨터 쓸 거야?
  B: Why? Do you need to use it? 왜? 네가 써야 돼?

  A: **Will** you **be staying** at home this afternoon? 오늘 오후에 집에 있을 거야?
  B: Yes. You can come over if you want. 응, 원하면 놀러 와도 돼.

| MORE TIPS | 미래진행시제는 확정된 미래나 오래 지속될 미래를 말할 경우, 또는 미래시제와 별 차이 없이도 우리가 알고 있는 이상으로 실생활에서 많이 쓰인다. 예를 들어 유명팝송 중에도 'I'll be loving you.' (by New Kids On The Block) 'I'll be missing you.' (by Puff Daddy) 등 미래진행시제를 사용한 제목이 많이 있다.

Unit Test

1. 괄호 안의 단어를 사용하여 미래진행형(will 사용) 문장을 완성하시오.

1. I __________________ (have) dinner at 7:30.
2. At 11:00 tomorrow, I __________________ (see) a movie with my friends.
3. Don't call me tomorrow morning. We __________________ (have) a meeting then.
4. The band __________________ (play) when you go in.
5. We __________________ (sit) on the bench for a while.
6. I'll give it back to Mary. I __________________ (see) her tonight.
7. Mark and I __________________ (lie) down on a beach this time next year.
8. "Can we meet tomorrow morning?" "I'm sorry, but I can't. I __________________. (work)"
9. What time __________________ Terry __________________ (arrive) tonight?
10. When __________________ Tom __________________ (leave) work?

2. 상대방의 계획을 물어보는 질문이다. 보기와 같이 미래진행시제를 사용하여 완성하시오.

보기 | Will you be going out tonight?

1. ________ you __________________ (use) your car today?
2. ________ you __________________ (work) tomorrow?
3. ________ you __________________ (stay) at home tonight?
4. ________ you __________________ (go out) for dinner?
5. How long ________ you __________________ (stay) here?

3. 우리말과 일치하도록 괄호 안의 단어를 알맞게 배열하시오.

1. 우리는 집에서 저녁을 먹고 있을 거야. (having dinner /will / we/ be/ at home)

   ____

2. 그는 그때 퇴근할 거야. (will/ he/ leaving work then/ be)

   ____

3. David은 그녀를 내일 만날 거야. (seeing/ David/ her tomorrow/ be/ will)

   ____

4. 너는 오늘 밤 집에 있을 거니? (at home/ staying/ you/ be/ will/ tonight/ ?)

   ____

5. 너는 얼마나 오래 네 컴퓨터를 쓸 거니? (using your computer/ you /will/ how long/ be/ ?)

   ____

Writing Pattern Practice | 미래진행시제

Pattern 1_ 「주어 + will + be + 동사~ing」 평서문(긍정문)

나는 일하고 있을 거야. ____________________

나는 너를 그리워할 거야. ____________________

나는 여기에서 서있을 거야. ____________________

나는 여기에서 앉아 있을 거야. ____________________

나는 여기에서 너를 기다리고 있을 거야. ____________________

나는 여기에서 아이스크림을 먹고 있을 거야. ____________________

나는 여기에서 전화통화 하고 있을 거야. ____________________

나는 소파에 누워 있을 거야. ____________________

그녀는 일본에서 영어를 가르치고 있을 거야. ____________________

그는 IBM에서 일할 거야.(work for) ____________________

내일 이맘 때 나는 스키타고 있을 거야.(This time tomorrow~)

____

다음 주 이맘때 나는 여행하고 있을 거야.(travel) ____________________

내년 이맘 때 나는 캐나다에 머무르고 있을 거야. ____________________

Pattern 2_ 「Will you be + ~ing?」 의문문

너는 오늘 네 차 사용할거니? ____________________

너는 내일 일할 거니? ____________________

너는 오늘밤 집에 있을 거니?(stay) ____________________

너는 저녁 먹으러 나갈거니?(go out) ____________________

너는 여기에 얼마나 오래 머무를 거니? ____________________

Unit

08 현재완료시제 _present perfect

● **Pattern** 주어 + have/has + 과거분사
● **Meaning** ~했다/ ~한 적 있다/~해왔다

Grammar in Practice

A: Look who's here! Jane Johnson!
B: Mark! Gosh, I haven't seen you *for ages! How have you been?
A: Terrific. How about you?
B: Well, the same old thing.

*for ages 오랫동안

Grammar in Use

1. 과거의 일이 현재에 영향을 미칠 때 쓰는 현재완료시제

● 과거 불특정한 시간에 일어난 일이 현재와 밀접한 관련이 있어서 두 상황을 동시에 생각하며 말할 때 현재완료를 쓴다. 형태는 「주어+have(has)+과거분사」이다.

예 I can't play baseball because I**'ve broken** my arm.

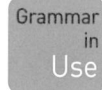

I've broken my arm.
I can't play baseball.

2. 현재완료시제의 숨은 뜻

I've forgotten his name. (=I can't remember his name now.)
나는 그의 이름을 잊어서 지금 생각이 안 난다는 뜻

I'm looking for Katie. **Have you seen her?** (=Do you know where she is?)
그녀가 어디 있는지 지금 알려줄 수 있냐는 뜻

Have you read the Bible? (=Do you know the Bible?)
성경책을 읽어본 적이 있어서 지금 그것에 대해서 알고 있느냐는 뜻

I've traveled in Australia a lot. (=I know Australia.)
호주를 여행해봐서 지금 호주에 대해 알고 있다는 뜻

3. 현재완료시제와 함께 쓰지 않는 부사(구)

- 명확하게 현재나 과거의 시점을 나타내는 부사(now, last night, two hours ago 등)와 함께 쓸 수 없다.

It has snowed last night.(X) → It **snowed** last night.(O)
The accident has happened two hours ago.(X)
→ The accident **happened** two hours ago.(O)

4. 현재완료시제와 함께 자주 쓰는 부사(구)

- 현재완료문장의 의미를 강조하거나 구체적으로 표현하기 위해 자주 쓰는 부사(구)는 다음과 같은 것들이 있다.

ever(한 번이라도)	never(전혀)	just(막)	yet(아직-부정문, 이제-의문문)
already(벌써)	since~(~이래로)	for~(~동안)	recently/lately(최근에) 등

Have you **ever** been to Italy? 이탈리아에 가 본 적이 있니?
I've **never** tried skydiving. 나는 스카이다이빙을 해본 적이 전혀 없어.
He's **already** cleaned the rooms. 그는 이미 방들을 치웠다.

5. 현재완료의 다양한 쓰임

- 아주 최근에 완료된 일을 말할 경우

I'**ve** just **had** a big dinner. 나는 금방 저녁을 잘 (많이) 먹었다.
Has it **stopped** snowing yet? (yet=until now) 지금 눈이 그쳤니?
*yet은 부정문과 의문문에서만 쓴다.

- 현재까지 계속 진행되어온 일을 말할 경우

It'**s rained** for a couple of days. 이삼 일 동안 비가 왔다.
"How long **have** you **known** her?" "I'**ve known** her for about three years." 너는 그녀를 얼마나 오래 알아왔니? 3년 정도 알아왔어.

- 지난 경험을 말할 경우

I'**ve been** to China twice. 나는 중국에 두 번 가봤다.
How often **have** you **been** in love in your life?
너는 이제까지 몇 번이나 사랑에 빠져봤니?

- '~해서 지금 …하다' 라는 뜻으로 결과를 강조하는 경우

"Is Tom there?" "No, he'**s gone** out." Tom 있어요? 아니오, 나가고 없어요.

| MORE TIPS | have been~은 '~에 가본 적 있다' 는 경험을 나타내고 have gone~은 '~에 가버리다' 라는 뜻으로 주어 I(나는)와 쓸 경우 어색하다.

- Ann **has gone** to Africa. Ann은 아프리카에 가고 없다.
- Ann **has been** to Africa. Ann은 아프리카에 가본 적이 있다.

Unit Test

1. **괄호 안의 단어를 이용하여 현재완료 의문문문장을 완성하시오.**

1. (you, ever, drive a car?) ______________________
2. (she, already, have lunch?) ______________________
3. (Ben, always, live, in Seoul?) ______________________
4. (how long, they, know, each other?) ______________________
5. (you, hear from Tom, lately?) ______________________

2. **둘 중 알맞은 것을 고르시오.**

1. Have you ever (been/ gone) to Italy?
2. "Is Mr. Kim there?" "No, he's (been/ gone) to work."
3. It's only 9. Has Jinny gone to bed (just/ already)?
4. I haven't finished my lunch (already/ yet).
5. Has it stopped raining (just/ yet)?

3. **보기와 같이 틀린 곳을 찾아 밑줄 치고 알맞게 고쳐 쓰시오.**

| 보기 | I'<u>ve tried</u> Mexican food yesterday. → <u>I tried</u> |

1. I have bought my car in 2000. → ______________________
2. Have you seen Monica on Tuesday? → ______________________
3. Molly has started her new job two days ago. → ______________________
4. Nina hasn't gone out with Ted last night. → ______________________
5. I've seen that movie yesterday. → ______________________

4. **우리말과 일치하도록 괄호 안의 단어를 알맞게 배열하시오.**

1. 너는 여행을 많이 해봤니? (a lot/ you/ have/ traveled/ ?)

____

2. 내 남동생은 핸드폰을 가져본 적이 없다. (a cell phone/ had/ my brother/ has never)

____

3. Tome은 막 출근했니? (Tom/ just/ has/ gone to work/?)

____

4. 나는 아침식사 이후로 아무 것도 안 먹었어. (eaten anything/ haven't / since breakfast/ I)

____

5. 우리는 Janet을 지난 달 이래로 본 적이 없어. (since/ haven't/ last month/ we/ seen Janet)

____

Writing Pattern Practice | 현재완료시제

Pattern 1_「주어 + have/has + 과거분사」 평서문(긍정문)

나는 금방 일어났다. ____________________

나는 그의 이름을 잊어버렸다. ____________________

나는 금방 저녁을 거하게 먹었다.(a big dinner) ____________________

나는 중국에 두 번 가봤다. ____________________

이삼 일 동안 비가 왔다.(a couple of) ____________________

Cindy는 이미 떠났다. ____________________

그는 나갔다.(나가고 없다) ____________________

Pattern 2_「Have/Has + 주어 + 과거분사?」 의문문

너는 그녀를 본 적 있니? ____________________

너는 일본에 가본 적 있니? ____________________

이제 눈이 그쳤니?(yet) ____________________

그들은 이미 나갔니? ____________________

Pattern 3_「의문사 + have/ has + 주어 + 과거분사?」 의문문

너는 (그동안) 어디에 있었니? ____________________

너는 (그동안) 어떻게 지냈니?(be) ____________________

너희는 얼마나 오래 서로 알아왔니? ____________________

Jack은 얼마나 자주 skydiving을 해봤니?(try) ____________________

얼마나 오래 비가 왔지? ____________________

그들은 얼마나 오래 서울에서 살아왔니? ____________________

Pattern 4_「주어 + haven't/ hasn't + 과거분사」 부정문

나는 그녀를 일주일동안 못 봤어. ____________________

나는 최근 잠을 잘 못 잤다.(lately) ____________________

너는 하루 종일 아무 것도 안 먹었다.(eat anything) ____________________

두 달 동안 비가 안 왔다. ____________________

그들은 아직 그들의 차를 팔지 않았다. ____________________

Unit

09 현재완료진행시제
_present perfect progressive

- **Pattern** 주어 + have(has) + been + 동사~ing
- **Meaning** ~를 해오고 있다

Grammar in Practice

A: It's been a long day. I'm exhausted.
B: You've been taking on too many projects lately.
A: I know.
B: Just get your *priorities in order and know your limits.

*priority 우선순위

Grammar in Use

1. 과거의 일이 현재까지 진행 중일 때 쓰는 현재완료진행시제

- 현재완료진행시제는 과거에 일어난 일이 현재까지 진행 중일 때, 또는 방금 전에 끝난 일이라도 현재에 영향을 미칠 때 쓴다. 형태는 「주어+have(has)+been+동사+~ing」이다.

It's **been raining** all day. 하루 종일 비가오고 있어.
I've **been waiting** for you for an hour. 나는 너를 1시간동안 기다리고 있어.
Where have you been? We've **been looking** all over for you. 어디 갔었어? 우리가 너를 여기저기 찾아다니고 있었잖아.
We**'ve been playing** badminton for two hours. 우리는 두 시간 동안 배드민턴을 치고 있어.
"What have you been doing?" I've **been vacuuming** and **doing** the laundry." 뭐하고 있었어? 진공청소기로 청소하고 빨래하고 있었어.

2. 현재완료진행시제와 현재완료시제 비교

- 현재완료진행과 현재완료시제의 '계속적 용법'은 내용상 큰 차이 없이 과거부터 지금까지 계속 되는 동작을 표현하는데, 단지 현재완료진행시제가 지금까지 일이 계속되고 있음을 더 강조한다.

[비교]
It**'s snowed** for a week. 일주일 동안 눈이 왔다.
It's **been snowing** for a week. 일주일 동안 눈이 오고 있다.

Henry **has worked** here for a long time. Henry는 여기에서 오랫동안 일해 왔다.
Henry **has been working** here for a long time. Henry는 여기에서 오랫동안 일해오고 있다.

You**'ve slept** all day. 너 하루 종일 잤구나.
You**'ve been sleeping** all day. 너 하루 종일 자고 있구나.

Unit Test

1. **괄호 안의 동사를 사용하여 현재완료진행형 문장을 완성하시오.**

1. I ________________________ (swim) all afternoon.
2. Mary and I ________________________ (play) tennis for two hours.
3. We ________________________ (learn) Spanish for six months.
4. It ________________________ (rain) for a couple of days.
5. It ________________________ (snow) since Tuesday.
6. They ________________________ (travel) since last month.
7. I ________________________ (work) very hard this week.
8. I ________________________ (teach) English since I was twenty-five.
9. My grandma ________________________ (garden) all afternoon.
10. You ________________________ (eat) all morning.

2. **평서문을 보기와 같이 의문문으로 바꾸시오.**

보기	He's been skiing all morning.→ **Has** he been skiing all morning? You've been learning English for years.→ **How long** have you been learning English?

1. Jane has been sleeping all day.
   → Has ________________________
2. You've been waiting for Terry.
   → Have ________________________
3. Her baby has been sleeping all afternoon.
   → How long ________________________
4. It's been raining for a week.
   → How long ________________________
5. She's been living in California for ten years.
   → How long ________________________

3. **우리말과 일치하도록 괄호 안의 단어를 알맞게 배열하시오.**

1. 하루 종일 비가오고 있다. (raining/ has/ it/ been/ all day)

   ____
2. 나는 8살 이래로 영어를 배우고 있다. (since/ have/ learning English/ been/ I/ I was eight)

   ____
3. 할머니가 정원 일을 오후 내내 하고 계시다. (has been/ my grandma/ all afternoon/ gardening)

   ____
4. 우리는 뉴욕에서 일 년 동안 살아오고 있다. (have/ we/ been/ in New York/ living/ for a year)

   ____
5. 얼마나 오랫동안 비가 오고 있는 거지? (has/ been/ how long/ it/ raining/?)

   ____

Writing Pattern Practice | 현재완료진행시제

Pattern 1_「주어 + have/has + been + 동사~ing」 평서문(긍정문)

하루 종일 비가오고 있어. ______________________

나는 너를 1시간동안 기다리고 있다. ______________________

일주일 동안 눈이 오고 있다. ______________________

우리가 너를 여기저기 찾아다니고 있었잖아.(look all over for)

____

우리는 두 시간 동안 배드민턴을 치고 있다. ______________________

Henry는 여기에서 오랫동안 일해오고 있다. ______________________

너 하루 종일 자고 있구나. ______________________

Mary와 그 때 이후로 테니스를 치고 있다. ______________________

우리는 스페인어를 여섯 달 동안 배우고 있다. ______________________

그들은 지난달 이래로 여행을 하고 있다. ______________________

나는 이번 주에 열심히 일하고 있다. ______________________

나는 스물다섯 살 부터 영어를 가르치고 있다.(since I was twenty-five)

____

우리 할머니는 오후 내내 정원 일을 하고 계시다.(garden)

____

Pattern 2_「(의문사) + have/has + 주어 + been + 동사~ing?」 의문문

너는 그를 (계속) 기다리고 있니? ______________________

비가 오랫동안 내리고 있니? ______________________

얼마나 오래 비가 내리고 있지? ______________________

너는 그를 얼마나 오래 기다리고 있니? ______________________

그들은 얼마나 오래 영어를 배우고 있니? ______________________

Unit

10 과거완료시제와 그 밖의 시제
_past perfect

● **Pattern** 주어 + had + 과거분사
● **Meaning** ~를 했었다, ~를 해왔었다

Grammar in Practice

A: How was your trip to Hawaii?
B: You know... It was the first time that I had been to Hawaii.
I had a lot of fun.

Grammar in Use

1. 과거와 과거보다 앞서 일어난 일을 구분 짓는 경우의 과거완료시제

● 형태는 「주어+had+과거분사」이다.

Janet **had** already **left.** | I got there.
과거완료 | 과거

Janet **had** already **left** when I got there. 내가 거기에 도착했을 때 Janet은 이미 떠났다.

| MORE TIPS | before, after 등 전후관계를 분명히 말해주는 접속사가 있는 경우 과거보다 앞서 일어난 일이라도 과거완료대신 과거시제를 쓸 수 있다.

- After I got home, I took a shower. 나는 집에 도착한 후 샤워를 했다.
- Before I went to bed, I gave him a call. 나는 잠자리에 들기 전 그에게 전화를 했다.

2. 과거이전의 일이 과거의 일과 밀접한 관련이 있을 경우의 과거완료시제

They had known each other for 10 years. | They got married.
과거완료 | 과거

When they got married, they **had known** each other for 10 years. 그들이 결혼했을 때 그들은 10년 동안 알고 지내왔었다.

3. 과거완료문장의 다양한 쓰임

The movie **had** already **begun** when I got there. 내가 도착했을 때 영화는 이미 시작했다.
It **had rained** for three weeks when I got to Seattle. 내가 Seattle에 도착했을 때 3주 동안 비가 왔었다.
"How was your trip to Florida?" "It was terrific. I **hadn't been** there before." Florida 여행 어땠어? 정말 좋았어. 전에 가본 적이 없었거든.

I had to get back to the store because I **had left** my umbrella there. 나는 우산을 두고 와서 가게에 돌아가야 했다.

4. 그 밖의 시제

● 과거완료진행시제(past perfect progressive)

과거완료진행시제는 과거보다 그 이전부터 진행 중이던 일이 끝나지 않고 계속될 때 쓴다. 형태는 「주어+had+been+동사~ing」이다.

Sarah fell ill because she **had been working** too hard. Sarah는 너무 열심히 일해서 아팠다.

We **had been walking** since sunrise, and we were very hungry. 우리는 해뜰 때부터 걸어서 몹시 배고팠다.

● 미래완료시제(future perfect)

미래완료시제란 현재의 시점에서 미래 어느 시점까지 완료될 사건을 예상하여 표현하는 시제이다. 형태는 「주어+will+have+과거분사」이다.

He'**ll have finished** the roof by Friday. 그는 지붕 일을 금요일까지 끝마칠 것이다.

We'**ll have been** married for ten years on December 1st. 12월 1일이면 결혼한 지 10년이 되는 거야.

Will he **have arrived** by the time we get there? 그가 우리가 갈 때까지 도착할까?

● 미래완료진행시제(future perfect progressive)

미래완료진행시제란 현재의 시점에서 미래 어느 시점까지 계속될 일을 예상하여 표현하는 시제이다. 형태는 「주어+will+have+been+동사~ing」이다.

Next month I'**ll have been teaching** for ten years.
다음 달이면 10년 동안 가르치게 된다.

Next year I'**ll have been working** at this company for twenty years.
내년이면 내가 이 회사에서 일한 지 20년이 된다.

WRAP-UP | 시제

12 시제	현재시제		과거시제		미래시제	
기본	현재	I study.	과거	I studied.	미래	I will study.
진행	현재진행	I am studying.	과거진행	I was studying.	미래진행	I will be studying.
완료	현재완료	I have studied.	과거완료	I had studied.	미래완료	I will have studied.
완료 진행	현재완료 진행	I have been studying.	과거완료 진행	I had been studying.	미래완료 진행	I will have been studying.

■ 매일 사용하는 기본시제 ▒ 상황에 따라 가끔 사용하는 시제 □ 자주 사용하지 않는 시제

Unit Test

1. 괄호 안의 동사를 사용하여 과거 또는 과거완료형 문장을 완성하시오.

1. Nobody ____________ (come) to the party because Anny ______________ (forget) to tell people about it.
2. The movie ______________ (already start) when we ______________ (arrive)
3. I couldn't find the book that you ______________ (lend) me.
4. When I came to my car, I realized that I ______________ (lose) my keys.
5. When we ______________ (paint) the kitchen, we ______________ (decide) to have a rest.

2. 다음 현재완료 문장을 괄호 안의 지시대로 바꾸어 쓰시오.

1. It has rained for a week.

(과거완료) ______________________________

(과거완료진행) ______________________________

(미래완료) ______________________________

(미래완료진행) ______________________________

2. I have lived in Italy for 10 years.

(과거완료) ______________________________

(과거완료진행) ______________________________

(미래완료) ______________________________

(미래완료진행) ______________________________

3. 다음 글을 읽고, 보기와 같이 질문에 답하시오.

On Sunday afternoon, everyone in my family was very busy. My father repaired his car; my mother did some gardening; Ted practiced his Taekwondo; Kate swam in the pool. I spent the afternoon cleaning my room.

보기	Who had dirt on her hands? Why? Mother, because she had been doing gardening.

1. Who had black *grease on his face and hands? Why? *grease 기름

____

2. Who was wearing a white uniform and a black belt? Why?

____

3. Who was all wet? Why?

____

Writing Pattern Practice | 과거완료시제와 그 밖의 시제

Pattern 1_ 「주어 + had + 과거분사」 과거완료시제

When I got there, Janet은 이미 떠났다.

When they got married, 그들은 서로 10년 동안 알아 왔었다.

When I got there, 영화는 이미 시작했다.(begin)

When I got to Seattle, 3주 동안 비가 왔었다.

나는 거기에 내 우산을 두고 와서, I had to get back to the store.(Because~)

Pattern 2_ 「주어 + had + been + 동사~ing」 과거완료진행시제

Sarah fell ill, 너무 열심히 일해오고 있어서.(because)

우리는 해뜰 때부터 걸어서 and we were very hungry.(since sunrise)

Pattern 3_ 「주어 + will + have + 과거분사」 미래완료시제

그는 지붕 일을 금요일까지 끝마칠 것이다.(finish the roof)

우리는 12월 1일에 결혼한 지 20년이 되는 거야.(be married)

그가 우리가 거기에 갈 때까지 도착할까?(~by the time we get there?)

Pattern 4_ 「주어 + will + have + been + 동사~ing」 미래완료진행시제

다음 달이면 10년 동안 가르치고 있는 게 된다.(Next month~)

내년이면 내가 이 회사에서 20년 동안 일하고 있는 게 된다.

REVIEW 1

1. **보기와 같이 술어전체에 밑줄을 치고 각 문장의 시제를 쓰시오.**

> 보기 | He <u>lives</u> in California. (현재)
> He <u>will live</u> in California. (미래)

1. He is living in California. (　　　　　　　)
2. He lived in California. (　　　　　　　)
3. He was living in California. (　　　　　　　)
4. He has lived in California. (　　　　　　　)
5. He has been living in California. (　　　　　　　)
6. He had lived in California before then. (　　　　　　　)
7. He had been living in California for 8 years. (　　　　　　　)
8. He will be living in California. (　　　　　　　)
9. He will have lived in California for 10 years next year. (　　　　　　　)
10. He will have been living in California for 10 years next year. (　　　　　　　)

2. **각 문장의 시제가 맞게 쓰였으면 T, 틀린 곳이 있으면 F를 쓰시오.**

1. I knew Mike since then. (　　)
2. She was out of breath. It was clear that she had been running. (　　)
3. That car is belonging to me. (　　)
4. I have a lot of work to do. (　　)
5. We have known each other for years. (　　)
6. We had been playing tennis for two hours when it started to rain. (　　)
7. I have had lunch at noon. (　　)
8. His hair was all wet. It had been raining. (　　)
9. Jane is wanting to get a wage rise. (　　)
10. You're always complaining about something. (　　)
11. I'll be seeing you one of these days. (　　)
12. Have you called me yesterday? (　　)
13. We've studied enough to pass the exam. (　　)
14. Have you ever seen a ghost before? (　　)
15. He has gone out two hours ago. (　　)
16. I'm hungry. I had not eaten anything since breakfast. (　　)
17. I didn't know who she was. I'd never seen her before. (　　)
18. "Was Cindy at the party when you got there?" "No, she has gone home." (　　)
19. That's a very old watch. How long do you have it? (　　)
20. Sally is a friend of mine. I've known her for a long time. (　　)

3. **의미가 통하도록 괄호 안의 표현 중 알맞은 것을 고르시오.**

1. Look out the window! (It snows./ It's snowing.)
2. Light (travels/ is traveling) about 300,000km per second.
3. We (didn't know/ weren't knowing) who she was.
4. David was waiting for me when I (arrived/ was arriving).
5. I (have thought/ thought) of moving to Paris since I was young.
6. I (know/ have known) her for years.
7. Peter and I (get married/ got married) in 2003.
8. "Have you seen Laura anywhere?" "I (saw/ have seen) her last night."
9. Tom (hurt his finger/ has hurt his finger) yesterday.
10. (Are you believing/ Do you believe) in God?

4. **문장을 괄호안의 지시대로 바꾸어 쓰시오.**

1. I start my new job.

(과거) ______________________________

(현재완료) ______________________________

(미래) ______________________________

(미래진행) ______________________________

2. I live in Boston.

(현재진행) ______________________________

(현재완료진행) ______________________________

(미래진행) ______________________________

(미래완료진행) ______________________________

3. Susan leaves for Seattle.

(현재진행) ______________________________

(과거) ______________________________

(과거진행) ______________________________

(과거완료) ______________________________

4. Jack works here for about a year.

(현재완료) ______________________________

(현재완료진행) ______________________________

(미래완료) ______________________________

(미래완료진행) ______________________________

REVIEW 2

[1-4] 다음 빈칸에 가장 적절한 것을 고르시오.

1. Brush your teeth before you ________ to bed.

① went
② have gone
③ go
④ will go

2. The Gulf War ________ in 1991.

① broke out
② has broken out
③ breaks out
④ will have broken out

3. Look out! We ____________________!

① are going to crash
② crash
③ have crashed
④ will have crashed

4. I ________ a computer class these days.

① am taking
② took
③ had taken
④ will take

5. 다음 글을 읽고, 괄호 안의 동사를 이용하여 미래진행시제문장을 완성하시오.

Mr. Watson, I'm going to be leaving the company soon. I have nothing but respect for this company, and have truly had a great time working here, but I've recently been offered a job that is just too good to refuse. I wanted to let you know as soon as possible so you won't have any problem finding a replacement. I ________________ (leave) in three weeks.

6. 다음 글을 읽고, 괄호 안에 들어갈 말로 알맞게 짝지어진 것을 고르시오.

Have you ever heard about Christopher Columbus? In 1492, nobody knew that there was America in the world. Most people thought the world was flat. "You will fall off the edge of the world if you go west." people said. However Christopher Columbus ________ the world was not flat. One day, Columbus sailed west to get to Asia with some sailors. Then one day they ________ land in front of them. But it wasn't Asia. It was America. They reached America instead of reaching Asia. This is how Columbus found America.

① thinks - saw
② thought - saw
③ has thought - have seen
④ thought - have seen

* Chapter 2 | 동사류

영어에서 동사는 문장에서 가장 중요한 핵심이다. 언어를 배운다는 것은 그 언어의 동사를 다루는 방법을 배우는 것이라 할 만큼, 영어에 있어서 동사와 관련된 부분은 문장 구조에 있어서 핵심적인 위치를 차지하고 있다. 문장의 뜻에 큰 영향을 미치는 시제, 부정문, 의문문도 동사나 조동사 중심으로 변화되어 쓰인다.

Unit

11 동작동사와 상태동사

● **Pattern** 주어 + 동사 (+목적어) ~
● **Meaning** ~는 …한다/…이다

Grammar in Practice

A: Are you going home? Do you want me to give you a ride?
B: Thanks, but I don't want to *put you out.
A: It's okay. I'm going past your place anyway.
B: I really appreciate it.

*put someone out ~에게 부담을 주다

Grammar in Use

1. 동작동사

대부분의 동작동사(go, come, eat, drink, cut, read, dance, study, write 등)는 사람의 행동을 주로 나타내며 단순시제와 진행시제 모두 쓸 수 있다. 동작동사가 현재시제로 쓰였을 경우 주로 습관이나 사실을 말한다.

[비교]
I **go** to church. 나는 교회에 다닌다.
I'**m going** to church. 나는 교회에 (지금) 가고 있다.

David **drinks** too much. David은 술을 너무 많이 마신다.
David **is drinking** too much. David은 (지금) 술을 너무 많이 마시고 있다.

2. 상태동사

상태동사는 사물의 상태나 구성, 사람의 지각, 마음의 움직임, 감정, 관계의 상태를 나타내는 동사를 말한다. 보통 진행형을 쓰지 않는다.

- 정신적인 활동과 관련된 동사: know, remember, realize, recognize, understand, believe, notice, suppose 등
  I **believe** in God. (I'm believing in God.→X) 나는 신을 믿는다.
  Do you **know** his phone number? (Are you knowing his phone number?→X) 그의 전화번호를 아니?

- 감정의 상태를 나타내는 동사: like, prefer, hate, want, desire, appreciate 등
  Which one do you **prefer?** (Which one are you preferring?→X) 어느 것이 더 좋니?

- 지각/ 감각동사: look, taste, smell, sound, feel, see 등
  Does the meat smell bad? (Is the meat smelling bad?→X) 고기 냄새가 안좋니?

- 그 밖의 상태 동사: belong, cost, fit, mean, own 등

This watch **costs** at least $1000. (This watch is costing at least $1000.→X) 이 시계는 적어도 1000달러는 나간다.

| MORE TIPS | 상태동사 중 다음 동사들은 의미가 달라지면(동작의 의미가 강해지는 경우) 진행형으로 쓸 수 있다는 사실에 주의한다.

taste	~맛이 나다	진행형 불가능	It **tastes** good. 그것은 맛이 좋다.
	맛을 보다	진행형 가능	Jane **is tasting** the soup. Jane은 수프를 맛보고 있다.
smell	~냄새가 나다	진행형 불가능	Something **smells** terrible. 뭔가 냄새가 지독하다.
	냄새를 맡다	진행형 가능	She's **smelling** the flowers. 그녀는 꽃들을 냄새 맡고 있다.
have	~을 가지고 있다	진행형 불가능	I **have** a boyfriend. 나는 남자친구가 있다.
	~을 먹다/ 마시다	진행형 가능	They'**re having** dinner. 그들은 저녁식사를 하고 있다.
	(파티 등)을 열다	진행형 가능	We'**re having** a party. 우리는 파티를 열고 있다.
think	~라는 의견이다	진행형 불가능	What do you **think** of the government? 정부에 대해 어떻게 생각해?
	~를 생각하다	진행형 가능	What **are** you **thinking** about? 뭐에 대해 생각하고 있니?
weigh	(무게가) 나가다	진행형 불가능	I **weigh** 60 kilos. 나는 60킬로 나간다.
	(무게를) 달다	진행형 가능	When I **was weighing** myself, the scares broke. 내 몸무게를 재고 있었을 때 저울이 고장났다.
see	~을 알다	진행형 불가능	I **see** what you mean. 무슨 의미인지 알아.
	~을 보다/ 만나다	진행형 가능	**Are** you **seeing** James? 너 James 만나니?

Unit Test

1. **다음 동사 중 동작동사를 골라 동그라미 하시오.**

know	eat	write	understand	belong	cost	walk

2. **다음 동사 중 상태동사를 골라 동그라미 하시오.**

notice	own 소유하다	read	study	like 좋아하다	cut	prefer	hate

3. **둘 중 알맞은 것을 고르시오.**

1. "What are you looking at?" "I (look/ am looking) at those beautiful flowers."
2. "How does it taste?" "It (tastes/ is tasting) like pizza."
3. Something (smells/ is smelling) good. Are you making dinner?
4. They (have/ are having) an important meeting now. You can't go in.
5. Sonny (has/ is having) a lot of money. He can afford to buy that car.

4. **틀린 곳을 찾아 밑줄치고 고쳐 쓰시오.**

1. This car is belonging to James.

→ ______________________________

2. My father is wanting a new car.

→ ______________________________

3. What am I doing? I have lunch now.

→ ______________________________

4. "What are they doing?" "They have a party."

→ ______________________________

5. Are you knowing his e-mail address?

→ ______________________________

5. **우리말과 일치하도록 괄호 안의 단어를 알맞게 배열하시오.**

1. 너는 너무 많이 먹고 있구나. (are/ too much/ you/ eating)

____

2. 너는 어떤 것을 더 좋아하니? (do/ which one/ prefer/ you/ ?)

____

3. Jason은 두 집을 소유하고 있다. (owns/ Jason/ two houses)

____

Writing Pattern Practice | 동작동사와 상태동사

Pattern 1_ 「주어 + 동사」 (동작동사/ 현재시제)

나는 공원에서 운동한다.

나는 샤워한다.

나는 아침을 먹는다.

나는 직장에 차를 몰고 간다.(drive)

나는 점심 후에 휴식을 취한다.

나는 퇴근 후 컴퓨터수업에 간다.(after work)

그는 학교에 간다.

그는 공부를 한다.

그는 그의 친구들과 점심을 먹는다.

그는 방과 후 축구를 한다.

그는 집에 간다.

Pattern 2_ 주어 + be동사 + ~ing」 (동작동사/ 현재진행시제)

나는 공원에서 운동을 하고 있다.

나는 샤워하고 있다.

나는 아침을 먹고 있다.

나는 직장에 차를 몰고 가고 있다.

나는 점심 후에 휴식을 취하고 있다.

나는 퇴근 후 컴퓨터수업에 가고 있다.(after work)

그는 학교에 가고 있다.

그는 공부를 하고 있다.

그는 친구들과 점심을 먹고 있다.

그는 방과 후 축구를 하고 있다.

그는 집에 가고 있다.

Pattern 3_ 「주어 + 동사」 (상태동사/ 현재시제)

나는 신을 믿는다.(believe in)

나는 남자친구가 있다.

너는 그의 전화번호를 아니?

너는 어느 것이 더 좋니?(Which one~)

이 시계는 적어도 1000달러는 나간다.

뭔가 냄새가 지독하다.(terrible)

Unit

12 사역동사

● Pattern	1. 주어 + make, have, let + 목적어 + 동사원형 2. 주어 + get + 목적어 + to 부정사
● Meaning	~에게 … 하게 하다

Grammar in Practice

A: Do you mind if I date John, Dad?

B: Go right ahead. He seems like a fine young man.

A: John and I are going to a party this evening. We might come home a little late.

B: Ok, I'll *let it slide this time but you should be back before 10:00.

*let it slide 봐주다, 눈감아주다

Grammar in Use

1. 사역동사

- '~에게 … 하게 하다' 라는 뜻으로 주로 5형식 형태 「주어+동사+목적어+목적격보어」로 쓴다. 동사에 따라 약간씩 의미의 차이가 있다.

He **made/had/let** me go. 그는 나를 가게 만들었다/했다/허락했다.
He **got** me to go. 그는 나를 가게 했다.

2. make

- '~에게 …을 하도록 만들다' 라는 뜻으로 「make+목적어+동사원형」 형태로 쓴다.

You always **make** me feel happy. 너는 항상 나를 행복하게 만든다.
My parents are trying to **make** me get married. 부모님은 나를 결혼하도록 만들려고 하신다.

3. have/ get

- '~에게 …을 하게 하다' 라는 뜻으로 각각 「have+목적어+동사원형」, 「get+목적어+to부정사」 형태로 쓴다.

I **had** Tom clean the house. 나는 Tom이 집을 치우게 했다.
I couldn't **get** Jane to change her mind. 나는 Jane이 마음을 바꾸도록 할 수 없었다.

4. let

- '~에게 …을 하게 허락하다' 라는 뜻으로 「let+목적어+동사원형」 형태로 쓴다.

Let me introduce myself. 제 소개 할게요.
That suitcase looks so heavy. **Let** me help you. 그 가방 무거워 보여. 내가 도와줄게.

| MORE TIPS | 목적어와 목적보어의 관계가 수동일 경우 목적보어는 과거분사를 쓴다.

- I got(=had) <u>my picture taken.</u> 나는 사진을 찍었다(찍게 했다). (my picture:목적어, taken:목적보어)
- I must **have** <u>my watch repaired.</u> 나는 내 시계를 고쳐야(고치게 해야) 한다. (my watch:목적어, repaired:목적보어)

Unit Test

1. **둘 중 알맞은 것을 고르시오.**

1. The police make him (confess/ to confess).
2. Let me (give/ to give) you some advice.
3. That sweater makes you (look/ to look) younger.
4. I had my brother (pick up/ to pick up) some milk on his way home.
5. I couldn't get David (give up/ to give up)

2. **틀린 곳을 찾아 밑줄치고 고쳐 쓰시오.**

1. Neil doesn't let anyone to read his secret diary. → ____________
2. I'll have the gardener to plant some trees. → ____________
3. That hat makes you looked prettier. → ____________
4. Those sunglasses make him to look younger. → ____________
5. Let me helped you. → ____________
6. Peter got me answer the door. → ____________
7. Please have Jack to call me back as soon as possible. → ____________
8. I can't get that child go to bed. → ____________
9. See if you can get the car starting. → ____________
10. I couldn't make John to change his mind. → ____________

3. **우리말과 일치하도록 괄호 안의 단어를 알맞게 배열하시오.**

1. 그 사람 들어오게 하세요. (him/ come in/ have)

____

2. 너는 우리를 항상 웃게 만든다. (smile all the time/ make/ us/ you)

____

3. 그 드레스는 너를 날씬해 보이게 한다. (makes/ that dress/ look thinner/ you)

____

4. 내가 여기에 있을 수 있게 해줘. (me/ let/ stay here)

____

5. 내가 잠시 그것에 대해 생각할 수 있게 해줘. (me/ think about it/ let/ for a while)

____

Writing Pattern Practice | 사역동사

Pattern 1_「주어 + make + 목적어 + 동사원형」 '~에게 …을 하도록 만들다'

너는 항상 나를 행복하게 만든다.(feel happy) ______________________

그는 나를 가게 만들었다. ______________________

그 드레스는 너를 더 날씬해 보이게 한다. (That dress, thinner)

____

내가 너를 당황하게 만들었니?(feel embarrassed) ______________________

내가 너를 피곤하게 만들었니?(feel tired) ______________________

Pattern 2_「주어 + have + 목적어 + 동사원형」 '~에게 …을 하게 하다'

나는 Tom이 집을 치우게 했다.(clean) ______________________

그 사람 들어오게 하세요.(him) ______________________

나는 내 여동생에게 내 숙제를 하도록 시켰다. ______________________

Pattern 3_「주어 + get + 목적어 + to 부정사」 '~에게 …을 하게 하다'

나는 Jane이 그녀의 마음을 바꾸도록 할 수 없었다. ______________________

나는 그를 설거지 하게 했다.(wash) ______________________

나는 Mary에게 우리를 돕게 했다. ______________________

Pattern 4_「주어 + let + 목적어 + 동사원형」 '~에게 …을 하게 허락하다'

제 소개할게요. ______________________

내가 도와줄게. ______________________

내가 여기에 있을 수 있게 해줘.(stay) ______________________

나는 그에게 내 차를 쓰게 했다. ______________________

Pattern 5_「주어 + make/have/get/let + 목적어 + 과거분사」 '~를 …되도록 만들다/ 시키다/ 허락하다'

나는 내 사진을 찍었다.(get) ______________________

나는 내 머리를 잘랐다.(have) ______________________

나는 내 귀를 뚫었다.(have, pierce뚫다) ______________________

Unit

13 감각, 지각동사

● Pattern 주어+감각동사+보어
주어+지각동사+목적어+동사원형/동사~ing

Grammar in Practice

A: What a beautiful dress!
B: Do you think it looks good on me?
A: Yes, and it goes well with your shoes.
B: It wasn't very expensive.
A: Really? It sure looks expensive.

Grammar in Use

1. 감각동사 look, feel, taste, smell, sound

감각동사는 사람의 오감으로 느껴지는 것을 표현할 때 사용하는 동사이다. 동사 다음에는 주로 '형용사' 나 'like+명사' 가 온다. taste, smell은 다음에 'of+명사' 를 쓰기도 한다.

look '~해 보이다'	"How do I **look**?" "You **look** great." 나 어때 보여? 너 좋아 보여. You **look** like Britney Spears. 너는 Britney Spears와 닮았어. *seem '~인 듯하다' 라는 뜻으로 쓰인다. He **seems** kind. 그는 친절한 듯하다.
feel '~한 느낌이 들다'	I always **felt** inferior when I was with her. 나는 그녀와 함께 있을 때 항상 열등감을 느꼈다. "How do you **feel**?" "I **feel** fine." 너는 기분이 어때? 좋아. Her fur coat **felt** so soft. 그녀의 털 코트는 촉감이 정말 부드러웠다.
taste '~한 맛이 나다'	"How does it **taste**?" "It **tastes** terrific." 맛이 어때? 훌륭해. This soup **tastes** mostly like(=of) garlic. 이 수프는 마늘 맛이 많이 난다.
smell '~한 냄새가 나다'	Those roses **smell** beautiful. 그 장미는 좋은 냄새가 난다. This soup **smells** funny. What's in it? 그 수프 냄새가 이상한데. 뭐 넣은 거야? *smell은 형용사 없이 그 자체로 '나쁜 냄새가 난다' 라는 뜻을 가질 때가 있다. Something **smells**. 뭔가 (안 좋은) 냄새 나. That dog **smells**. 그 개 (안 좋은) 냄새 나.
sound '(내용이/소리가) ~하게 들리다'	You **sound** unhappy. What's the matter? 너 목소리가 안 좋은데. 무슨 일이야? Your idea **sounds** great. 네 생각이 좋은 것 같아. You **sound** like my mother. 너 우리 엄마같이 말하는구나. "Let's go on a picnic this weekend." "That **sounds** like a good idea." 이번 주말에 피크닉 가자. 좋은 생각같이 들리는데.

2. 지각동사 see, watch, hear, feel 등

지각동사는 보고, 듣고, 느끼는 동사를 말하며 그 대상인 목적어, 그리고 그 목적어(대상)의 움직임을 표현하는 목적보어가 따라온다.

- 목적어와 목적보어의 관계가 능동일 경우 「주어+동사+목적어+목적보어(동사/동사~ing)」
  I **saw** you walk/walking down the street. 나는 네가 길을 걷는 것을 봤어.
  Did you **see** me dance/dancing? 내가 춤추는 것을 봤니?
  I like **watching** you eat/eating. 나는 네가 먹는 것을 지켜보는 게 좋아.
  I **heard** you yell/yelling at her. 나는 네가 그녀에게 소리치는 것을 들었어.
  Did you **hear** them fight/fighting? 너는 그들이 싸우는 것을 들었니?
  I **felt** someone move/moving in the kitchen. 나는 누군가 부엌에서 움직이는 것을 느꼈다.
  I suddenly **felt** an insect crawl/crawling up my leg. 나는 갑자기 벌레가 내 다리를 기어 올라오는 것을 느꼈다.

| MORE TIPS | 목적보어 자리에 '동사원형' 대신 '동사~ing'를 쓰는 경우는 동작의 진행을 강조할 때이다.

- 목적어와 목적보어의 관계가 수동일 경우 「주어+동사+목적어+목적보어(과거분사)」
  I **saw** the house painted. 나는 그 집이 페인트칠 되어 있는 것을 봤다.
  She **felt** her face touched. 그녀는 얼굴이 누군가에 의해 만져지는 것을 느꼈다.

Unit Test

1. **둘 중 알맞은 것을 고르시오.**

1. You look (happy/ happily).
2. Does it smell (good/ like good)?
3. That hairdo makes you look (pretty/ like pretty).
4. It tastes (good/ well).
5. Does it sound (a good idea/ like a good idea)?

2. **틀린 곳을 찾아 밑줄치고 고쳐 쓰시오.**

1. David saw me to dance. → ______
2. Did you see me cheated? → ______
3. I felt someone walked up to me. → ______
4. I watched them to play tennis. → ______
5. She felt her face touching. → ______

3. **우리말과 일치하도록 괄호 안의 단어를 알맞게 배열하시오.**

1. 너는 네 언니와 닮았어. (like/ look/ you/ your sister)

______

2. 뭔가 (안 좋은) 냄새가 나. (smells/ something)

______

3. 이 빵 마늘 맛이 나. (tastes/ this bread/ garlic/ like(of))

______

4. 그거 좋은 생각 같이 들린다. (like/ sounds/ it/ a good idea)

______

5. 너 우리 엄마같이 말하는구나. (like/ sound/ you/ my mother)

______

6. 나는 네가 학교에 뛰어 가고 있는 것을 봤다. (you/ saw/ I/ running to school)

______

7. 너는 John이 수업시간 내내 조는 것을 봤니? (see/ John/ doze over the class/ you/ did/ ?)

______

8. 나는 네가 춤추는 것을 지켜보는 게 좋아. (watching/ like/ I/ you/ dance)

______

9. 나는 그녀가 울고 있는 것을 느꼈다. (felt/ her/ crying/ I)

______

10. 나는 초인종이 울리는 것을 들었다. (heard/ I/ the doorbell/ ring)

______

Writing Pattern Practice | 감각, 지각동사

Pattern 1_ 「주어 + look + 보어」 …해 보이다

너 좋아 보여.(great) ______________________________

너 네 엄마와 꼭 닮았다.(just like) ______________________________

Pattern 2_ 「주어 + feel + 보어」 …한 느낌이 들다

나는 기분 좋아.(fine) ______________________________

그녀의 털 코트는 촉감이 정말 부드러웠다.(so) ______________________________

Pattern 3_ 「주어 + taste + 보어」 …한 맛이 나다

그것 맛이 좋아?(good) ______________________________

그거 맛이 정말 좋아.(terrific) ______________________________

Pattern 4_ 「주어 + smell (+ 보어)」 …한 냄새가 나다

이 수프 냄새가 이상한데.(funny) ______________________________

뭔가 (안 좋은) 냄새 나. ______________________________

그 개 (안 좋은) 냄새 나.(That dog~) ______________________________

Pattern 5_ 「주어 + sound + 보어」 …하게 들리다

너 목소리가 안 좋은데.(unhappy) ______________________________

네 생각이 좋은 것 같아.(great) ______________________________

너 우리 엄마같이 말하는구나.(You sound~) ______________________________

Pattern 6_ 「주어 + see/watch +목적어 + 목적보어」 ~가 …하는 것을 보다/지켜보다

나는 네가 길을 걷는 것을 봤다. ______________________________

너는 내가 춤추는 것을 봤니? ______________________________

나는 네가 먹는 것을 지켜보는 게 좋아.(watching) ______________________________

Pattern 7_ 「주어 + hear/feel +목적어 + 목적보어」 ~가 …하는 것을 듣다/느끼다

나는 네가 그녀에게 소리치는 것을 들었다.(yell at) ______________________________

너는 그들이 싸우는 것을 들었니? ______________________________

나는 누군가 부엌에서 움직이는 것을 느꼈다. ______________________________

나는 갑자기 벌레가 내 다리를 기어 올라오는 것을 느꼈다.(an insect, crawl/crawling up)

____

Unit

14 변화동사

- **Pattern** 주어 + become, get, go, come, grow, turn + 보어
- **Meaning** ~하게 되다

Grammar in Practice

A: A man kept calling and hung up on me all night.
B: Oh, my. Didn't you get his number from the caller ID on your phone?
A: It showed 'caller ID unavailable.' I'm going *insane.
B: Why don't you report it to the police?

*insane 정신이 나간, 미친

Grammar in Use

1. become : 「become + 형용사/명사」

- become은 상태의 변화를 나타내거나 시간이 흐른 후 어떻게 되었는지 말하고 싶을 때 쓴다.

It was **becoming** dark. 어두워지고 있었다.
What do I have to do to **become** a pilot? 파일럿이 되려면 어떻게 해야 하지?

2. go : 「go + 형용사」

- go는 색의 변화 또는 질적으로는 나쁜 쪽으로 변화할 경우 쓴다.

My mother **went** white with anger. 엄마는 화가 나서 얼굴이 하얘지셨다.
Everything **went** black and I passed out. 모든 것이 깜깜해지고 나는 기절했다.
*그 외 표현: go mad/ go crazy/ go insane/ go deaf/ go blind/ go grey/ go bald(대머리가 되다)/ go stale(상하게 되다)/ go flat(펑크 나다) 등

3. come : 「come + 형용사」

- come이 '~되다'의 뜻으로 쓰일 경우 대표적인 표현으로 come true, come right이 있다.

Your dream will **come** true. 네 꿈은 이루어질 거야.
You've got to trust me. Everything will **come** right in the end. 너는 나를 믿어야 해. 모든 게 결국은 잘 될 거야.

4. grow : 「grow + 형용사」

- grow는 서서히 시간을 두고 변해가는 느낌을 말할 때 쓴다.

The weather **grew** colder. 날씨가 추워졌다.
It's **growing** dark. 점점 어두워지고 있다.

5. turn : 「turn + 형용사」, 「turn into + 명사」

- turn은 눈에 띄는 확실한 변화를 말할 때 주로 쓴다.

The leaves are **turning** red. 잎들이 붉게 물들고 있다.
Tadpoles **turn into** frogs. 올챙이는 개구리가 된다.

6. stay, keep, remain : 「stay, keep, remain + 형용사」, 「keep + 동사~ing」

- stay, keep, remain은 '~ 상태를 유지하다' 라는 뜻으로 쓴다.

Stay awake. 계속 깨어있어.
Debbie **stayed** single. Debbie는 독신으로 있었다.
They **remained** silent. 그들은 (계속) 조용히 있었다.
Mary **kept** quiet. Mary는 (계속) 조용히 있었다.
I **keep** forgetting it's December. 나는 12월이라는 것을 계속 잊어버린다.

7. get : 「get + 형용사」, 「get to + 동사원형」

- get은 '~하게 되다' 라는 뜻으로 상태의 변화를 말할 때 구어체(informal)에서 가장 많이 쓰는 동사이다.

It was **getting** cold. 추워지고 있었다.
You **get** prettier every day. 너는 매일 더 예뻐지는구나.
Jack and Mary **got** married in 2002 and **got** divorced three years later.
Jack과 Mary는 2002년에 결혼하고 3년 후에 이혼했다.
David is nice when you **get to** know him. David은 알게 되면 좋은 사람이다.

동사 get의 다양한 쓰임 | Grammar Point |

동사 get은 일상생활에서 가장 많이 쓰는 동사 중에 하나로 문장에서 변화동사외에 여러 가지 역할을 한다.

1.「get+명사/대명사」 '~을 받다/ 얻다/ 이해하다' 등의 뜻이다.

I **got** a present from my friend. 나는 친구에게 선물을 받았다.
I **got** the picture. 감 잡았다.

2.「get+형용사」 '~되다' 의 뜻으로 상태의 변화를 나타낸다.

As you **get** older, your memory gets worse. 나이가 들수록 기억력은 나빠진다.

3.「get+과거분사」 우리에게 스스로 어떤 행위를 하게 되는 경우 쓴다.

예 get dressed/ get lost/ get engaged/ get married/ get divorced 등
I **got** married two months ago. 나는 두 달 전에 결혼했다.

4.「get+과거분사」 수동의 의미로 쓴다.

예 get broken/ get arrested/ get invited/ get paid 등
I **get** paid on 25th. 나는 25일에 월급을 받는다.

Unit Test

1. **둘 중 문맥상 알맞은 것을 고르시오.**

1. A prince (turns/ grows) into a frog in this cartoon fairy tale.
2. Anny (became/ got) a doctor.
3. David is nice when you (get to/ grow to) know him.
4. We (got/ grew) married in 2005.
5. My mother (went/ came) white with anger.

2. **빈칸에 들어갈 가장 알맞은 말을 보기에서 골라 시제에 맞게 써 넣으시오.**

보기 | keep, come, turn, become, get

1. I ________ to know a famous singer last night. 나는 어제 밤 유명한 가수를 알게 되었다.
2. Your dream will ________ true. 네 꿈은 이루어질 거야.
3. Mary ________ quiet. Mary는 계속 조용히 있었다.
4. What do I have to do to ________ a pilot? 파일럿이 되려면 어떻게 해야 하지?
5. That toy could ________ into a robot. 그 장남감은 로봇으로 변신할 수도 있다.

3. **우리말과 일치하도록 괄호 안의 단어를 알맞게 배열하시오.**

1. 그는 교수가 되기를 원한다. (wants to/ he/ a professor/ become)

____

2. 잎이 빨갛게 물들고 있다. (are/ turning/ the leaves/ red)

____

3. 점점 더워지고 있었다. (was getting/ hot/ it)

____

4. 네 꿈은 이루어질 거야. (will/ your dream/ come true)

____

5. 나는 두 달 전에 결혼했다. (two months ago/ got married/ I)

____

6. 모든 게 결국 잘 될 거야. (in the end/ come right/ everything will)

____

7. 세 블럭을 계속 가세요. (for three blocks/ going straight/ keep)

____

Writing Pattern Practice | 변화동사

Pattern 1_「become + 형용사/명사」

어두워지고 있었다. ______________________

파일럿이 되려면 내가 어떻게 해야 하지?(have to) ______________________

Pattern 2_「go + 형용사」

엄마는 화가 나서 (얼굴이) 하얘지셨다.(with anger) ______________________

모든 것이 깜깜해지고 나는 기절했다.(pass out) ______________________

Pattern 3_「come + 형용사」

네 꿈은 이루어질 거야. ______________________

모든 게 결국은 잘 될 거야.(in the end) ______________________

Pattern 4_「grow + 형용사」

날씨가 더 추워졌다.(colder) ______________________

점점 어두워지고 있다. ______________________

Pattern 5_「true + 형용사」, 「turn into + 명사」

잎들이 붉게 물들고 있다. ______________________

올챙이는 개구리가 된다.(Tadpoles~) ______________________

Pattern 6_「stay, keep, remain + 형용사」, 「keep + 동사~ing」

계속 깨어있어.(Stay~) ______________________

Debbie는 (계속) 독신으로 있었다.(stay) ______________________

Mary는 (계속) 조용히 있었다.(keep quiet) ______________________

그들은 (계속) 조용히 있었다.(remain silent) ______________________

계속 뛰어라.(Keep~) ______________________

Pattern 7_「get + 형용사」, 「get to + 동사원형」

점점 추워지고 있었다. ______________________

Jack과 Mary는 2002년에 결혼했다. ______________________

우리는 진실을 알게 되었다.(the truth) ______________________

Unit

15 능력의 조동사

- **Pattern** 주어 + 조동사 + 동사원형
- **Meaning** ~를 할 수 있다

Grammar in Practice

A: I have the *hiccups. I can't stop hiccupping.
B: Hold your breath for as long as you can.
A: I tried that, but it didn't *work. They keep coming back.
B: Then sip some water. That'll fix it.

*hiccups 딸꾹질, work 효과있다

Grammar in Use

1. can

- '~할 수 있다'는 능력을 말한다. 부정문은 cannot(can't), 의문문은 「Can+주어+동사원형?」 형태를 쓴다.

"**Can** you drive?" "Yes, I **can**, but I **can't** drive a truck."
운전할 수 있니? 응, 할 수 있어. 하지만 트럭은 못해.

2. be able to

- can 대신 be able to를 쓰기도 한다. 이때 be able to는 좀 더 딱딱한 느낌의 표현이다.

Jane **is able to** speak a few foreign languages. Jane은 외국어 몇개를 구사할 수 있다.

3. can 대신 반드시 be able to가 와야 하는 경우

- 조동사 다음에 올 때
  I'll **be able to** get there on time. 나는 정각에 거기에 도착할 수 있을 거야.

- to부정사와 함께 쓸 때
  I want to **be able to** get this report done by tonight. 나는 오늘밤까지 이 보고서를 끝마칠 수 있기를 원한다.

- 완료시제일 때
  I haven't **been able to** sleep well recently. 최근에 잘 잘 수 없었다.

4. can, be able to의 과거형

- can과 be able to의 과거형은 could 또는 was/were able to를 쓴다.

I **could** read when I was four. 나는 네 살 때 글을 읽을 줄 알았다.
I **wasn't able to** call you last night. 나는 지난밤에 너에게 전화할 수 없었다.

MORE TIPS 과거시제 긍정문에서 was/were able to가 could보다 특정한 상황에서 '겨우 ~할 수 있었다'라는 느낌이 강하다. 현재시제나 부정문에서는 별 의미차이 없이 쓰인다.

- I **could** ride a bicycle when I was five. 나는 다섯 살 때 자전거를 탈 수 있었다.
- A fire broke out in that building, but everybody **was able to** escape. 저 빌딩에서 화재가 발생했지만 모두 피할 수 있었다.

Unit Test

1. **be able to 또는 be not able to를 사용하여 문장을 완성하시오.**

1. Don't worry. I might ________________ make it to the meeting.
2. You'll ________________ speak English well if you do your best.
3. I'm busy working now. I ________________ be with you.
4. I want to ________________ make a lot of money.
5. Flowers ________________ survive without water.

2. **둘 중 내용상 알맞은 것을 고르시오.**

1. I'm afraid I (can/ can't) come to your birthday party.
2. Anyone (can/ can't) do it. It's simple and easy.
3. I (can/ can't) understand why you did it. I've never been able to understand you.
4. I was sick yesterday. I (could/ couldn't) eat well.
5. I lost my book. I looked everywhere, but I (could/ couldn't) find it.
6. I was sitting at the back of the classroom and (could/ couldn't) hear well.
7. We must (be able to/ can) speak three foreign languages to get that job.
8. Tim will (be able to/ can) come here tomorrow morning.
9. Ask Kathy about your problem. She might (be able to/ can) help you.
10. Terry may (be able to/ can) lend you that much money.

3. **우리말과 일치하도록 괄호 안의 단어를 알맞게 배열하시오.**

1. 너는 외국어를 말할 수 있니? (you/ speak/ can/ any foreign languages/ ?)

____

2. 나는 BMW를 살 여유는 없었다. (afford/ wasn't able to/ I/ a BMW)

____

3. 내 얘기 들리니? (you/ can/ hear me/ ?)

____

4. 내가 어떻게 이 복사기를 사용하지? (I/ how can/ this copy machine/ use?)

____

5. James got into the house, and 그는 가스냄새를 맡을 수 있었다. (smell/ he/ gas/ could)

____

Writing Pattern Practice | 능력의 조동사

Pattern 1_ 「주어 + can + 동사원형」 '…할 수 있다'

나는 운전할 수 있어. ____________________

나는 영어를 잘 말할 수 있어. ____________________

나는 너를 내일 아침 볼 수 있어. ____________________

Parker 씨는 12시에 당신을 만날 수 있어요. ____________________

나는 금요일에 너를 못 봐.(see) ____________________

Pattern 2_ 「주어 + am/are/is able to + 동사원형」 '…할 수 있다'

나는 정각에 거기에 도착할 수 있을 거야.(get) ____________________

그녀는 몇 주 후면 걸을 수 있을 거야.(in a few weeks)

____

나는 오늘밤까지 이 보고서를 끝마칠 수 있기를 원한다.(get this report done)

____

Jane은 외국어 몇개를 구사할 수 있다.(a few foreign languages)

____

나는 최근에 잘 잘 수 없었다.(sleep well) ____________________

Pattern 3_ 「주어 + could + 동사원형」 '…할 수 있었다'

나는 네 살 때 (글을) 읽을 줄 알았다. ____________________

나는 다섯 살 때 자전거를 탈 수 있었다.(I~) ____________________

Jane은 배드민턴을 잘 쳤지만 나를 이기지는 못했다.(beat(이기다))

____

그는 매표소를 찾을 수 없었다.(the ticket office) ____________________

Pattern 4_ 「주어 + was/were able to + 동사원형」 '…할 수 있었다'

나는 지난 밤에 너에게 전화할 수 없었다. ____________________

우리는 그를 설득할 수 있었다.(persuade) ____________________

저 빌딩에서 화재가 발생했지만 모두 피할 수 있었다. (A fire~, break out, escape)

____

Unit

16 허가의 조동사

● Pattern 주어 + 조동사 + 동사원형
● Meaning ~를 해도 좋다

Grammar in Practice

A: Bill. May I be excused a little early today?
B: No problem. Just be sure you have everything all *sorted out for tomorrow's meeting.
A: It's done already. The files are on your desk.
B: Great. I will see you tomorrow then.

*sort out 정리하다

Grammar in Use

1. 상대방에게 어떤 일을 허락할 경우 can, may

● You can~, You may~는 '~를 해도 좋다'는 뜻으로 상대방에게 어떤 일을 허락할 때 쓴다.
You **can(=may)** park here. 여기에 주차해도 좋아요.
You **can(=may)** give it back to me tomorrow. 그것을 내일 돌려줘도 좋아요.

2. 상대방의 허락을 구하는 경우 can, could, may

● Can I ~? Could I ~? May I ~? 는 상대방에게 허락을 구할 때 쓴다.
Can I take this book home? 이 책 집에 가져가도 될까?
Could I use your phone? 당신 전화를 써도 될까요?
May I help you with those bags? 그 가방 들어 드릴까요?

| MORE TIPS | 상대방의 허락을 구할 경우 다른 표현으로 'Do you mind if I~?' 'Would you mind if I~?' 등을 쓸 수 있다. 이때 긍정의 답을 할 경우 거절의 답임을 유의한다.
• "Do you mind if I smoke here?" "Yes, I do." 제가 여기서 담배 피는 것을 꺼리시나요? 네, 꺼립니다.

3. 상대방에게 불허하는 경우 cannot(can't), may not

● You cannot(can't)~, You may not~은 상대방에게 '~를 하면 안 된다'라고 할 때 쓴다.
You **cannot(can't)** go in. They're having an important meeting now. 들어가서는 안돼요. 중요한 회의가 있어요.
You **may not** smoke here. 여기에서 담배필 수 없어요.

| MORE TIPS | 규칙이나 허가 조항을 말할 경우 can(not)이나 may(not) 대신에 'be (not) allowed to~'를 쓸 수 있다.
• You're allowed to smoke here. 여기에서는 담배를 펴도 좋아요.
• You're not allowed to drink. You're underage. 너는 술을 마셔서는 안 된다. 너는 미성년자야.

Unit Test

보기	
	I'd like to use your phone. (could)
	→ Could I use your phone?
	Are children allowed to go inside? (can)
	→ Can children go inside?
	Swim here if you want to. (may)
	→ You may swim here if you want to.

1. **다음 문장을 보기와 같이 괄호 안의 지시대로 can, could, may를 사용하여 바꿔 쓰시오.**

1. I'd like to pay you tomorrow. (can)

→ ______

2. I'd like to have something to drink. (can)

→ ______

3. I'd like to *take a day off. (could) *take a day off 하루 쉬다

→ ______

4. I'd like to take it back to you tomorrow. (could)

→ ______

5. I'd like to take a coffee break. (may)

→ ______

6. I'd like to borrow your book. (may)

→ ______

7. Are we allowed to see that movie? (can)

→ ______

8. Are students allowed to use this library? (can)

→ ______

9. Are we allowed to smoke in this building? (could)

→ ______

10. Give it back to me tomorrow. (can)

→ ______

11. Use my car if you want to. (can)

→ ______

12. Go inside and wait. (may)

→ ______

Writing Pattern Practice | 허가의 조동사

Pattern 1_ 「You can/may + 동사원형」 '당신은 …를 해도 좋다'

당신은 여기에 주차해도 좋아요. ______

당신은 그것을 내일 내게 돌려줘도 좋아요.(give it back)

______

당신은 내 전화를 써도 좋아요. ______

당신은 내 자전거를 가져가도 좋아요.(take) ______

당신은 비디오를 봐도 좋아요.(watch) ______

Pattern 2_ 「Can/Could/May I ~?」 '내가 …를 해도 될까?'

이 책을 집에 가져가도 될까?(Can~, take) ______

네게 질문 하나해도 될까?(Can~) ______

당신 전화를 써도 될까요?(Could~) ______

내가 여기에 앉아도 될까요?(Could~) ______

그 가방들 도와 드릴까요?(May~, help you with~) ______

제가 도와드릴까요?(May~) ______

Pattern 3_ 「You cannot(can't)/ may not ~」 '당신은 …를 할 수 없다'

당신은 들어가서는 안돼요.(can't) ______

당신은 이 전화를 사용할 수 없어요.(can't) ______

당신은 여기에서 담배필 수 없어요.(may not) ______

Pattern 4_ 「You are/aren't allowed to ~」 '당신은 …를 해도 된다/ 안 된다'

당신은 여기에서는 담배를 펴도 좋아요. ______

당신은 그 컴퓨터를 써도 좋아요.(that computer) ______

당신은 술을 마셔서는 안돼요. ______

당신은 들어가서는 안돼요.(go in) ______

Unit

17 추측/가능성의 조동사

● **Pattern** 주어 + 조동사 + 동사원형
● **Meaning** ~일지도 모른다, ~임에 틀림없다

Grammar in Practice

A: What's good here, Ann?
B: Pasta and pizza.
A: Why don't we get 2 pizzas and 2 pastas? Oh, and a salad.
B: John, your eyes may be bigger than your stomach. You might need a *doggy bag.

*doggy bag 남은 음식을 싸가는 용기나 봉투

Grammar in Use

1. could ~일 수도 있다

That story **could** be true. 그 이야기는 사실일 수도 있다.
(=Possibly that story is true.)
David **could** be at the library. David은 도서관에 있을 수도 있다.
(=Possibly David is at the library.)

2. might, may ~일 지도 모른다

Take your umbrella. It **might** rain in the afternoon. 우산 가져가. 오후에 비 올지도 몰라.
(=Perhaps it will rain in the afternoon.)
Your parents **may** understand what you did. 네가 한 행동에 대해 네 부모님은 아마 이해하실 거야. (=Perhaps your parents understand what you did.)

| MORE TIPS | might과 may는 약한 추측의 뜻으로 쓸 경우 의문문에서 잘 쓰지 않는다. 대신 「Be+주어+likely to~?」 또는 「Do you think+주어+may/might ~?」를 쓰는 편이 자연스럽다.
예) 이번 겨울에 파리에 갈 것 같니?
• May/Might you go to Paris this winter? →X
• Are you likely to go to Paris this winter? →○
• Do you think you may/might go to Paris this winter? →○

3. should ~일 것이다, 보통 이론적인 배경이나 근거가 있을 때 쓴다.

Leo **should** be at work at this hour. Leo는 이 시간이면 직장에 있을 거야.
(=I have good reasons to believe that Leo is at work.)
Jessie **should** get here soon - she left home at six. Jessie는 여기에 곧 도착할 거야. 여섯시에 떠났거든. (=I have good reasons to believe that Jessie will get here soon.)
My boss is away, but he **should** be back tomorrow morning. 사장님은 안계시지만 내일 아침에는 돌아오실 거야. (=I have good reasons to believe that he will be back tomorrow morning.)

4. have(has) got to, must ~임에 틀림없다

You fell in love with David? You'**ve got to** be kidding. David과 사랑에 빠졌다구? 너 농담하고 있음에 틀림없어. (=I bet[=I'm sure] you're kidding.)

Susie **must** have a problem. She keeps crying. Susie에게 문제가 있음에 틀림없어. 계속 울잖아. (=I bet[=I'm sure] Susie has a problem.)

● **긍정추측** | Grammar Point |

말하는 사람의 확신의 정도에 따라 다음과 같이 구분하여 쓴다.

could < might < may < should < have(has) got to < must

0% 100%
불확실 .... 확실

예

She **could** be married. 그녀는 결혼했을 수도 있다.
She **might** be married. 그녀는 결혼했을 지도 모른다.
She **may** be married. 그녀는 결혼했을 지도 모른다.
She **should** be married. 그녀는 결혼했을 거다.
She **has got to** be married. 그녀는 결혼했을 거다.
She **must** be married. 그녀는 결혼했음에 틀림없다

5. might not, may not/ must not(mustn't)/ cannot(can't) ~가 아닐지도 모른다/ ~가 아님에 틀림없다/ ~일 리 없다

might not과 may not은 약한 추측에 대한 부정이고, must not(mustn't), cannot(can't)은 강한추측에 대한 부정으로 쓴다.

They **might(=may)** not know you're in Busan. 그들은 네가 부산에 있다는 것을 아마 모를 거야. (=It is possible that they don't know you're in Busan)

She isn't answering the phone. She **must not(mustn't)** be at home. 그녀가 전화를 안 받아. 집에 없음에 틀림없어. (=I bet[=I'm sure] she isn't at home.)

Sarah only left the office ten minutes ago. She **cannot(can't)** be home yet. Sarah는 단지 10분전에 사무실을 떠났어. 아직 집에 와 있을 리 없어. (=It is impossible that she is home.)

● **부정추측** | Grammar Point |

말하는 사람의 확신의 정도에 따라 다음과 같이 구분하여 쓴다.

might not 〈 may not 〈 must not(mustn't) 〈 cannot(can't)

0% 100%
불확실 .... 확실

예

She **might not** be sick. 그녀는 아프지 않을 지도 모른다.
She **may not** be sick. 그녀는 아프지 않을 지도 모른다.
She **must not(mustn't)** be sick. 그녀는 아프지 않음에 틀림없다.
She **cannot(can't)** be sick. 그녀는 아플 리가 없다.

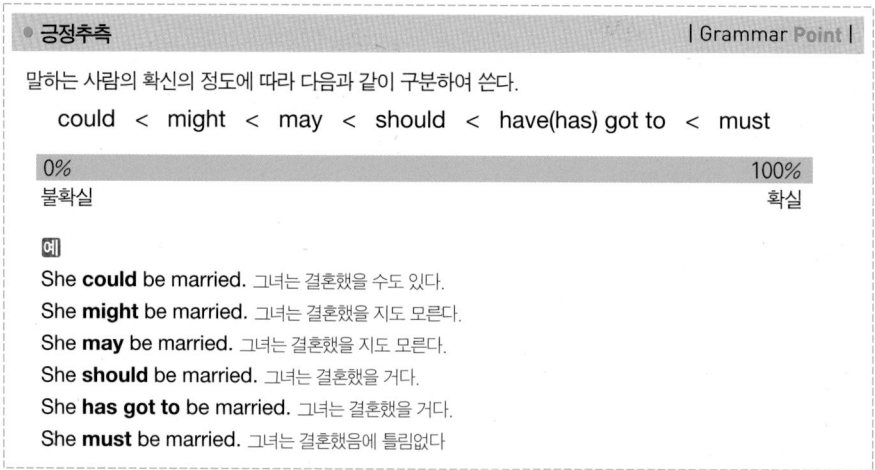

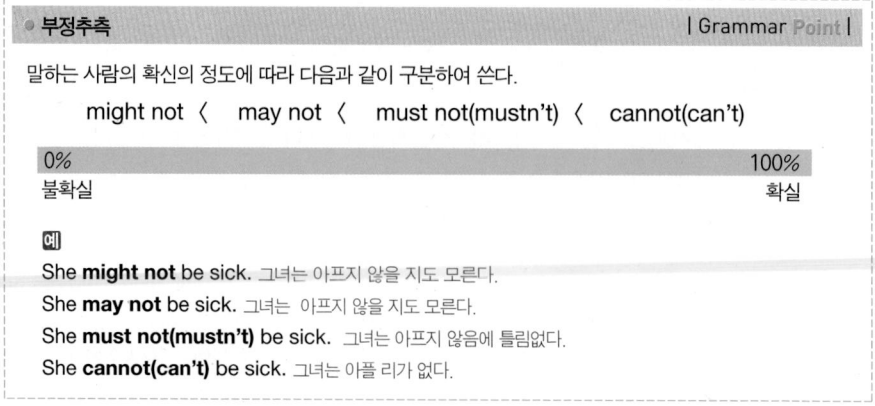

Unit Test

1. 보기와 같이 might를 사용하여 고쳐 쓰시오.

보기	Possibly Liz is at home. → Liz might be at home.

1. Possibly Bob is in his office. → ____________________
2. Possibly she knows where Jane is. → ____________________
3. Possibly it is David. → ____________________
4. Possibly she is working. → ____________________
5. Possibly he is taking a shower. → ____________________

2. 보기와 같이 must를 사용하여 고쳐 쓰시오.

보기	I'm sure Debbie is sick. → Debbie must be sick.

1. I'm sure you are tired. → ____________________
2. I'm sure you are joking. → ____________________
3. I'm sure your watch is expensive. → ____________________
4. I'm sure Jane is out. → ____________________
5. I'm sure that restaurant is very good. → ____________________

3. 보기와 같이 might not을 사용하여 고쳐 쓰시오.

보기	It is possible that she is not married. → She might not be married.

1. It is possible that this watch isn't cheap.
   → ____________________
2. It is possible that she isn't working. → ____________________
3. It is possible that he doesn't want to see me.
   → ____________________
4. It is possible that Elizabeth doesn't know the truth.
   → ____________________
5. It is possible that Bob isn't busy working.
   → ____________________

4. 보기와 같이 cannot(can' t)을 사용하여 고쳐 쓰시오.

보기	It is impossible that they are home. → They can't be home.

1. It is impossible that you are serious. → ____________________
2. It is impossible that this restaurant is good.
   → ____________________
3. It is impossible that he is hungry. → ____________________
4. It is impossible that there is misunderstanding between us.
   → ____________________
5. It is impossible that those shoes are expensive.
   → ____________________

Writing Pattern Practice 추측의 조동사

Pattern 1_「주어 + could + 동사원형」…일 수도 있다

그 이야기는 사실일 수도 있다.(That~) ____________________

David은 도서관에 있을 수도 있다. ____________________

Pattern 2_「주어 + might/may + 동사원형」…일 지도 모른다

오후에 비가 올지도 몰라.(might) ____________________

네가 한 행동에 대해 네 부모님은 아마 이해하실 거야.(may, what you did)

____

Pattern 3_「주어 + should + 동사원형」…일 것이다

Leo는 이 시간이면 직장에 있을 거야.(at work, at this hour)

____

Jessie는 여기에 곧 도착할 거야.(get) ____________________

Pattern 4_「주어 + have(has) got to + 동사원형」…임에 틀림없다

너는 농담하고 있음에 틀림없어.(kid) ____________________

그는 의사임에 틀림없어. ____________________

Pattern 5_「주어 + must + 동사원형」…임에 틀림없다

Susie는 문제가 있음에 틀림없어. ____________________

네 여동생은 60kg 넘게 (몸무게가) 나감에 틀림없다.(weigh, over)

____

그들은 축구를 하고 있음에 틀림없다. ____________________

Pattern 6_「주어 + might not/ may not + 동사원형」…가 아닐지도 모른다

그들은 네가 부산에 있다는 것을 아마 모를 거야. ____________________

Cindy는 아마 거기에 있지 않을 거야. ____________________

Pattern 7_「주어 + must not(mustn't) + 동사원형」…가 아님에 틀림없다

그녀는 집에 없음에 틀림없어.(at home) ____________________

그것들은 네 신발이 아님에 틀림없어. ____________________

Pattern 8_「주어 + cannot(can't) + 동사원형」…일 리 없다

그녀가 아플 리가 없어. ____________________

그가 지금 일하고 있을 리가 없어. ____________________

Unit

18 충고/경고의 조동사

- **Pattern** 주어 + 조동사 + 동사원형
- **Meaning** ~를 해야 한다, ~를 하는 게 좋다

Grammar in Practice

A: John, are you all right? You look a bit pale.
B: Does it show? I'm coming down with a cold.
A: I think you should see a doctor after work.
B: Yes, I guess so.

Grammar in Use

1. should, ought to ~해야 한다 〈충고, 의무〉

- should와 ought to 두 표현의 의미차이는 거의 없다.

"What **should** I do?" "You really **should** quit smoking. It's bad for your health." 내가 어떻게 해야 하지? 너는 정말 담배를 끊어야해. 건강에 나빠.
Everybody **should** wear car seat belts. 모든 사람들은 안전벨트를 매야 한다.
People **ought to** drive carefully. 사람들은 조심스럽게 운전해야 한다.

| MORE TIPS | 회화체에서 should는 상대방에게 충고할 경우 「I think+주어+should~」, 「I don't think+주어+should~」 형태의 구문으로 좀 더 부드럽게 표현할 수 있다.
- I think you should drive more carefully. 운전을 좀 더 조심스럽게 해야겠어.
- I don't think you should go and apologize to Katie. 네가 Katie에게 가서 사과를 해야 한다고 생각하지는 않아.

2. had better ~하는 편이 낫다, ~해야 한다 〈경고〉

- should와 ought to보다 경고성이 강한 표현이다.

You'**d better** turn that music down before your mother gets angry. 네 어머니가 화내시기 전에 음악 볼륨을 낮추는 게 좋아.
It's freezing out there. You'**d better** bundle up. 밖에 매우 추워. 껴입는 게 좋아.
We'**d better** stop for gas soon. 우리는 연료를 넣으러 멈춰야 해.

| MORE TIPS | had better는 경고성이 강하므로 본인보다 지위가 높은 사람이나 낯선 사람에게 사용하면 무례하게 들릴 수 있다. had better를 경고의 의미없어 부드럽게 표현하려면 「It would be good to~」를 쓰는 편이 좋다.
- It would be good to go and see the police. 경찰을 만나보러 가는 게 좋겠어.
- It would be good to thank him. 그에게 고마워하는 게 좋겠어.

| MORE TIPS | had better와 비슷하게 생긴 would rather는 선택의 상황에서 쓰는 말로 '차라리/그냥 ~하겠다' 라는 뜻이다. had better와 구분하여 사용해야 한다.
- I don't feel like going out. I would rather stay home. 나길 기분이 아니야. 치리리 집에 있을래.

3. should not(shouldn't) ~ 해서는 안 된다 〈충고, 의무〉

- should와 ought to의 부정은 주로 should not(shouldn't)를 쓴다. ought not to(oughtn't)는 흔히 쓰는 표현이 아니다. 「I don't think 주어+should~」 형태로 좀 더 부드럽게 표현할 수 있다.

People **shouldn't** drink and drive. 사람들은 음주운전을 해서는 안 된다.

I don't think you **should** work so hard. 네가 그렇게 열심히 일해야 한다고 생각하지 않아.

I don't think the government **should** raise taxes. 정부가 세금을 인상해야 한다고 생각하지 않는다.

4. had better not ~하지 않는 게 낫다, ~해서는 안 된다 〈경고〉

You'**d better not** bother Kate today. She's not in a good mood. 오늘은 Kate를 귀찮게하지 마라. 그녀는 기분이 안 좋아.

| MORE TIPS | 상대방에게 충고와 제안을 할 경우 「I suggest that 주어+동사원형」 형태를 쓰기도 한다.

- **I suggest that** you take a vacation. 나는 네가 휴가를 갖기를 권한다.
- **Mary suggested that** I buy some new clothes. Mary는 나에게 새 옷을 좀 사라고 권했다.
- **They suggested that** I get a job in a bank. 그들은 나에게 은행에서 직장을 구하라고 권했다.

Unit Test

1. should 또는 shouldn't 중 내용상 알맞은 것을 골라 써 넣으시오.

1. We _________ drive too fast on the highway.
2. You look tired. I think you _________ take a vacation.
3. Drivers _________ use their cell phones when they drive.
4. I don't think you _________ go on a diet. You're skinny enough.
5. You really _________ stop smoking. It's bad for you.

2. had better 또는 had better not 중 알맞은 것을 골라 써 넣으시오.

1. You look pale. You _________________ see a doctor right now.
2. It's freezing out there. You _________________ go out.
3. You _________________ listen to what I'm saying. It's very important.
4. We _________________ leave now. It's getting late.
5. You _________________ speed up. You're going to crash that car.

3. should를 사용하여 보기와 같이 의문문을 완성하시오.

보기 | how much butter to buy → <u>How much butter should I buy?</u>

1. how long to wait → ______________________
2. where to put my bike → ______________________
3. what to do on the weekend → ______________________
4. when to return this book → ______________________
5. how to cook a crab → ______________________

4. 보기와 같이 각자의 생각을 적어보시오.

보기 | I think people should <u>exercise.</u>

1. I think people should ______________________
2. I don't think people should ______________________
3. I think children should ______________________
4. I don't think children should ______________________
5. I think my father/ mother should ______________________

Writing Pattern Practice | 충고/ 경고 조동사

Pattern 1_「주어 + should + 동사원형」…해야 한다

나는 하루에 한 번 이 약을 먹어야 한다.(take) ____________________

너는 정말 담배를 끊어야해.(quit) ____________________

너는 사과해야해. ____________________

너는 이 일에 지원해야해.(apply for) ____________________

너는 잠자리에 들어야해. ____________________

너는 운전을 좀 더 조심스럽게 해야겠어.(I think~) ____________________

Pattern 2_「주어 + ought to + 동사원형」…해야 한다

사람들은 조심스럽게 운전해야 한다. ____________________

너는 부츠를 신어야해. ____________________

우리는 그것을 명심해야 한다.(keep that in mind) ____________________

Pattern 3_「주어 + had better('d better) + 동사원형」…하는 편이 낫다

네 어머니가 화내시기 전에 노래 볼륨을 낮추는 게 좋아.(turn that music down)

____

너는 껴입는 게 좋아.(bundle up) ____________________

너는 조용히 하는 게 좋아. ____________________

Pattern 4_「주어 + should not(shoudn't) + 동사원형」…해서는 안 된다

너는 회의에 늦어서는 안 된다.(late for) ____________________

사람들은 너무 많이 먹어서는 안 된다. ____________________

그들은 결혼해서는 안 된다.(I don't think~) ____________________

Pattern 5_「주어 + had better not('d better not) + 동사원형」…하지 않는 게 낫다

너는 늦지 않는 게 좋아. ____________________

너는 밤새지 않는 게 좋아.(stay up all night) ____________________

너는 그를 방해하지 않는 게 좋아.(bother) ____________________

Unit

19 의무의 조동사

- **Pattern** 주어 + 조동사 + 동사원형
- **Meaning** ~를 해야 한다

Grammar in Practice

A: Are you free on Saturday?
B: Yeah, I'm not tied up with anything. Why?
A: Why don't we go to the amusement park? I've got two free passes.
B: That sounds interesting, but I have to say no. I don't like riding on a roller coaster.

Grammar in Use

1. **have to/ has to ~을 해야 한다 〈의무〉**
I can't meet you tonight. I **have to** work late. 오늘밤 너를 못 만나. 늦게까지 일 해야 해.
Ann really **has to** cut down on sweets. Ann은 정말 단 음식을 줄여야한다.
Do I **have to** clean all the rooms? 내가 모든 방을 치워야하니?

2. **have got to/ has got to ~을 해야 한다 (=have to/has to) 〈의무〉**
I**'ve got to** go home right now. It's already 11:00. 나는 지금 당장 가야해. 벌써 11시야.
Tom can't come to work tomorrow morning. He**'s got to** see the dentist.
Tom이 내일 아침 회사에 못 와. 치과에 가야하거든.
Have you **got to** leave this early? 이렇게 일찍 가야해?

3. **must ~을 꼭 해야 한다 〈의무〉**
This is a terrible party. I really **must** go home. 끔찍한 파티다. 정말 집에 가야 되겠어.
Must you watch me eating like that? 그렇게 내가 먹고 있는 거 봐야하니?

4. **don't/ doesn't have to ~을 할 필요 없다 〈불필요〉**
I **don't have to** wear a tie at work. 나는 직장에서 넥타이를 맬 필요가 없다.
Tomorrow is a holiday. I **don't have to** work. 내일은 휴일이야. 나는 일할 필요가 없어.
It's rained a lot. We **don't have to** water the garden. 비가 많이 왔어. 우리는 정원에 물을 줄 필요가 없어.

5. must not(mustn't) ~을 해서는 안 된다 〈금지〉

You **must not** make a U-turn here. 너는 여기에서 U턴을 해서는 안 된다.

Residents **must not** hang washing out of the windows. 주민들은 빨래를 창 밖에 널어서는 안 된다.

You **must not** bother your father while he's working. 너는 네 아버지가 일하시는 동안 방해를 해서는 안 된다.

6. 미래형 ~을 해야 할 것이다

- will must는 불가능하므로 미래형은 보통 will have to를 사용한다. 하지만 이미 정한 일이라면 그냥 have (got) to를 쓸 수 있다.

  Next year I'**ll have to** get a job. 나는 내년에 직장을 구해야한다.

  I don't feel well. I **have (got) to** see a doctor tomorrow. 몸이 안 좋아. 내일 병원에 가야겠어.

| MORE TIPS | must는 지켜야할 규칙이나 지시사항을 말할 경우 미래문장에서 쓰인다.

• You can borrow this book, but you **must** bring it back tomorrow. 이 책을 빌려가도 좋지만 내일 가져와야 해.

7. 과거형 ~을 해야 했다

- must와 have got to는 과거형이 없으므로 had to를 쓴다.

  Edward **had to** stay up late last night. Edward는 어제 밤늦게 잠들어야 했다.

  Did you **have to** work yesterday? 어제 일해야 했어?

| MORE TIPS |

have to(have got to)와 must의 비교

have to(have got to)	must
1. 필요와 의무 I **have to(have got to)** study English.	1. 필요와 의무 강조 (보다 긴급한/ 중요한 상황) I **must** study English.
2. 객관적인 의무를 강조 I **have to(have got to)** stop smoking. (의사선생님이나 건강상의 이유로 담배를 끊어야 하는 경우) Do you **have to** wear a tie? (넥타이를 매야하는 규칙이 있는지 묻는 경우)	2. 말하는 사람이나 듣는 사람의 주관적인 느낌과 강한 의지 강조 I **must** stop smoking. (내가 담배를 끊기를 정말 원하는 경우) **Must** you wear that tie? (네가 그 넥타이를 매기를 정말 원하는지 질문하는 경우)

Unit Test

1. **보기와 같이 평서문을 의문문으로 바꾸시오.**

보기		
	I have to leave now.	→ Do I have to leave now?
	You have got to work hard.	→ Have you got to work hard?
	He must park here.	→ Must he park here?

1. I have to go to the hospital. → ______________________
2. Jack has to work late. → ______________________
3. We must get to the store before 8. → ______________________
4. She's got to visit her aunt. → ______________________
5. They had to stay up all night. → ______________________

2. **긍정문을 don't/ doesn't have to를 사용하여 부정문으로 바꾸시오.**

1. We must hurry up.

→ ______________________

2. Kimberly has to get up early tomorrow morning.

→ ______________________

3. You must get a visa to go to the United States.

→ ______________________

3. **have to, has to 또는 had to 중 알맞은 것을 골라 써 넣으시오.**

1. "You're wearing a suit." "I __________ go for a job interview now."
2. There was nobody to help John. He __________ do everything by himself.
3. I can't talk to you now. I __________ make an important phone call right away.
4. Susan __________ see the dentist. Her tooth really hurts.
5. I left before the end of the class. I __________ go home early.

4. **don't have to, doesn't have to 또는 mustn't 중 알맞은 것을 골라 써 넣으시오.**

1. Jack works from Monday to Friday. He ______________ work on Saturdays.
2. I don't want anyone to know. You ______________ tell anyone.
3. You ______________ be a good player to enjoy a game of soccer.
4. The plane is taking off. People ______________ walk around.
5. Tomorrow is Sunday. Sally ______________ get up early.

Writing Pattern Practice | 의무의 조동사

Pattern 1_ 「주어 + have to + 동사원형」 …을 해야 한다

나는 늦게까지 일 해야 해. ______

Ann은 정말 단 음식을 줄여야한다.(cut down on sweets)

______

내가 모든 방들을 치워야하니? ______

Pattern 2_ 「주어 + have got to + 동사원형」 …을 해야 한다

나는 지금 당장 가야해.(right now) ______

그는 치과에 가야해.(see the dentist) ______

너는 이렇게 일찍 가야하니? ______

Pattern 3_ 「주어 + must + 동사원형」 …을 꼭 해야 한다

나는 정말 집에 가야 되겠어. ______

너는 그 넥타이를 매야하니?(wear that tie) ______

Pattern 4_ 「주어 + don't/ doesn't have to + 동사원형」 …을 할 필요 없다

나는 직장에서 넥타이를 맬 필요가 없어.(wear a tie at work)

______

우리는 정원에 물을 줄 필요가 없어.(water) ______

Pattern 5_ 「주어 + must not(mustn't) + 동사원형」 …을 해서는 안 된다

너는 여기에서 U턴을 해서는 안 된다.(make) ______

너는 네 아버지가 일하시는 동안 방해를 해서는 안 된다.(bother, while)

______

Pattern 6_ 「주어 + will have to + 동사원형」 …을 해야 할 것이다

나는 내년에 직장을 구해야 할 거야.(get) ______

너는 오늘 오후에 Jack을 만나야 할 거야. ______

Pattern 7_ 「주어 + had to + 동사원형」 …을 해야 했다

Edward는 어제 밤늦게 잠들어야 했다.(stay up late)

______

너는 어제 일해야 했니? ______

Unit
20 부탁/제안의 조동사

- Pattern 조동사 + 주어 + 동사원형?
- Meaning ~해줄래(요)?, ~할까(요)?

Grammar in Practice

A: Would you mind taking our picture?
B: Not at all. How does it work?
A: Just press the button on the top of the camera.
B: All right. Here we go. Cheese!

Grammar in Use

1. 부탁하기

상대방에게 부탁할 때 can, will, could, would 등의 조동사를 써서 표현한다.

less polite
Can you give me a hand? 도와줄래?
Will you be quiet, please? 좀 조용히 해 줄래?
Could you help me with this bag? 이 가방 좀 들어줄래요?
Would you watch the children for a few minutes? 잠시 아이들 봐 주실래요?
more polite
Would you mind taking our picture? 사진 좀 찍어주실래요?

부탁	Can you ~?/ Will you ~?/ Could you~?/ Would you~?	
답변	〈긍정〉 Sure./ Certainly./ Yes, I'd love to.	〈부정〉 I'm sorry, but I can't./ I'd love to, but I can't.

* Would you mind ~ing?의 질문에 "Yes."는 거절의 답이므로 긍정의 대답을 할 경우 "No," "Not at all," "Of course not" 등을 쓴다는 점을 유의한다.

2. 제안하기

상대방에게 '~하자' 또는 '우리 ~ 하는 게 어때?' 라고 제안하는 말이다.

Let's go for a walk. 산책가자.
Why don't we go out for dinner? 우리 저녁 나가서 먹을까?
How about seeing a movie tonight? 오늘밤 영화 보는 게 어때?

제안	Let's ~/ Why don't we ~?/ How (What) about ~ing?	
답변	〈긍정〉 That sounds good. That would be nice.	〈부정〉 I'm sorry, but I can't. I'd love to, but I can't.

| MORE TIPS | Why don't we~?, Why don't you~?, Why don't I~?는 각각 '우리 ~ 하는 게 어때?', '너 ~ 하는 게 어떠니?', '나 ~ 할까?' 라는 뜻으로 의미가 서로 다르다.

[비교]
Why don't we go out for a walk? 우리 산책 나가는 게 어떨까?
Why don't you buy some new clothes? 너 새 옷을 사는 게 어때?
Why don't I just skip the class? 나 그냥 수업 빼먹을까?

Unit Test

1. **보기와 같이 괄호 안의 단어를 사용하여 바꿔 쓰시오.**

보기 | I want you to lend me some money.(can) → Can you lend me some money?

1. I want you to pass the salt. (can)

→ ______________________________

2. I want you to pick me up. (could)

→ ______________________________

3. I want you to give me a ride to the airport. (will)

→ ______________________________

4. I want you to explain it to me again. (would)

→ ______________________________

5. I want you to open the window. (would ~ mind)

→ ______________________________

2. **보기와 같이 괄호 안의 단어를 사용하여 바꿔 쓰시오.**

보기 | I want to go to the amusement park with you. (let's) → Let's go to the amusement park.

1. I want to go to see a movie with you. (let's)

→ ______________________________

2. I want to take a coffee break with you. (why don't we)

→ ______________________________

3. I want to go on a picnic with you. (how about)

→ ______________________________

3. **다음은 두 사람의 대화다. why don't we ~?와 why don't you ~? 중 적절한 표현을 빈칸에 써 넣으시오.**

1. "I'm hungry. I feel like eating something." "____________________ eat some cake?"
2. "Tomorrow is Susan's birthday. What should I buy?" "____________________ buy a necklace?"
3. "The weather is nice.____________________ go on a picnic together?" "Sounds good."
4. "I have a toothache. it really hurts." "____________________ see the dentist right away?"
5. "Let's do something fun. I'm a little bored." "____________________ rent a movie?"

Writing Pattern Practice | 부탁/제안의 조동사

Pattern 1_ 「Can you + 동사원형?」 …해줄래(요)?

도와줄래?(give me a hand) ______________________

부탁 들어줄래?(do me a favor) ______________________

Pattern 2_ 「Will you + 동사원형?」 …해줄래(요)?

조용히 해 줄래?(, please?) ______________________

문 열어줄래? ______________________

Pattern 3_ 「Could you + 동사원형?」 …해줄래요?

이 가방을 들어줄래요?(help me with) ______________________

내게 돈 좀 빌려줄래요? ______________________

Pattern 4_ 「Would you + 동사원형?」 …해줄래요?

아이들 봐주실래요?(watch) ______________________

내게 소금을 건네주시겠어요? ______________________

Pattern 5_ 「Would you mind + 동사~ing?」 …해줄래요?

우리 사진 좀 찍어주실래요? ______________________

창문을 열어주시겠어요? ______________________

Pattern 6_ 「Let's + 동사원형」 …하자

산책가자.(go for) ______________________

영화 빌리자.(rent) ______________________

Pattern 7_ 「Why don't we + 동사원형?」 우리 …하는 게 어때?

우리 저녁 나가서 먹을까?(go out) ______________________

우리 오렌지 주스 좀 마실까? ______________________

Pattern 8_ 「How about + 동사~ing?」 우리 …하는 게 어때?

오늘밤 영화 보는 게 어때? ______________________

쇼핑가는 거 어때? ______________________

Unit

21 과거습관/필요의 조동사

__ used to, would, need

● **Pattern** 주어 + 조동사 + 동사원형
● **Meaning** ~하곤 했다/ ~할 필요가 있다

Grammar in Practice

A: I used to drive to work but now I take the bus.
B: Good for you. It's better for your health.

Grammar in Use

1. used to

used to는 '~하곤 했다, ~이었었다' 라는 뜻으로 과거의 습관이나 지속되었던 상태를 나타내며 '현재는 더 이상 그렇지 않다' 라는 뜻이 내포되어 있다. 부정문은 「never used to」,「didn't use to」, 「used not to」를 쓸 수 있지만 「used not to」는 비교적 딱딱한 표현으로 흔히 사용하지 않는다. 의문문은 「Did+주어+use to~?」 형태로 쓴다.

I **used to** smoke a lot, but I've stopped. 나는 담배를 많이 피웠었지만 지금은 끊었다.
I **never used to** like horror movies. 나는 공포영화를 좋아하지 않았었다.
Did you **use to** exercise in the morning? 너는 아침에 운동을 하곤 했니?

2. used to와 would

과거의 습관에는 used to, would를 같이 쓸 수 있다. 단지 중요한 것은 과거의 상태를 나타내거나 음주나 흡연과 같은 버릇을 말할 경우 used to만 가능하다.

[비교]

There **used to** be a tall building here.→O 여기 큰 건물이 있었는데.
There **would** be a tall building here.→X
I **used to** smoke.→O 나는 담배를 피곤했었어. I **would** smoke.→X
When we were children, we **would** go skating every winter.→우리가 어렸을 때 겨울마다 스케이트를 타러 갔었지.

3. need

need는 '~할 필요가 있다' 라는 뜻으로 조동사일 경우 인칭/수에 따라 그 형태가 변하지 않으며 의문/부정문에서 do동사가 필요 없음을 유의한다. 미국영어에서는 일반동사 need를 주로 쓴다.

조동사 need
평서문 He **need** pay now.
의문문 **Need** he pay now?
부정문 He **need not**(needn't) pay now.

[비교]

need가 일반동사로 쓰일 경우 의미는 같지만 목적어로 to부정사가 온다는 점과 의문문과 부정문에서 do 동사가 필요하다는 점이 조동사 need와 구분된다.

일반동사 need
평서문 He **needs to** pay now.
의문문 **Does** he **need to** pay now?
부정문 He **doesn't need to** pay now.

Unit Test

1. **다음 문장을 보기와 같이 used to를 사용하여 다시 쓰시오.**

> 보기 | There was a bank on the corner, but there is a bookstore now.
> → <u>There used to be a bank on the corner.</u>

1. I exercised every morning, but I don't exercise now.

→ ______________________________

2. I liked opera, but I don't like opera any more.

→ ______________________________

3. I smoked a lot, but I've stopped.

→ ______________________________

4. She worked for Samsung, but she works for LG now.

→ ______________________________

5. They loved each other, but they broke up.

→ ______________________________

2. **둘 중 알맞은 것을 고르시오. 둘 다 가능할 경우 모두 동그라미 하시오.**

1. James (used to/ would) be very healthy when he was young.
2. I (used to/ would) drink a lot, but I've stopped.
3. There (used to/ would) be a nice restaurant here two years ago.
4. My father and I (used to/ would) exercise in the morning when we lived in Seattle.
5. You (used to/ would) be very skinny before.

3. **다음은 일반동사 need이다. 괄호 안의 지시대로 바꿔 쓰시오.**

1. You need help. (의문문)

____

2. She needs to keep awake. (부정문)

____

3. He doesn't need to say that again. (긍정문)

____

Writing Pattern Practice | 과거 습관/ 필요 조동사

Pattern 1_「주어 + used to + 동사원형」 …하곤 했다, …이었었다

나는 담배를 많이 피웠었다. ____________________

너 매우 날씬했었는데.(very skinny) ____________________

너 그를 안 좋아했었잖아. ____________________

나는 단 것을 안 먹었었다.(sweets) ____________________

여기에 은행이 있었는데. ____________________

여기 큰 건물이 있었는데. ____________________

Pattern 2_「주어 + would + 동사원형」 …하곤 했다

When I was a child, 나는 공원에서 운동을 했었다.

____

When I was a child, 나는 여동생과 아침에 조깅을 갔었다.

____

Pattern 3_「주어 + 조동사 need + 동사원형」 …할 필요가 있다 (very formal)

나는 지금 가야한다. ____________________

그는 지금 가야한다. ____________________

내가 지금 가야하니? ____________________

나는 지금 가야할 필요가 없다. ____________________

그는 지금 갈 필요 없다. ____________________

그는 지금 가야하니? ____________________

Pattern 4_「주어+ 일반동사 need(s) + to 동사원형」 …할 필요가 있다

나는 지금 돈을 내야한다.(pay) ____________________

그는 지금 돈을 내야한다. ____________________

내가 지금 돈을 내야하니? ____________________

그는 지금 돈을 내야하니? ____________________

나는 지금 돈을 낼 필요가 없다. ____________________

그는 지금 돈을 낼 필요 없다. ____________________

Unit

22 조동사 + have + 과거분사

- **Pattern** 주어 + 조동사 + have + 과거분사
- **Meaning** 과거에 대한 후회, 추측

Grammar in Practice

A: What happened to Sue? She was supposed to be here an hour ago.
B: Have you phoned her on her cell?
A: Of course, I have tried more than ten times, but her phone's been off.
B: Either something *came up or she must've forgotten it somewhere.

*come up (어떤 일이) 일어나다

Grammar in Use

1. 「should/ could/ might(may)/ must have + 과거분사」

과거에 있었던 일을 통해 현재의 심리를 표현하는데 과거와 현재가 연결되어 있는 표현이다.

2. 「should have(should've) + 과거분사」

'~했어야 했는데' 라는 뜻으로 과거사실에 대한 유감을 나타낸다.

I **should have studied** hard. 열심히 공부했어야 했는데.
It's raining outside. I **should have brought** my umbrella. 밖에 비와. 우산을 가져왔어야 했는데.

3. 「could have(could've) + 과거분사」

'~할 수도 있었는데' 라는 뜻으로 과거사실에 대한 가능성을 나타낸다.

I **could have made** a lot of money. 돈을 많이 벌수도 있었는데.
You **could have helped** me. 너는 나를 도와줄 수 있었잖아.

| MORE TIPS | 「could have+과거분사」는 「might(may) have+과거분사」와 비슷하게 과거에 대한 약한 추측을 나타내는 경우도 있다.

4. 「might(may) have(might've) + 과거분사」

'~했을지도 모른다' 라는 뜻으로 과거사실에 대한 추측을 나타낸다.

I **might have left** my keys in the office. 아마 사무실에 열쇠를 두고 온 것 같아.
James **might have missed** the bus. James는 버스를 놓쳤을 지도 몰라.

5. 「must have(must've) + 과거분사」

'~했었음에 틀림없다' 라는 뜻으로 과거사실에 대한 강한 추측을 나타낸다.

Tina **must have forgotten** our appointment. Tina는 우리 약속을 잊었음에 틀림없어.
It **must have been** love. 그것은 사랑이었음에 틀림없다.

Unit Test

1. 다음 문장을 조동사 should를 사용하여 보기와 같이 바꿔 쓰시오.

보기	You didn't come, but it would have been good to come. →You should have come.

1. You didn't have lunch, but it would have been good to have lunch.

→

2. I didn't bring my umbrella, but it would have been good to bring my umbrella.

→

3. He didn't come on time, but it would have been good to come on time.

→

2. 다음 문장을 조동사 might를 사용하여 보기와 같이 바꿔 쓰시오.

보기	Perhaps she was asleep. →She might have been asleep.

1. Perhaps you left your cell phone in the car.

→

2. Perhaps he forgot our appointment.

→

3. Perhaps Jenny was in a bad mood.

→

3. 다음 문장을 조동사 must를 사용하여 보기와 같이 바꿔 쓰시오.

보기	Surely they went out for dinner. →They must have gone out for dinner.

1. Surely I dropped my keys in my office.

→

2. Surely the movie was boring.

→

3. Surely she was out of her mind.

→

Writing Pattern Practice | 조동사+have+과거분사

Pattern 1_「주어 + should have + 과거분사」 …했어야 했는데

나는 열심히 공부했어야 했는데. ______

나는 내 우산을 가져왔어야 했는데. ______

너는 왔어야 했어. ______

너는 더 일찍 잠자리에 들었어야 했어.(earlier) ______

Pattern 2_「주어 + could have + 과거분사」 …할 수도 있었는데

나는 돈을 많이 벌수도 있었는데.(a lot of) ______

너는 나를 도와줄 수 있었잖아. ______

그녀는 그 직업을 얻을 수 있었다.(get) ______

그들은 여기에 정시에 올 수도 있었다.(on time) ______

Pattern 3_「주어 + might/may have + 과거분사」 …했을지도 모른다

나는 아마 사무실에 내 열쇠를 두고 온 것 같아.(my keys, in my office)

______

James는 버스를 놓쳤을 지도 몰라. ______

그녀는 집에 있었을 지도 몰라.(at home) ______

그들은 퇴근 했을지도 몰라.(leave work) ______

Pattern 4_「주어 + must have + 과거분사」 …했었음에 틀림없다

Tina는 우리 약속을 잊었음에 틀림없어. ______

그것은 사랑이었음에 틀림없어. ______

공원에 사람이 많이 있었음에 틀림없다.(a lot of) ______

그녀는 늦게 일어났음에 틀림없어. ______

WRAP-UP | 조동사

조동사별 의미정리	
will	1. 미래, 예정 : ~할 것이다 I **will** see a movie tonight. 오늘밤 영화 볼 거야. 2. 부탁 : ~해 줄래요? **Will** you do me a favor? 부탁 좀 들어줄래요?
would	1. 공손한 부탁, 제안 : ~해 줄래요? **Would** you show me the way to the bank? 은행까지 길 좀 알려주실래요? **Would** you mind standing up for a moment? 잠시만 일어서 주실래요? **Would** you like coffee, or would you prefer tea? 커피를 드실래요, 차를 드실래요? 2. 과거의 반복되는 행동 : ~하곤 했었다 I **would** go skating every winter when I was a child. 어렸을 때 겨울마다 스케이트를 타러가곤 했었지.
should	1. 충고 : ~하는 게 좋다 You **should** see the dentist. 너는 치과에 가보는 게 좋아. 2. 추측 : ~일거야 John **should** be there soon. He left an hour ago. Jon이 곧 도착할 거야. 한 시간 전에 떠났거든.
can	1. 능력 : ~할 수 있다 I **can** swim well. 나는 수영을 잘 해. 2. 허가 : ~해도 좋다 You **can** park here. 여기에 주차해도 좋아요. 3. 부탁 : ~해도 되요? **Can** I have your e-mail address? 내가 네 이메일 주소를 알 수 있을까?
be able to	능력 : ~할 수 있다 I'**m able to** drive. 나는 운전할 수 있어.
could	1. 과거능력 : ~할 수 있었다 I **could** ride a bike when I was five. 나는 5살 때 자전거를 탈 수 있었다. 2. 공손한 부탁 : ~해줄래요? **Could** you help me with my homework? 내 숙제를 도와줄래요? 3. 약한 추측 : ~일 수도 있다 She **could** be at home. 그녀는 집에 있을 수도 있다.
may	1. 허가 : ~해도 좋다 You **may** go in. 들어가셔도 좋아요. 2. 공손한 부탁 : ~해도 되나요? **May** I ask you a question? 질문 하나해도 될까요? 3. 약한 추측 : 아마 ~일 거다 Tina **may** be in her room. Tina는 자기 방에 아마 있을 거예요.

WRAP-UP | 조동사

조동사별 의미정리	
might	약한 추측 : ~일지도 모른다 It **might** rain in the afternoon. 오후에 비가 좀 올지도 몰라.
need	필요 : ~할 필요가 있다 You **need** do the work. 너는 그 일을 할 필요가 있어.
have to(have got to)	1. 의무/필요 : ~해야 한다 I **have got to** go. 나는 가야해. 2. 강한 추측 : ~임에 틀림없다 He'**s got to** be a lawyer. 그는 변호사임에 틀림없다.
must	1. 의무 : ~를 꼭 해야 한다 I **must** go on a diet. 나는 다이어트를 (꼭) 해야해. 2. 강한 추측 : ~임에 틀림없다 You **must** be joking. 너는 농담하고 있음에 틀림없어.
used to	과거의 반복되는 행동/상태 : ~하곤 했었다/ ~이었다 I **used to** live in Tokyo. 나는 동경에 살았었다. I **used to** have a BMW. 나는 BMW를 가지고 있었었다. We **used to** have a pet. 우리는 애완동물을 길렀었다. Where did you **used to** spend your vacations? 너는 어디에서 방학을 보내곤 했니?
had better	경고 : ~하는 게 좋다/~해야 한다 You **had better** take off now. 너는 지금 떠나는 게 좋을 거야.
would rather	선택 : 차라리 ~하겠다 I don't feel like going out. I **would rather** stay home. 나갈 기분이 아니야. 차라리 집에 있을래.
조동사+have+과거분사	과거 추측/ 후회 「should/could/might/must+have+과거분사」 ~했어야 했다/~했을 수도 있다/~했을 지도 모른다/~했음에 틀림없다 I **should have studied** English hard. 나는 영어를 열심히 공부했어야 했어. You **could have made** a lot of money. 너는 돈을 많이 벌 수 있었어. Jane **might have been** late for work. Jane은 아마 직장에 늦었을 거야. David **must have forgotten** our appointment. David은 우리 약속을 잊었음에 틀림없어.

REVIEW 1

1. **문장이 맞게 쓰였으면 T, 틀린 곳이 있으면 F를 쓰시오.**

1. I'm believing in God. (　　　)
2. Do you know his phone number? (　　　)
3. Which one are you preferring? (　　　)
4. You look just like your mother. (　　　)
5. This watch is costing at least $1000. (　　　)
6. Are you understanding what I'm saying? (　　　)
7. David always drinks too much. (　　　)
8. I'm looking at myself in the mirror. (　　　)
9. We're going to school. (　　　)
10. This car is belonging to James. (　　　)
11. This pie is smelling good. (　　　)
12. I couldn't recognize you. (　　　)
13. I'm supposing that you are right. (　　　)
14. What are you wanting to eat? (　　　)
15. I'm talking on the phone now. (　　　)

2. **둘 중 알맞은 것을 고르시오.**

1. You always make me (smile/ to smile).
2. Did I make you (feel/ to feel) embarrassed?
3. I had john (pick up/ to pick up) some milk on his way home.
4. Have him (call/ to call) me back.
5. Get her (answer/ to answer) the door.
6. I could get Jenny (change/ to change) her mind.
7. Let her (go/ to go) out.
8. I won't let it (happen/ to happen) again.
9. I had my hair (cut/ cutting).
10. Did you get your ears (pierce/ pierced)?
11. I must have my watch (repair/ repaired).
12. I had my picture (take/ taken).
13. You (look/ look like) great.
14. Does it (smell/ smell of) garlic?
15. Her fur coat (felt/ felt like) soft.
16. This cake (tastes/ taste like) sweet.
17. Those roses (smell/ smell like) beautiful.
18. That (sounds/ sounds like) a good idea.
19. I saw you (walk/ walked) down the street.
20. I felt an insect (crawl/ crawled) up my leg.

REVIEW 2

[1-4] 빈칸에 들어갈 가장 알맞은 말은?

1. After the years of his efforts, his dream ________ true.

① turned
② went
③ grew
④ came

2. After leaving school, he ____________ a professional soccer player.

① turned
② went
③ grew
④ became

3. I think I'll _________ get there on time.

① can
② be able to
③ may
④ might

4. I _________ speak three foreign languages when I was eight.

① might
② could
③ should
④ must

[5-10] 빈 칸에 들어가기 어색한 말은?

5. I'd like to have something to drink. ________ I drink some water?

① Can
② Could
③ May
④ Will

6. "Do you know where Tom is?" "He ______ be downstairs."

① had better
② may
③ should
④ might

7. "I have a cold." "You _______ take some medicine and get some sleep."

① had better
② will
③ have got to
④ should

8. French fries can cause cancer. You ______ eat them.

① had better not
② will not
③ should not
④ must not

9. This suitcase is too heavy. ________ you give me a hand?

① Can
② Could
③ Would
④ Should

10. "You're wearing a suit." "I _________ go for a job interview."

① have to
② have got to
③ had better
④ am about to

REVIEW 2

11. 다음 글을 읽고, 빈칸에 차례로 들어갈 알맞은 말을 고르시오.

Learn To Be A Professional Photographer!

Have you ever dreamed of seeing your photographs in a magazine? If so, now your dream can _______ true!

We'll teach you to _______ a professional photographer - at home, in your spare time!

Here are just a few of the topics covered:
Cameras, lenses, film, lighting, and composition
Developing and printing film and slides
Working with models
Starting a photo business

* Train at home - beginner to advanced!
* All lessons, videotapes, and audiotapes included!
* Success guaranteed!

For more information about our courses, visit us online at: www.photoinstitute.org

① come - get
② go - turn
③ come - become
④ go - grow

12. 다음 글을 읽고, 빈칸에 들어갈 가장 알맞은 말을 고르시오.

Americans today get less sleep than they did a century ago. In 1900, the average American slept 8.5 hours a night. Today, according to a recent poll, that figure has dropped to 6.5 hours. A small number of companies have instituted nap policies, and have even set up nap rooms for workers. According to researchers at the NSC, a 15-minute nap is enough to recharge a person's batteries for the next three or four hours. "I think it's fair to say that napping is an essential biological need." says Dr. Sue Serby, director of research at the NSC. "I hope that businesses continue to recognize that a 15-minute nap can play a vital role in increasing a worker's productivity and overall health. All of us _______ encourage this nap policies." said Dr. Serby.

① should
② can
③ might
④ are able to

13. 다음 글을 읽고, 빈칸에 들어갈 가장 알맞은 말을 고르시오

FOR SALE

Moving and _________ sell! Large white refrigerator, perfect for dorm room / bedroom / basement. In excellent condition, only used 1 1/2 school years. Paid $170, asking for $60. Call or e-mail me if interested. katie92@ti.com ***-****

① might ② had better
③ could ④ must

* Chapter 3 | 명사류

문장은 주부와 술부로 나뉜다. 술부의 핵심이 동사라면 주부의 핵심은 명사의 몫이다. 그러므로 명사는 동사와 더불어 문장의 뼈대역할을 한다는 것을 알 수 있다. 이러한 명사는 문장 안에서 주어 이외에도 목적어, 보어, 전치사의 목적어 역할 또한 할 수 있다.

Unit

23 셀 수 있는 명사

● Pattern a(n)/the + 명사/ 명사-(e)s

Grammar in Practice

A: What's your favorite snack?

B: It's a sandwich with meat, vegetables, and honey.

A: How do you make it?

B: Well, first put the meat and vegetables on one of the slices of bread. Then pour some honey over them and put the other slice of bread on top. That's it.

Grammar in Use

1. 명사

사람이나 사물의 이름 또는 개념을 나타내는 말을 명사라고 하는데, '하나, 둘…'로 셀 수 있는 명사와 개체수가 많거나 모양이 일정하지 않아 셀 수 없는 명사로 대분된다.

셀 수 있는 명사	단독으로 쓰이지 않고 관사 'a(n) 또는 the'를 붙이거나 복수형 '-(e)s'으로 쓴다. **[셀 수 있는 명사의 예]** a chair – chairs　an idea – ideas　a boy – boys a woman – women　a child – children　a tooth – teeth 등
셀 수 없는 명사	복수형을 쓰지 않으며 정관사 'the'는 상황에 따라 붙여 쓸 수 있지만 부정관사 'a(n)'는 쓸 수 없다. **[셀 수 없는 명사의 예]** English, water, bread, love, money, happiness 등

[셀 수 있는 명사와 셀 수 없는 명사 모두 가능한 명사]

paper (종이) **Paper** is made from wood.
a paper (신문) I'm going out to buy **a paper.**

coffee (커피) I drink **coffee** a lot. [tea/beer/Coke]
a coffee (커피 한잔-주문할 때) I'll have **a** (cup of) **coffee**, please. [a tea/a beer/a Coke]

glass (유리) This vase is made of **glass.**
a glass (유리잔) I need **a glass.**

chicken (닭고기) Do you want **chicken** or beef? [fish/lamb/turkey]
a chicken (닭) There's **a chicken** in the garden. [a fish/a lamb/a turkey]

wine (와인) Jane never drinks **wine.**
wines (와인의 종류) France produces some wonderful **wines.**

time (시간) Time flies when you're having hun.
times (~번) I called him more than ten **times** yesterday.

2. 셀 수 있는 명사의 복수형 만드는 법

● 규칙	
• 대부분의 명사에 -s를 붙인다	day→days, week→weeks, month→months, year→years
• -s, -x, -sh, -ch, -o로 끝나는 명사는 -es를 붙인다	bus→buses, box→boxes, dish→dishes, church→churches, potato→potatoes, tomato→tomatoes, echo→echoes 예외: pianos, photos, radios 등
• 「자음+y」로 끝나는 명사는 y를 i로 고치고, -es를 붙인다 단, 「모음+y」로 끝나는 명사는 -s만 붙인다는 점을 유의한다	century→centuries, baby→babies, lady→ladies, dictionary→dictionaries 예외: keys, guys, boys 등
• -f, -fe는 v로 바꾸고 -es를 붙인다	life→lives, shelf→shelves, leaf→leaves, wife→wives, thief→thieves 예외: belief→beliefs, proof→proofs, roof→roofs 등
● 불규칙	
• 모음이 변한다	tooth→teeth, man→men, woman→women, foot→feet, goose→geese, mouse→mice, crisis→crises, oasis→oases
• 어미에 -(r)en을 붙인다	child→children, ox→oxen
• 단수, 복수가 같다	fish→fish, deer→deer, sheep→sheep, trout→trout, Japanese→Japanese, Swiss→Swiss

3. 복수형(-(e)s)이지만 단수 취급하는 명사

● -ics로 끝나는 명사

economics(경제학), electronics(전자학), gymnastics(체육학), mathematics(수학), physics(물리학), politics(정치학) 등

Mathematics is my favorite subject. 수학은 내가 좋아하는 과목이다.

● 돈의 액수, 기간, 거리 등을 하나로 볼 때

Two weeks wasn't enough holiday. 두 주는 충분한 휴가가 아니었다.

Ten miles is a long way to walk. You'd better take the bus. 10마일은 걷기에 멀어. 버스를 타는 게 좋아.

● news, the United States(미국), Athens(아테네), measles(홍역), 「one of+복수명사」 등

The news was so shocking. 그 뉴스는 충격적이었다.

The United States is smaller than Canada. 미국은 캐나다보다 작다.

One of my friends works for IBM. 친구 중 하나가 IBM에서 일한다.

4. 항상 복수형(-(e)s)이고 복수 취급 하는 명사

pants, jeans, slacks, shorts, trousers, pajamas, glasses, scissors 등은 짝이 있어야 하나의 사물이 되는 명사로 a pair of, two pairs of로 센다.

My **jeans** are too tight. 내 청바지가 너무 껴.

"Where are my **glasses**?" "They are on the desk." 내 안경 어디 있지? 책상위에 있어.

Have you got **a pair of nail-scissors?** 손톱가위 있니?

5. 단수형이지만 복수 취급하는 명사

(the) police, people, cattle 등

Do you think the **police** are well paid? 경찰이 월급을 많이 받을 것 같니?

Most **people** are interested in movies. 대부분의 사람들은 영화에 관심이 있다.

6. 의미에 따라 단수, 복수 취급하는 명사

family, team, club, staff 등의 단어는 하나의 단위로 쓸 경우 단수취급, 그 안에 속한 하나하나의 개인이나 사물을 가리킬 경우는 주로 복수취급한다.

How are your **family?**(복수) 가족들은 어때?

The average **family** has 3.5 members. It's smaller than 50 years ago.(단수) 평균 가족은 3.5명이다. 50년 전보다 줄어들었다.

| MORE TIPS | 미국식 영어에서는 명사를 하나의 단위로 쓰거나 하나하나의 개인으로 보거나 모두 단수취급을 하기도 한다.

- How **is** your family? 가족들은 어때?
- My family **is** my life. 내 가족은 내 삶이다.

● 명사 말하기 | Grammar Point |

영어에서 셀 수 있는 명사는 그 명사만 혼자 사용하는 경우는 없다. 어떤 형태로든 그 명사의 뜻을 구체화시켜주는 말을 붙여야 한다. 그러므로 '차' (car)를 말할 때 그냥 '차' (car)라고 하지 않는다. '한대의 차' (a car), '이 차' (this car), '저 차' (that car), '그 차' (the car), 또는 '차들' (cars) 등 구체적으로 정확하게 표현해 주어야 한다.

Unit Test

1. 다음 명사의 복수형을 쓰시오.

month → ________	bus → ________	piano → ________	photo → ________
potato → ________	tomato → ________	centry → ________	lady → ________
life → ________	leaf → ________	proof → ________	tooth → ________
foot → ________	woman → ________	mouse → ________	fish → ________
deer → ________	sheep → ________	child → ________	ox → ________

2. 둘 중 알맞은 것을 고르시오.

1. One of my friends (has/ have) lost a shoe.
2. Time (flies/ fly) when you're having hun.
3. I called you more than ten (time/ times) yesterday.
4. Economics (is/ are) my favorite subject.
5. Two kilos (is/ are) pretty small for a newborn baby.
6. Five weeks (is/ are) a long time to wait.
7. The news (was/ were) very shocking.
8. The United States (is/ are) quite a big country.
9. My jeans (is/ are) too tight.
10. Have you got a pair of (nail-scissor/ nail-scissors)?
11. The police in Britain (wear/ wears) blue uniforms.
12. A lot of people (has/ have) complained about the noise.

3. 괄호 안의 명사를 적당한 형태로 빈칸에 써 넣으시오.(명사, a/an+명사, 명사(e)s 중 택일)

1. There's __________ in the garden. (chicken)
2. Do you want __________ or beef? (chicken)
3. Three __________, please. (beer)
4. __________ makes you fat. (beer)
5. __________ goes so quickly. (time)
6. She called Katie ten __________ yesterday. (time)
7. Do you often drink __________ ?(wine)
8. Spain produces some wonderful __________. (wine)
9. This vase is made of __________. (glass)
10. I need __________ to drink some water. (glass)

Writing Pattern Practice | 셀 수 있는 명사

Pattern 1_ 셀 수 있는 명사와 셀 수 없는 명사 모두 가능한 명사 「a+명사/ 명사」

나는 커피를 많이 마신다.(a lot) ______________________

저는 커피 한잔을 마실 거예요.(have) ______________________

닭고기를 원하나요, 소고기를 원하나요? ______________________

정원에 닭이 한 마리 있다. ______________________

Jane은 wine을 마시지 않는다.(never) ______________________

프랑스는 좋은 와인을 생산한다.(some wonderful wines)

____

Pattern 2_ 복수형이지만 단수취급 명사 「명사(e)s + is~ 」

수학은 내가 좋아하는 과목이다. ______________________

10마일은 걷기에 먼 길이야.(to walk) ______________________

그 뉴스는 충격적이었다.(shocking) ______________________

미국은 캐나다보다 더 작다.(smaller) ______________________

내 친구들 중 하나가 IBM에서 일한다.(work for) ______________________

Pattern 3_ 항상 복수형이고 복수취급 명사 「명사(e)s + are~」

내 청바지가 너무 껴. ______________________

내 안경 어디 있지? ______________________

Pattern 4_ 단수형이지만 복수취급 명사 「명사 + are~」

경찰이 한 남자를 심문하고 있다.(question) ______________________

대부분의 사람들은 영화에 관심이 있다.(movies) ______________________

Pattern 5_ 의미에 따라 단수/ 복수취급 명사 「명사 + is~/ 명사 + are~」

네 가족은 어때?(가족구성원 모두의 안부를 물을 때) ______________________

평균 가족은 3.5명이다.(The average~) ______________________

Unit

24 셀 수 없는 명사

● Pattern a(n) + 명사/ (the +) 명사

Grammar in Practice

A: Mom, I think something is burning.
Smoke is coming out of the oven.
B: Oh, my! Turn it off with care.

Grammar in Use

1. 셀 수 없는 명사

셀 수 없는 명사는 보통 부정관사(a/an)를 붙이지 않고 복수형으로도 쓰지 않는다.

2. 고유명사

특정한 사람이나 장소 또는 사물의 이름을 말하며 첫 글자를 대문자로 시작한다.
Africa, Iraq, September, Sunday, Christmas, Easter, Central Park 등
Katie left for **Las Vegas** on **September** 20. Katie는 9월 20일에 Las Vegas로 떠났다.

| MORE TIPS | 고유명사는 보통 관사 a/an/the를 붙이지 않지만 예외가 있다.
1. the Bushes 복수형인 경우 가족을 나타내는 집합적인 의미이므로 the를 붙임.
2. the United States 여러 주를 합쳐놓은 국가로 복수형으로 쓰이는 집합적인 의미를 가진 국가명은 the를 붙임.
예 the Philippines, the Netherlands, the Bahamas 등

3. 집단(한 덩어리) 명사

특정한 명사를 지칭하지 않고 여러 개를 포함하는 덩치가 큰 명사를 가리키는 경우로 셀 수 없는 명사이다. 단 각 집단 안에 속하는 특정한 명사는 셀 수 있는 명사이다.

전체(셀 수 없음)	부분(셀 수 있음)
furniture(가구)	desks, chairs, tables, beds 등
mail(우편물)	letters, postcards, parcels소포 등
luggage/baggage(짐)	suitcases, bags 등
clothing(의류)	shirts, pants, vests 등
fruit(과일)	apples, bananas, grapes 등

4. 물질 명사

물질의 이름을 나타내며 한개, 두개로 단위를 나누어 세기 애메하기나 작은 것이 모여서 전체를 이루는 것들이 이에 속한다.
water, coffee, tea, ice, smoke, weather, meat, cheese, smoke 등

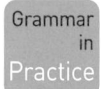

"What would you like to drink?" "I'd like some **water.**" 뭐 마시고 싶어요? 물마시고 싶어요.

| MORE TIPS | 일상 회화에서 일부 셀 수 없는 명사를 복수형으로 쓰기도 한다.
• We'll have **two hamburgers** and **two coffees.** 우리는 햄버거 두 개와 커피 두 잔 먹을게요.

5. 추상명사

구체적인 모양이 없는 것으로 감정, 개념, 운동, 질병 등을 나타내는 말이다.
beauty, luck, experience, shame부끄러움, happiness, courage용기, advice, information, intelligence, measles홍역 등

Beauty is but skin-deep. 미모는 단지 겉모습일 뿐이다.
It wasn't your fault. It was bad **luck.** 네 잘못이 아니야. 운이 나빴어.
Experience teaches. 경험은 가르침을 준다.

6. a + 셀 수 없는 명사

셀 수 없는 명사지만 일반적인 경우가 아니라 특정한 상황이라면 부정관사(a/an)를 사용한다. 보통 명사 앞에 꾸며주는 형용사가 있는 경우가 많다.
I don't usually have **a big lunch.** 나는 보통 점심을 거하게 먹지 않는다.
Have **a good time.** 좋은 시간 보내.
You've been **a great help.** 네가 도움이 많이 되었어.
You need **a good sleep.** 너는 잘 자야해.
My parents wanted me to have **a good education.** 부모님은 내가 좋은 교육을 받기를 원하셨다.

7. 셀 수 없는 명사를 셀 수 있게 해주는 어구

a piece/slice (two pieces/slices) of cake
a piece/sheet (two pieces/sheets) of paper
a bar (two bars) of chocolate
a loaf (two loaves) of bread
a glass (two glasses) of water/juice
a cup (two cups) of coffee/tea
a bottle (two bottles) of beer/soda
a jar (two jars) of jam
a carton (two cartons) of milk
a bag (two bags) of flour
a box (two boxes) of cereal
a kilo (two kilos) of cheese
a pound (two pounds) of butter/pork
a meter (two meter) of cable

Unit Test

1. 둘 중 알맞은 것을 고르시오.

1. (Mozart/ a Mozart) was a great composer.
2. I bought some (fruit/ fruits).
3. Cake is made from (sugar/ a sugar) and flour.
4. (Kelly/ The Kelly) left for Las Vegas on September 20.
5. I don't usually have (big/ a big) lunch.
6. This is (nice/ a nice) room.
7. I was in a hurry this morning. I didn't have (time/ a time) to eat breakfast.
8. Bad news (doesn't/ don't) make people happy.
9. Susan gave us some useful (advice/ advices)
10. (Her hair is/ Her hairs are) too short.

2. 틀린 곳을 찾아 밑줄치고 고쳐 쓰시오.

1. I put two slice of cheese in the sandwich.

→

2. You should not drink more than three cups of coffees a day.

→

3. Two spoonful of sugar will make it too sweet.

→

4. Give us two glass of orange juice.

→

5. I drink almost ten glasses of waters a day.

→

3. 우리말과 일치하도록 괄호 안의 단어를 알맞게 배열하시오.

1. 나는 보통 점심을 거하게 먹지 않는다. (a big lunch/ don't usually/ I/ have)

2. 좋은 시간 보내. (a/ time/ have/ good)

3. 네가 도움이 많이 되었어. (been/ you've/ a great help)

4. 너는 잘 자야해. (sleep/ need/ you/ a good)

5. 부모님은 내가 좋은 교육을 받기를 원하셨다. (wanted me to/ a good education/ my parents/ have)

Writing Pattern Practice │ 셀 수 없는 명사

Pattern 1_ 고유명사

12월 25일은 크리스마스이다. ______

Tom과 Mary는 파리에서 만났다. ______

Kate은 아프리카를 향해 떠났다. ______

Pattern 2_ 집단(한 덩어리) 명사

포도와 사과는 과일이다.(grapes) ______

의자와 테이블은 가구다. ______

편지와 엽서는 우편물이다.(postcards) ______

Pattern 3_ 물질명사

Jack은 맥주 두 병을 마셨다. ______

내게 종이 한 장 줘.(piece) ______

빵 한 덩어리와 우유 한 잔이 내 아침식사이다. ______

Pattern 4_ 추상명사

경험은 가르침을 준다.(teach) ______

저는 당신의 친절에 감사합니다.(appreciate) ______

그것은 나쁜 운이었다.(운이 나빴어) ______

Pattern 5_ 「a + 셀 수 없는 명사」

나는 보통 점심을 거하게 먹지 않는다.(usually, big) ______

좋은 시간 보내.(good) ______

(그동안) 네가 도움이 많이 되었어.(a great help) ______

너는 잘 자야해.(need, good) ______

Unit

25 수량을 나타내는 표현

● Pattern 수량표현 + 셀 수 있는/셀 수 없는 명사

Grammar in Practice

A: Where are you going?
B: I'm going to my band practice.
A: I didn't know you played in a band.
B: I just started it a couple of weeks ago.

Grammar in Use

1. 수를 나타내는 few/ a few/ a couple of/ several/ many/ a number of

few 거의 없는	There were **few** people in the park. 공원에 사람이 거의 없었다.
a few 약간의	There are **a few** things you have to know. 네가 알아야 할 것이 몇 가지 있어.
a couple of 둘 셋의	Can you stay **a couple of** days longer? 이삼일 더 머무를 수 있어?
several 몇몇의	**Several** students didn't come to class. 몇몇 학생이 수업에 오지 않았다.
many 많은	"Are there **many** opera houses in Korea?" "No, not many." 한국에는 오페라 하우스가 많이 있나요? 아니오, 많이 없어요.
a number of 수많은	**A number of** people disagree. 많은 사람들이 반대한다.

| MORE TIPS |

1. few

few는 '(수가) 거의 없는' 이라는 뜻으로 셀 수 있는 명사 앞에 오면서 부정의 뜻을 지니고 있음을 유의한다.
• There are few eggs in the fridge. 냉장고에 계란이 거의 없다.
• Few people think that prices will get stabilized. 물가가 안정될 거라고 생각하는 사람들은 거의 없다.

2. a number of 와 the number of 비교

「a number of+복수명사」는 '많은 수의 ~' 라는 뜻으로 복수취급하며 「the number of+복수명사」는 '~의 수' 라는 뜻으로 단수취급한다.
• A number of languages are used in the world. 세계적으로 많은 언어가 쓰여지고 있다.
• The number of languages used in the world is not known exactly. 세계적으로 쓰이는 언어의 수는 정확히 알려지지 않았다.

2. 양을 나타내는 little/ a little/ much/ a great deal of

little 거의 없는	Cactuses need **little** water. 선인장은 물이 거의 필요 없다.
a little 약간의	Give the roses **a little** water every other day. 그 장미꽃은 이틀에 한 번 물을 조금씩 주어라.
much 많은	I didn't eat **much** breakfast. 나는 아침식사를 많이 먹지 않았다.
a great deal of 다량의	We need **a great deal of** time to finish the project. 그 프로젝트를 완성하기 위해 우리는 많은 시간이 필요하다.

| MORE TIPS |

1. much는 부정문에서 더욱 자연스럽다. 긍정문에는 a lot of(lots of)를 주로 쓴다.

〔비교〕

- I spent **a lot of** money. 나는 많은 돈을 썼다.
- I didn't spend **much** money. 나는 많은 돈을 쓰지 않았다.

2. a number of와 함께 a great deal of는 딱딱한 표현으로 구어체에서 자주 쓰이는 표현은 아니다.

3. 수와 양을 모두 나타내는 no/ some/ any/ a lot of/ lots of/ plenty of

no not a/ not any	Sorry, I've got **no** time. 미안하지만, 시간이 없어. **No** cigarette is completely harmless. 완전히 무해한 담배는 없다. He has **no** brothers. 그는 형제가 없다.
some 약간의 (긍정문, 상대방에게 Yes라는 대답을 기대하는 의문문) any 약간의 (부정문, 의문문, 조건문) *긍정문에서 '어떤 ~라도'라는 강조의 의미로 any를 사용할 수 있다.	Mary has got **some** interesting ideas. Mary는 흥미로운 의견을 가지고 있다. Could I have **some** coffee? 제가 커피 좀 마실 수 있을까요? I don't need **any** help. 나는 아무런 도움도 필요하지 않다. Do you know **any** good jokes? 재미있는 농담 좀 아니? If you find **any** mistakes, let me know. 실수를 발견하면 알려줘요. I'm prepared to take **any** advice. 나는 어떤 충고라도 받아들일 준비가 되어 있다.
a lot of/ lots of 많은	I have **a lot of** friends to hang around with. 나는 어울리는 친구들이 많다. You have **lots of** work to do. 너는 할일이 많아.
plenty of 많은	There are **plenty of** nice restaurants in this city. 이 도시에는 좋은 음식점이 많이 있다. Have you got **plenty of** time? 시간 많이 있니?

Unit Test

1. 둘 중 알맞은 것을 고르시오.

1. Ann isn't very popular. She has (few/ little) friends.
2. He's very lucky. He has (few/ little) problems.
3. The weather has been very dry these days. We've had (few/ little) rain.
4. Ted spoke (little/ few) Korean, so it was difficult to communicate.
5. There was (little/ a lot of) traffic on my way here, so it took only 10 minutes to get here.
6. I don't know much French. I know (a few/ a little) words.
7. How've you been? I haven't seen you for (a few/ a little) months.
8. "When was the last time you saw a movie?" "(A few/ A little) days ago."
9. "Do you know Italy?" "Not really. I haven't been there for (many/ much) years."
10. In Korea, (many/ much) people drive fast.
11. I went shopping yesterday, but I didn't spend (many/ much) money.
12. This is a very interesting place to live. There are (many/ much) things to do.
13. Hurry up. We don't have (many/ much) time.

2. 맞는 문장은 동그라미하고 틀린 문장은 틀린 곳을 찾아 밑줄치고 고쳐 쓰시오.

1. I haven't decided it yet. I need little time to think. → ______
2. I have plenty of money to spend. → ______
3. Do you mind if I ask you few questions? → ______
4. There is a number of food here. → ______
5. He has no friends here. → ______

3. 괄호 안의 단어를 사용하여 보기와 같이 의문문을 완성하시오.

> 보기 | How <u>many letters</u>(letter) did you get?
> How <u>much money</u>(money) did you spend?

1. How ______ (time) do you need?
2. How ______ (people) were there in the party?
3. How ______ (money) did it cost?
4. How ______ (sugar) do you want in your coffee?
5. How ______ (tourists) were there?

Writing Pattern Practice | 수량을 나타내는 표현

Pattern 1_「수를 나타내는 표현 + 셀 수 있는 명사(복수형)」

공원에 사람이 거의 없었다. ______________________

네가 알아야 할 것이 몇 가지 있어.(you have to know)
____

너는 이삼일 더 머무를 수 있니?(Can~, a couple of)
____

몇몇 학생이 수업에 오지 않았다.(Several~) ______________________

한국에는 오페라 하우스가 많이 있나요?(many) ______________________

많은 사람들이 반대한다.(A number of~) ______________________

Pattern 2_「양을 나타내는 표현 + 셀 수 없는 명사」

선인장은 물이 거의 필요 없다.(Cactuses~) ______________________

나는 약간의 시간이 필요하다. ______________________

나는 아침식사를 많이 하지 않았다.(eat much) ______________________

그 프로젝트를 완성하기 위해 우리는 많은 시간이 필요하다.(a great deal of)
____

Pattern 3_「수와 양을 나타내는 표현 + 셀 수 있는/ 셀 수 없는 명사」

미안하지만, 시간이 없어.(Sorry,~) ______________________

그는 형제가 없다.(brothers) ______________________

Mary는 흥미로운 의견을 좀 가지고 있다.(ideas) ______________________

제가 커피 좀 마실 수 있을까요?(Could I have~) ______________________

너는 재미있는 농담 좀 아니? (good jokes) ______________________

나는 아무런 도움도 필요하지 않다. ______________________

너는 할일이 많아.(a lot of) ______________________

이 도시에는 좋은 음식점이 많이 있다.(plenty of) ______________________

Unit

26 그 밖의 수량표현

● **Pattern** both, either, neither, all, every, half, each, another, other, most+명사

Grammar in Practice

A: Can I still get tickets for tonight's *performance?
B: The front balcony is still available.
A: Aren't there any other seats?
B: No, I'm afraid not.

*performance 공연

1. both (of)/ either (of)/ neither (of)

*ⓓ determiners – a, the, my, this와 같은 명사 앞에 붙는 한정사를 뜻함.

「both (of) + ⓓ + 복수명사」 둘 다	**Both (of)** my parents were born in Seoul. 우리 부모님 두 분 모두 서울에서 태어나셨다. **Both (of)** the films were very good. 두 편의 영화가 모두 다 좋았다.
「either + 단수명사」 「either of + ⓓ + 복수명사」 둘 중 하나	Come on Monday or Tuesday. **Either** day is OK. 월요일이나 화요일에 와요. 아무 날이나 좋아요. You can use **either of** the phones. 두 전화 중 아무거나 사용해도 좋아요.
「neither + 단수명사」 「neither of + ⓓ + 복수명사」 둘 다 ~아니다	"Can you come on Saturday or Sunday?" "I'm afraid **neither** day is possible." 토요일이나 일요일에 올 수 있니? 유감이지만 둘 다 안돼. **Neither of** my friends came to see me. 내 친구들 중 아무도 나를 보러 오지 않았다.

2. another/ other

「another + 단수명사」 (또) 다른~(=additional, extra)	**Another** day has gone. 또 하루가 지나갔다. Could I have **another** piece of bread? 빵 한 조각 더 먹을 수 있을까요?
「other + 복수명사」 다른~ *other 앞에 one, every 등이 오는 경우 단수명사와 같이 쓰기도 한다	Can you show me some **other** shoes? 다른 신발 보여줄래요? Where are the **other** people? 다른 사람들은 어디 있어? We meet **every other** week. 우리는 격주로 만난다.

| MORE TIPS | another 다음에 'few' 나 '숫자' 가 올 경우 다음에 복수명사가 올 수 있다.
• I'm staying for **another** few weeks. 나는 몇 주 동안 더 머무를 거야.
• I'm staying for **another** three weeks. 나는 3주 동안 더 머무를 거야.

3. all/ every/ half/ each

「all + 셀 수 있는/없는 명사」 모든 「all (of) + ⓓ + 셀 수 있는/없는 명사」 ~의 모두 *명사에 따라 단수/복수취급	**All** men are equal. 모든 사람은 평등하다. I drank **all (of)** the milk. 나는 우유를 다 마셨다.
「every + 셀 수 있는 명사의 단수형」 모든 *항상 단수취급	**Every** light was out. 모든 전기가 나갔다. **Every** room is being used. 모든 방이 사용 중이다.
「half (of) + ⓓ + 셀 수 있는/없는 명사」 절반의	**Half (of)** my friends got married. 내 친구 중 절반은 결혼했다. *양이나 거리를 나타낼 때는 of를 쓰지 않는다. Give me **half** a glass of water. 물 반잔 줘. Give me **half** of a glass of water.(X)
「each + 단수명사」 「each of + ⓓ + 복수명사」 각각(의) *항상 단수취급	I enjoy **each** moment. 나는 매순간을 즐긴다. I write to **each of** my friends a couple of times a month. 나는 한 달에 두 세 번씩 각각 친구에게 편지를 쓴다.

4. most (of)

「most + 셀 수 있는/없는 명사」 대부분(의) 「most of + ⓓ + 셀 수 있는/없는 명사」 ~의 대부분	**Most** Swiss people understand French. 대부분의 스위스 사람들은 불어를 이해한다. **Most** cheese is made from cow's milk. 대부분의 치즈는 소의 젖으로 만들어진다. **Most of** my friends live in San Francisco. 내 친구들 중 대부분은 샌프란시스코에 산다. We've eaten two sandwiches and **most of** a cold chicken. 우리는 샌드위치 두개와 식은 닭고기를 거의 다 먹었다.

| MORE TIPS | 보통 수량표현 all이나 most는 뒤에 불특정한 명사가 오면 of를 붙이지 않고 the, this, that, my, your 등의 한정을 받는 특정한 명사가 와서 의미가 제한되는 경우 of를 붙인다.

- All children like chocolate. 모든 아이들은 초콜릿을 좋아한다.
- All of the children like chocolate. 그 아이들 모두는 초콜릿을 좋아한다.
- Most people like shopping. 대부분의 사람들은 쇼핑을 좋아한다.
- Most of the people like shopping. 그 사람들 중 대부분이 쇼핑을 좋아한다.

Unit Test

1. **빈칸에 of가 필요하면 쓰고 필요하지 않으면 X표 하시오.**

1. Saturday or Sunday. Either _______ day is fine with me.
2. You can eat here or take it home. Either _______ way is possible.
3. Either _______ the students will get the prize.
4. Neither _______ my friends came to see me.
5. At first, neither _______ man could speak.
6. Every _______ room is being used.
7. All _______ men are equal.
8. All _______ people were scared to death.
9. Give me half _______ a glass of water.
10. Most _______ my friends are married.

2. **둘 중 알맞은 것을 고르시오.**

1. Both my sisters (live/ lives) in Hawaii.
2. You can use either of the (phone/ phones).
3. Neither of the (story/ stories) was true.
4. I enjoyed every (minute/ minutes) of my stay in Rome.
5. If this doesn't work out, there is (another/ other) solution.
6. (All/ All of) men are equal.
7. Show me another (one/ ones).
8. (Most/ Most of) vegetables contain *fiber. *fiber 섬유질
9. Each (student/ students) had a different solution to the problem.
10. I often write to each of my (friend/ friends).

3. **우리말과 일치하도록 괄호 안의 단어를 알맞게 배열하시오.**

1. 또 한해가 지났다. (year/ another/ has gone)

____

2. 나머지 사람들은 어디 있어? (the other/ where are/ people/?)

____

3. 나는 모든 음식을 먹었다. (ate/ I/ the food/ all)

____

4. 학생들은 그의 말 한 마디 한 마디에 귀를 기울였다. (his every word/ the students/ listened to)

____

5. 대부분의 사람들은 과일 먹는 것을 좋아한다. (people/ like to eat fruit/ most)

____

Writing Pattern Practice | 그 밖의 수량표현

Pattern 1_ 「both (of) + ⓓ + 복수명사」 둘 다

우리 부모님 두 분 모두 서울에 사신다. ______________________

Pattern 2_ 「either + 단수명사」, 「either of + ⓓ + 복수명사」 둘 중 하나

당신은 두 전화 중 아무거나 사용해도 좋아요.(You can~) ______________________

Pattern 3_ 「neither + 단수명사」, 「neither of + ⓓ + 복수명사」 둘 다 ~아니다

내 남동생들 중 아무도 여기에 오지 않았다. ______________________

Pattern 4_ 「another + 단수명사」 (또) 다른~

내게 다른 것으로 보여줘요. ______________________

Pattern 5_ 「other + 복수명사」 다른~

나는 다른 약속은 없어.(no, appointments) ______________________

Pattern 6_ 「one, every...+ other + 단수명사」 다른~

나는 2주마다 집에 갔었다.(week) ______________________

Pattern 7_ 「all + 셀 수 있는/없는 명사」 모든, 「all (of) + ⓓ + 셀 수 있는/없는 명사」 ~의 모두

그 차들 모두가 중고다.(used ones) ______________________

Pattern 8_ 「every + 셀 수 있는 명사의 단수형」 모든

모든 방이 사용 중이다.(being used) ______________________

Pattern 9_ 「half (of + ⓓ) + 셀 수 있는/없는 명사」 절반의

내 친구 중 절반은 미혼이다. (single) ______________________

Pattern 10_ 「each + 단수명사」, 「each of + ⓓ + 복수명사」 각각(의)

식사 후마다 네 이를 닦아라.(Brush~each meal) ______________________

Pattern 11_ 「most + 셀 수 있는/없는 명사」 대부분(의), 「most of + ⓓ + 셀 수 있는/없는 명사」 ~의 대부분

대부분의 사람들은 쇼핑을 좋아한다. ______________________

Unit

27 부정관사

● Pattern a(an) + 명사

Grammar in Practice

(At a hotel)

A: Do you have a single room for two nights?

B: We only have a small suite.

A: What's the rate?

B: $120 a night, including breakfast.

Grammar in Use

1. 부정관사 a, an

부정관사 a는 셀 수 있는 명사의 단수형 앞에 쓴다. 이 때 명사의 발음이 a, e, i, o, u로 시작하면 부정관사 an을 붙인다. 철자가 모음으로 시작하더라도 발음이 모음이 아닐 경우 부정관사 a를 써야 하는 것을 유의한다.

예 an umbrella, an interesting book, an hour, an honest boy, an MP(Military Police 헌병), an SOS, a useful book, a university, a one-way conversation 등

2. 막연한 '하나' 또는 분명한 '하나'

We live in **an** old house. 우리는 오래된 집에 산다.

I have **a** sister and two brothers. 나는 언니가 한명 오빠가 두명이다.

3. 종족의 대표

A fox is a very cunning animal. 여우는 매우 교활한 동물이다.

| MORE TIPS | 대표명사를 나타내는 방법은 주로 「a+단수명사」,「복수명사」,「무관사+셀 수 없는 명사」 등이다.

4. '~마다'

Heather works eight hours **a** day, five days a week. Heather는 하루에 여덟 시간, 일주일에 5일 일한다.

5. 직업이나 종류

Mark is **a** mechanic. Mark는 기계 수리공이다.

A glider is **a** plane with no engine. 글라이너는 엔진이 없는 비행기이디.

Tennis is **a** sport. 테니스는 스포츠의 한 종류이다.

6. 특정한 상황의 명사 앞에

I had **a** big lunch. 나는 점심을 많이(잘) 먹었다.

We had **a** wonderful time. 우리는 멋진 시간을 보냈다.

Unit Test

1. 빈칸에 알맞은 부정관사 a 또는 an을 써 넣으시오.

________ umbrella	________ one-way conversation	________ hour
________ honest boy	________ MP	________ SOS
________ useful book	________ university	________ interesting book

2. 부정관사가 필요한 곳에 a 또는 an을 써 넣으시오. (필요 없는 곳에는 X표 하시오.)

1. We live in ______________ old house.
2. Let's see ______________ movie.
3. A fox is ______________ very cunning animal.
4. We've waited for you for ______________ hour.
5. I work ______________ five days ______________ week.
6. This is ______________ useful book.
7. Hawaii is ______________ island.
8. A glider is ______________ plane with no engine.
9. Tennis is ______________ sport.
10. I had ______________ big lunch.
11. Do you have ______________ sisters?
12. It's raining out there. I need ______________ umbrella.

3. 밑줄 친 부분을 「a + 단수명사」 형태의 대표명사로 바꿔 문장을 다시 쓰시오.

보기	Dogs are faithful animals. → A dog is a faithful animal.

1. Foxes are cunning animals. → ______________________________
2. Elephants can swim very well. → ______________________________
3. Doctors must like people. → ______________________________
4. Islands are surrounded by water. → ______________________________
5. Flowers smell good. → ______________________________

Writing Pattern Practice | 부정관사

Pattern 1_ 막연한 '하나'와 분명한 '하나'의 「a/an + 명사」

우리는 오래된 집에 산다. ______________________

영화 보자.(see) ______________________

나는 언니가 하나 있다. ______________________

Pattern 2_ 종족의, 대표의 「a/an + 명사」

여우는 매우 교활한 동물이다.(cunning) ______________________

악어는 수영을 잘 할 수 있다.(Crocodiles~) ______________________

개는 충직한 동물이다.(faithful) ______________________

Pattern 3_ '~마다'의 「a/an + 명사」

나는 일 년에 한번 씩 여행을 한다.(travel) ______________________

나는 한 달에 두세 번 영화를 본다.(a couple of times)

____

Heather는 하루에 여덟 시간, 일주일에 5일 일한다. ______________________

Pattern 4_ 직업이나 종류의 「a/an + 명사」

Mark는 기계 수리공이다.(a mechanic) ______________________

글라이더는 엔진이 없는 비행기이다.(with no engine) ______________________

테니스는 스포츠의 한 종류이다. ______________________

그녀는 영어선생님이다. ______________________

Pattern 5_ 특정한 상황의 명사 앞에 「a/an + 명사」

나는 점심을 많이(잘) 먹었다.(have, big) ______________________

우리는 멋진 시간을 보냈다.(wonderful) ______________________

정말 더운 날이다.(It's~, extremely) ______________________

Unit

28 정관사

● Pattern the + 명사

Grammar in Practice

(On the bus)

A: Does this bus go to the Hayatt?

B: No. You'll have to get off at the bank and take the number 83.

A: How long is the ride?

B: About half an hour.

Grammar in Use

1. 정관사 the

명사 앞에서 특정한 것을 나타낼 때 쓴다. 명사의 발음이 a, e, i, o, u로 시작하면 the /ðə/를 the /ði:/로 읽는다.

2. 문맥상 알 수 있는 명사를 지칭하는 경우

[비교]

I'm going to **the** bank. (듣는 사람이 어느 은행인지 알고 있을 경우)
Is there a bank near here? (특정한 은행을 가리키지 않을 경우)

Did you wash **the** clothes? (듣는 사람이 어느 옷인지 알고 있을 경우)
I need to buy clothes. (특정한 옷을 가리키지 않는 경우)

Could you open **the** window? 창문 열어줄래요?
Ann is in **the** kitchen. Ann은 부엌에 있어.
Did you feed **the** dogs? 개들 밥 줬니?
Did you enjoy **the** party? 파티는 즐거웠니?

3. 앞에서 언급한 명사를 다시 말할 경우

Lucy bought a car. She showed us **the** car today. Lucy는 차를 샀다. 그녀는 우리에게 오늘 그 차를 보여줬다.
She's got a son. **The** boy is nine years old. 그녀는 아들이 있다. 그 소년은 9살이다.

4. 수식어구가 있어서 한정 받을 경우

Who is **the** girl over there with Terry? Terry와 함께 저쪽에 있는 그 소녀는 누구지?
The man in black is my boss. 검정 옷을 입은 그 남자가 내 상사다.

5. 세상에 유일한 것을 말할 경우

예 the sun, the moon, the Earth, the world, the universe 등

People used to think that **the** Earth was flat. 사람들은 지구가 평평하다고 믿었었다.
I haven't seen **the** sun for days. 해를 못 본지 며칠 되었다.

6. 최상급, next, same, only 앞

My grandma is **the** oldest in my family. 할머니가 우리 가족 중에 가장 나이 드셨다.
Ken and I went to **the** same high school. Ken과 나는 같은 고등학교에 다녔다.

7. 신체의 일부분을 말할 경우

She kicked him on **the** knee. 그녀는 그의 무릎을 찼다.
He hit me on **the** head. 그는 내 머리를 때렸다.

8. 사람들의 일상에 친숙한 주변 환경을 말할 경우

예 the town, the city, the country, the mountains, the sea, the seaside, the wind, the rain, the weather, the sunshine 등

I like listening to **the rain.** 나는 비오는 소리 듣는 것을 좋아한다.
British people talk about **the weather** a lot. 영국 사람들은 날씨에 대해 많이 이야기한다.
Susan likes **the seaside**, but I prefer **the mountains.** Susan은 해변을 좋아하고 나는 산을 더 좋아한다.

9. 「the + 고유명사」

예 바다와 강: the Pacific, the Atlantic, the Indian, the Han, the Nile
산맥, 제도, 반도: the Alps, the Philippines, the Korean Peninsula
유명기관, 건물, 호텔, 박물관: the Empire State Building, the Chrysler Building
배, 언론사: the Titanic, the L.A. Times, the Digest
복수 국가명: the United States of America, the United Kingdom, the Netherlands

Have you ever been to **the Philippines?** 필리핀에 가본 적 있니?
The Empire State Building is one of the tallest buildings in the United States. 엠파이어 스테이트 빌딩은 미국에서 가장 높은 건물 중 하나다.

Unit Test

1. **둘 중 알맞은 것을 고르시오.**

1. I lay down on (a/ the) ground.
2. There're a lot of stars in (a/ the) sky.
3. The sun is (a/ the) star.
4. "Did you have (a/ the) nice vacation?" "Yes, it was (a/ the) best vacation I've ever had."
5. Your shirt is (a/ the) same color as mine.
6. I bought a book. (A/ The) book is about love.
7. Have you ever been to (a/ the) Empire State Building?
8. I have (a/ the) good idea. Let's go bowling this afternoon.
9. I kissed him on (a/ the) cheek.
10. The Earth goes around the sun once (a/ the) day.

2. **다음 문장을 읽고 the가 필요한 자리에 ✓표 하시오.**

1. I like listening to rain.
2. Alaska is largest state in the United States.
3. Earth is a planet.
4. I'm fed up with doing same thing everyday.
5. Does this bus go to Hayatt?
6. He hit me on head.
7. Do you want to live in country?
8. You're only person that I trust.
9. Look at woman wearing sunglasses.
10. Have you ever been to Philippines?

3. **우리말과 일치하도록 괄호 안의 단어를 알맞게 배열하시오.**

1. 할머니가 우리 가족 중에 가장 나이 드셨다. (the oldest/ My grandma is/ in my family)

   ____

2. Ken과 나는 같은 고등학교에 다녔다. (went to/ the same high school/ Ken and I)

   ____

3. 그녀는 그의 무릎을 찼다. (kicked him/ she/ on the knee)

   ____

Writing Pattern Practice | 정관사

Pattern 1_ 문맥상 알 수 있는 명사를 지칭하는 경우의 「the + 명사」

(그) 창문 열어줄래요?(Could~?) ______

Ann은 (그) 부엌에 있어. ______

(그) 파티는 즐거웠니?(enjoy) ______

Pattern 2_ 앞에서 언급한 명사를 다시 말할 경우의 「the + 명사」

Lucy bought a car. 그녀는 우리에게 오늘 그 차를 보여줬다. ______

She's got a son. 그 소년은 9살이다. ______

Pattern 3_ 수식어구가 있어서 한정 받을 경우의 「the + 명사」

Terry와 함께 저쪽에 있는 소녀는 누구지?(over there) ______

검정 옷을 입은 남자가 내 상사다.(in black) ______

Pattern 4_ 세상에 유일한 것을 말할 경우의 「the + 명사」

사람들은 지구가 평평하다고 믿었었다.(used to think that, flat) ______

나는 며칠 동안 해를 못 봤다.(for days) ______

Pattern 5_ 최상급, next, same, only 앞의 「the + 명사」

할머니가 우리 가족 중에 가장 나이 드셨다. ______

Ken과 나는 같은 고등학교에 다녔다. ______

Pattern 6_ 신체의 일부분을 말할 경우의 「the + 단수명사」

그녀는 그의 무릎을 찼다. ______

그는 내 머리를 때렸다. ______

Pattern 7_ 사람들의 일상에 친숙한 주변 환경을 말할 경우의 「the + 명사」

나는 비오는 소리 듣는 것을 좋아한다.(listening) ______

영국 사람들은 날씨에 대해 많이 이야기한다.(British people~, a lot) ______

Pattern 8_ 「the + 고유명사」

태평양	______	인도양	______
알프스 산맥	______	L.A. 타임즈	______
엠파이어스테이트 빌딩	______	타이타닉(호)	______
미국	______	네덜란드	______

Unit

29 관사의 생략

● Pattern 무관사 + 명사

Grammar in Practice

(Making a reservation)

A: I'd like to fly to Dallas on Sunday, the 21st.

B: Just a minute and I'll see if there are any flights.

A: I'd like to travel first class.

B: OK. We have a nonstop flight leaving at 8:30 PM.

Grammar in Use

1. 장소를 나타내는 명사가 그 본래의 목적으로 쓰일 때 관사 생략

규칙적으로 반복해서 찾는 곳이나 상황을 전체적으로 추상화시키는 경우 관사를 쓰지 않고 표현하는 것들이 있다.

to/at/from **school**, **university**, **church**, **work**(직장)
at/from **home**
to/in/out of **bed**, **hospital**, **prison**(감옥)

School starts at 9:00. 학교는 9시에 시작한다.

She's in **prison**. 그녀는 수감되어 있다.

You should be in **bed**. 너는 (침대에서) 쉬어야해.

*명사본래의 목적에서 벗어난 뜻으로 쓰일 경우 the를 생략하지 않는다.

[비교]

Tom is **in hospital.** Tom은 병원에 있다.(입원했다.)

Tom works as a cook **in the hospital.** Tom은 병원에서 조리사로 일한다.

Susie is **in bed.** Susie는 침대에서 자고/쉬고 있다.

Susie found her earings **in the bed.** Susie는 침대에서 귀걸이를 발견했다.

| MORE TIPS |

정관사(the)를 생략하는 장소명	정관사(the)를 붙이는 장소명
• 대륙, 대부분의 나라이름 Africa, Japan • 주, 도시이름 Wisconsin, Chicago • 대부분의 거리/공원이름 Main Street, Fifth Avenue, Central Park, Broadway • 호수, 섬, 대부분의 산 이름 Lake Victoria, Hawaii, Everest	• 대양, 바다, 강, 산맥, 사막 이름 the Atlantic, the Red Sea, the Nile, the Rocky Mountains, the Sahara • 호텔, 극장, 박물관 이름 the Hyatt (Hotel), the Playhouse, the Louvre • 나라의 공식 이름/복수국가명 the United States, the Netherlands, the Philippines

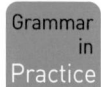

2. 식사/ 요일/ 달/ 명절 이름 앞에서 생략

have **breakfast/ lunch/ dinner**	on **Monday/ Thursday**
in **January/ February**	at **Christmas/ Easter**

I've just had **lunch.** 나는 금방 점심을 먹었어.
Let's meet on **Monday.** 월요일에 만나자.
What do you usually do at **Christmas**? 크리스마스에는 보통 뭐하니?

3. 「by + 교통수단」의 경우 생략

구체적인 차량을 가리키는 경우가 아니라 일반적인 교통수단을 말할 경우 관사를 생략한다.

by **bus/ taxi/ bike/ plane/ car/ train/ subway**	on **foot**

I usually go to school **by bus.** 나는 보통 버스를 타고 학교에 다닌다.
It takes an hour **on foot.** 걸어서 1시간 걸려.

4. 반복되거나 대조되는 「명사 + 명사」의 경우 생략

한 명사가 반복되거나 대조적인 두 명사로 이루어진 고정적인 표현은 관사를 생략한다.

arm in arm 팔짱을 끼고	**with knife and fork** 나이프와 포크로
day after day 날마다	**night after night** 밤마다
inch by inch 조금씩	**from top to bottom** 위에서 아래까지

Korean can be written **from top to bottom** or from left to right. 한국어는 위부터 아래쪽으로 또는 왼쪽에서 오른쪽으로 쓰여질 수 있다.
The couple were walking **arm in arm.** 두 사람은 팔짱을 끼고 걷고 있었다.

5. 「Mr./ Mrs./ Doctor/ President/ Aunt 등 + 이름」 앞에서 생략

Mr. Smith	**Doctor Smith**	**Uncle Tom**	**Aunt Janet**
Prince Charles	**Professor Kim**		

Uncle Tom visited us. Tom 삼촌이 우리를 방문했다.

6. 관용적인 관사 생략

on **TV** 텔레비전에서	in **fact** 사실상	on **fire** 화재가 나서

What's **on TV?** TV에서 뭐하니?
The bakery is **on fire.** 빵집에 불났다.

Unit Test

1. 다음 중 주로 무관사로 쓰이는 명사를 골라 동그라미 하시오.

Africa	Hyatt	Tokyo	Main Street	Nile 나일강
January	United States	Rocky Mountains	Portugal	

2. 빈칸에 the가 필요한 곳에는 the를 쓰고, 필요하지 않은 곳에는 X표 하시오.

1. I haven't had ________ dinner yet.
2. What is ________ longest river in________ world?
3. We usually go to school by ________ bus.
4. What time do you usually go to ________ work?
5. Do you come from ________ United States?
6. What's on ________ TV?
7. The bakery is on ________ fire.
8. Tom works as a cook in ________ hospital.
9. Your shirt is on ________ bed.
10. What do you usually do at ________ Christmas?
11. Your sweater is ________ same color as mine.
12. What did you have for ________ breakfast?
13. We visited France and ________ United Kingdom.
14. We called ________ Doctor White.
15. Who is ________ Captain Johnson?
16. What is the name of the ocean between ________ Africa and ________ Australia?
17. The couple were walking ________ arm in ________ arm.
18. It takes about an hour by ________ subway.
19. Queen Elizabeth had dinner with ________ President Bush.
20. I've been to ________ Vancouver twice.
21. ________ Hilton hotel is on ________ Main Street.
22. My favorite place in New York is ________Central Park.
23. Korea is smaller than ________ Netherlands.
24. Korean can be written from ________top to ________ bottom or from left to right.
25. Where is ________ school located?

Writing Pattern Practice | 관사의 생략

Pattern 1_ 장소를 나타내는 명사가 그 본래의 목적으로 쓰일 때 관사생략

> to/at/from school, university, church, work(직장)
> at/from home
> to/in/out of bed, hospital, prison(감옥)

학교는 9시에 시작한다. ______________________

그녀는 수감되어 있다. ______________________

너는 (침대에서) 쉬어야해.(should be) ______________________

Pattern 2_ 식사/ 요일/ 달/ 명절 이름 앞에서 관사생략

> have breakfast/ lunch/ dinner   on Monday/ Thursday
> in January/ February   at Christmas/ Easter

나는 금방 점심을 먹었어.(I' ve~, have) ______________________

월요일에 만나자. ______________________

1월에는 눈이 많이 온다.(It~, a lot) ______________________

너는 크리스마스에는 보통 뭐하니? ______________________

Pattern 3_ 「by + 교통수단」의 경우 관사생략

> by bus/ taxi/ bike/ plane/ car/ train/ subway
> on foot

나는 보통 버스를 타고 학교에 다닌다. ______________________

우리는 부산에 기차를 타고 갔다. ______________________

걸어서 1시간 걸려.(take) ______________________

Pattern 4_ 반복되거나 대조되는 「명사 + 명사」의 경우 관사생략

> arm in arm 팔짱을 끼고   with knife and fork 나이프와 포크로   day after day 날마다
> night after night 밤마다   from top to bottom 위에서 아래까지   inch by inch 조금씩

두 사람은 팔짱을 서로 끼고 걷고 있었다.(The couple~)

____

그들은 나이프와 포크로 먹는다. ______________________

Writing Pattern Practice | 관사의 생략

Pattern 5_ 「Mr./ Mrs./ Doctor/ President/ Aunt 등 + 이름」 앞에서 관사생략

Mr. Smith, Doctor Smith, Uncle Tom, Aunt Janet, Prince Charles, Professor Kim

Tom 삼촌이 우리를 방문했다. ________________

나는 오늘 저녁 Doctor Johnson을 만나기로 되어 있다.(be supposed to)

____

누가 Professor Kim이에요? ________________

Pattern 6_ 관용적인 관사생략

on TV 텔레비전에서, in fact 사실상, on fire 화재가 나서

TV에서 뭐하니? ________________

사실상 우리는 충분한 돈이 없다. ________________

빵집에 불났다. ________________

Unit

30 인칭대명사와 it

● Pattern
1. 1인칭 I(나)/we(우리)
2. 2인칭 you(너/너희)
3. 3인칭 he(그)/she(그녀)/it(그것)/they(그들)

Grammar in Practice

A: Cindy, I'd like you to meet my sister Mary.
B: It's nice to meet you.
C: Nice to meet you, too. How do you like Minnesota so far?
B: It's very cold and I'm still feeling a little homesick.
C: You're bound to feel that way at first, I think. It always takes time to get used to a new place.

Grammar in Use

1. 인칭대명사

인칭대명사는 사람이나 사물을 가리키는 명사 대신 쓰는 대명사다. 말하는 사람(1인칭)과 상대방(2인칭), 그리고 다른 사람, 사물, 사건(3인칭)으로 나눌 수 있다.

- 「주격인칭대명사 + 동사」
  I love Paris. 나는 파리를 좋아한다.
- 「동사 + 목적격인칭대명사」
  Tell **me** what to do. 무엇을 할 지 말해줘.
- 「전치사 + 목적격인칭대명사」
  Look **at** us. 우리를 봐.
- 「be동사 + 목적격인칭대명사」
  "Who is it?" "It's **me**." 누구세요? 저예요.

2. 인칭대명사의 순서

대명사 또는 명사를 두 개 이상 열거할 경우 상대방을 존중하는 의미로 2, 3인칭을 1인칭보다 먼저 쓴다.

Jack and I are close friends. Jack과 나는 친한 친구다.
My sister and I have a lot of things in common. 언니와 나는 공통점이 많다.

3. 「as/ than/ but/ except + me(or I)」

as/than/but/except 다음은 의미상 주어자리라 해도 구어체(informal)인 경우 목적격 인칭대명사를 주로 쓴다.

I can speak English better **than her**. 나는 그녀보다 영어를 더 잘 할 수 있다.
Everybody **except him** can come. 그를 제외한 모두가 올 수 있다.

4. 시간, 날씨, 요일, 날짜, 거리, 상황 등을 나타내는 it

'it'이 시간, 날씨, 요일, 날짜, 거리, 상황 등을 나타내는 경우 비인칭 또는 무인칭 주어라고 하는데 이 때 it은 해석하지 않는다.

It's nine thirty. 9시 30분이다.

It's freezing out there. 밖이 몹시 춥다.

It's Monday again. 또 다시 월요일이다.

It's January 1st. 1월 1일이다.

It's ten miles to the nearest bank. 가장 가까운 은행까지 10마일이다.

"How is **it** going?" "Terrific." 어떻게 지내니? 아주 좋아.

5. 가주어, 가목적어 역할을 하는 it

주어나 목적어 자리에 부정사 또는 절 형태가 와서 길어질 때 it을 대신 쓰고 진짜 주어나 목적어를 뒤로 보낸다. 이때 it 역시 해석하지 않는다.

It's nice to talk to you. 너랑 얘기해서 좋아.

It was surprising you made it to the first class. 네가 1교시 제때에 갔다니 놀랍다.

We found **it** strange that she was absent for two weeks. 우리는 그녀가 두 주 동안 결석한 것은 이상하다고 생각했다.

Jack made **it** very clear that he was in love with her. Jack은 그가 그녀와 사랑에 빠져 있는 것을 매우 확실하게 했다.

6. it을 이용한 관용표현 「it's worth ~ing」, 「it's no use ~ing」

각각 '~할 가치가 있다', '~해도 소용없다'라는 뜻으로 이 때 it은 가주어역할을 한다.

It's worth visit**ing** Italy. 이탈리아는 방문할 가치가 있다.

It's worth buy**ing that car.** 그 차를 살 가치가 있다.

It's no use cry**ing** over spilt milk. 지나간 일은 후회해도 소용없다.

Unit Test

1. **1번과 같이 밑줄 친 it의 쓰임이 같은 것을 보기에서 고르시오.**

1. It's sunny out there. (C)
2. It's ten to five. ( )
3. It was surprising you made it to the first class. ( )
4. How far is it to your school? ( )
5. How did it go? ( )
6. Is it Sunday today? ( )
7. His bad leg made it a problem to walk. ( )

보기	
	A. I find it interesting to hear her stories.
	B. It's nice to talk to you.
	C. It's cold outside.
	D. It's twenty miles from here.
	E. How is it going?
	F. It's Saturday.
	G. It's eleven thirty.

2. **어색한 곳을 찾아 밑줄치고 고쳐 쓰시오.**

1. Tell I what to do. → ______________________
2. Look at we. → ______________________
3. I and my mother have little in common. → ______________________
4. Why is she with he? → ______________________
5. He gave some flowers to me and Jane. → ______________________

3. **우리말과 일치하도록 괄호 안의 단어를 알맞게 배열하시오.**

1. 우리를 봐. (at/ look/ us)

____

2. Jack과 나는 가까운 친구다. (and/ I/ Jack/ close friends/ are)

____

3. 그를 제외한 모두가 올 수 있다. (him/ everybody except/ can come)

____

4. 파리는 방문할 가치가 있다. (worth/ it's/ visiting Paris)

____

5. 설명하려고 노력해봐야 소용없다. (trying to explain/ no use/ it's)

____

Writing Pattern Practice | 인칭대명사와 it

Pattern 1_ 주격 인칭대명사, 목적격 인칭대명사

「주격인칭대명사 + 동사」

나는 그녀를 그리워한다. ____________________

「동사 + 목적격인칭대명사」

무엇을 할 지 내게 말해줘.(what to do) ____________________

「전치사 + 목적격인칭대명사」

우리를 봐. ____________________

「be동사 + 목적격인칭대명사」

"Who is it?" 저요. ____________________

Pattern 2_ 「I/me를 제외한 인칭대명사 + I/me」

Jack과 나는 가까운 친구다. ____________________

그것은 Peter와 나의 문제야.(That's a matter for~) ____________________

Pattern 3_ 「as/ than/ but/ except + me(or I)」

나는 그녀보다 영어를 더 잘 할 수 있다. ____________________

그를 제외한 모두가 올 수 있다. ____________________

Pattern 4_ 시간, 날씨, 요일, 날짜, 거리, 상황 등을 나타내는 it

9시 30분이다. ____________________

밖에 몹시 춥다.(freezing) ____________________

다시 월요일이다. ____________________

1월 1일이다. ____________________

가장 가까운 은행까지 10마일이다.(the nearest) ____________________

어떻게 지내니?(it) ____________________

Pattern 5_ 가주어, 가목적어 역할을 하는 it

너랑 얘기해서 좋아.(nice, talk) ____________________

우리는 그녀가 두 주 동안 결석을 한 것은 이상하다고 생각했다. (find, absent)

____

Pattern 6_ 「it's worth ~ing」, 「it's no use ~ing」

이탈리아는 방문할 가치가 있다. ____________________

지나간 일 후회해도 소용없다.(cry over spilt milk)

____

Unit

31 소유격과 소유대명사

● Pattern
1. my/your/his/her/its/our/their+명사
2. mine/yours/his/hers/ours/theirs

Grammar in Practice

A: Is that your phone ringing?
B: Not mine. Mine is in silent mode.
A: We're in the library.
B: Yeah, right. I just hate people who don't turn off their phones in the library.

Grammar in Use

1. 인칭대명사의 소유격

인칭대명사의 소유격 my/your/his/her/its/our/their는 명사구의 맨 앞에 위치한다.

This is **my younger sister.** 얘가 내 여동생이야.

May I ask **your phone number?** 전화번호를 여쭤 봐도 될까요?

2. 이중소유격

a/an, some, this, that, no 등이 명사 앞에 올 경우 소유격을 같이 쓰지 않는다. 이때는 「a/an, some, this, that, no+명사+of+소유대명사」 형태의 이중소유격을 쓴다.

Laura is **a friend of mine.** (a my friend→X) Laura는 내 친구 중 하나이다.(=Laura is one of my friends.)

Can I borrow **some books of yours?** (some your books→X) 네 책들 중 몇 권을 빌릴 수 있을까? (=Can I borrow some of your books?)

3. 명사의 소유격

- 명사의 소유격은 사람, 동물인 경우 명사에 's를 붙인다.

  Emily is **Ted's** sister. Emily는 Ted의 여동생이다.

  Where is the **manager's** office? 지배인 사무실이 어디죠?

- 조직이나 단체(a group of people) 또는 장소명(places)일 경우 's나 of 둘 다 쓸 수 있다.

  That is **the government's** decision.(=the decision of the government) 그것이 정부의 결정이야.

  Do you know **the world's** population?(=the population of the world) 세계인구가 얼마인지 알고 있니?

  That is **America's** influence.(=the influence of America) 그것이 미국의 영향이다.

- -s로 끝나는 명사일 경우, 뒤에 apostrophe(')만 붙인다.

  This is my **parents'** car. (parents's→X) 이것은 부모님 차다.
  This is my **sisters'** room. (sisters's→X) 이것은 내 여동생들의 방이다.

- 복수명사라 하지라도 -s로 끝나지 않을 경우 's를 붙인다.

  These are **children's** backpacks. 이것들은 아이들의 가방이다.

- 시간이나 단위를 나타내는 명사일 경우 이중소유격 대신 's를 사용하여 소유격을 만든다.

  yesterday's news 어제 뉴스
  last Saturday's match 지난 토요일의 경기
  three dollars' worth of popcorn 3달러어치의 팝콘
  six hours' sleep 6시간의 수면

  Do you have **today's** newspaper? 너 오늘 신문 있니?
  We need at least **seven hours'** sleep a night. 우리는 하루에 적어도 7시간의 수면이 필요하다.

4. 무생물 명사의 소유격

명사가 무생물일 경우 주로 's 대신 of를 사용한다.

the name **of** this street 이 거리의 이름
the title **of** this song 이 노래의 제목
the roof **of** this house 집의 지붕
the top **of** the page 페이지 윗부분

5. 소유대명사

소유대명사 mine/yours/his/hers/ours/theirs는 「소유격+명사」를 대신 쓰는 말이다. 명사의 소유대명사인 경우 명사's 를 쓴다.

That's **my car.** → That's **mine.**
Which is **your bag?** → Which is **yours?**
Those are **Karen's** shoes. → Those are **Karen's.**

Can I use your phone? I can't find **mine.** 네 전화 써도 되니? 내 것을 찾을 수가 없어.
This isn't my pen. It's **Selly's.** 이것은 내 펜이 아니야. Selly 거야.

Unit Test

1. 다음 두 단어를 보기와 같이 's 또는 of를 이용하여 연결하시오.

> 보기 | (the car, my father) → my father's car
> (the end, the month) → the end of the month

1. (the beginning, the movie) → ____________
2. (the car, my parents) → ____________
3. (the newspaper, yesterday) → ____________
4. (the roof, this house) → ____________
5. (the name, your boyfriend) → ____________

2. 틀린 곳이 없으면 OK, 틀린 곳이 있으면 찾아서 밑줄치고 고쳐 쓰시오. 보기를 참고하시오.

> 보기 | Who is the singer of this song? → OK
> Where is the bag of Jessie? → Jessie's bag

1. What's the name of this street? → ____________
2. Look at the top of the page. → ____________
3. We need eight hours's sleep a night. → ____________
4. The hair of Jean is beautiful. → ____________
5. What color is Kelly's hair? → ____________
6. I've never met the son of Karen. → ____________
7. Do you still have yesterday's newspaper? → ____________
8. This is my parents' room. → ____________
9. Laura is a my friend. → ____________
10. Can I borrow some books of yours? → ____________

3. 밑줄 친 것을 보기와 같이 소유대명사를 이용해 바꾸시오.

> 보기 | That's my car. → That's mine.

1. Which is your bag? → ____________
2. Are those his sunglasses? → ____________
3. Those are Karen's shoes. → ____________
4. This is Cindy's cell phone. → ____________
5. This is my sister's room. → ____________

Writing Pattern Practice | 소유격과 소유대명사

Pattern 1_ 인칭대명사의 소유격 「my/ your/ his/ her/ its/ our/ their + 명사」

얘가 내 여동생이야. ______________________

당신의 전화번호를 여쭤 봐도 될까요? ______________________

Pattern 2_ 이중소유격 「a/an, some, this, that, no + 명사 + of + 소유대명사」

Laura는 내 친구 중 하나이다. ______________________

네 것들 중 책 몇 권을 빌릴 수 있을까?(Can I~, some)

____

Pattern 3_ 명사의 소유격 「명사's」

Emily는 Ted의 여동생이다. ______________________

지배인 사무실이 어디죠?(the manager's) ______________________

이것은 내 부모님 차다. ______________________

이것은 내 여동생들의 방이다. ______________________

이것들은 아이들 가방이다.(backpacks) ______________________

너 오늘 신문 있니? ______________________

우리는 하루에 적어도 7시간의 수면이 필요하다.(a night)

____

Pattern 4_ 무생물 명사의 소유격 「명사 + of + 명사」

너는 이 거리의 이름을 아니? ______________________

내게 이 노래의 제목을 말해줘. ______________________

Pattern 5_ 소유대명사 「mine/yours/his/hers/ours/theirs 또는 명사's」

그것은 내거야. ______________________

어느 것이 네것이니? ______________________

그것들은 Karen거야. ______________________

Unit

32 지시대명사

● **Pattern** this/these, that/those

Grammar in Practice

A: I'd like to have this *prescription filled.
B: I'll take care of it right away.
A: And I'd like something for a *sunburn.
B: Try this. It's a new product.

*prescription 처방전, sunburn 화상

Grammar in Use

1. 지시대명사 this/these, that/those

this/those는 가까이, that/those는 멀리 있는 사람/사물/상황을 가리키거나 소개할 때 쓴다.

This is my cap. 이것은 내 모자다.
These are sunglasses. 이것은 선글라스다.
This is my wife. 이 사람은 내 처입니다.
That is my computer. 저것은 내 컴퓨터야.
What are **those?** 저것들은 뭐니?
That is my daughter. 쟤가 내 딸이야.

| MORE TIPS | 지시대명사 that/those는 명사의 반복을 피하기 위해 쓰기도 한다.
- The population of China is much larger than **that** of Korea. 중국의 인구는 한국(의 인구)보다 훨씬 많다.
- Prices in New York are higher than **those** in Texas. 뉴욕의 물가는 텍사스(의 물가) 보다 높다.

2. 지시형용사 this/these, that/those

명사를 꾸며주는 형용사 역할을 하기도 한다.

I'll be busy **this** weekend. 이번 주말에는 바쁠 거야.
These scissors are awfully heavy. 이 가위가 매우 무겁다.
What is **that** loud noise? 저 시끄러운 소리는 뭐야?

3. 부사 this, that

this는 '이만큼', '이 정도로'의 뜻으로 that은 '그만큼', '그 정도로'의 뜻으로 쓴다.

I didn't expect you to come **this** early. 네가 이렇게 일찍 오리라 예상하지 못했어.
I can't eat **that** much. 나는 그렇게 많이 못 먹어.
His English is not **that** good. 그의 영어는 그렇게 훌륭하지 않아.

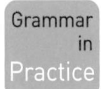

Unit Test

1. **밑줄 친 지시대명사 that의 쓰임이 비슷한 것끼리 연결하시오.**

1. That is my computer.
2. What is that loud noise?
3. His English is not that good.

a. That girl is my sister.
b. She's not that pretty.
c. That is what I'm talking about.

2. **빈칸에 지시형용사 this 또는 these를 쓰시오.**

1. "Do you like ________ flowers?" "Yes, I really like them."
2. "Is ________ what you want?" "Yes, it is."
3. "Do you feel like eating ________?" "Yes, I really want to eat it."
4. ________ music is kind of boring, isn' t it?
5. ________ boys are willing to go out to play soccer.

3. **빈칸에 지시형용사 that 또는 those를 쓰시오.**

1. Who's ________ boy over there?
2. Look at ________ shoes. They are very nice.
3. ________ girl is Jane who I'm working with.
4. "Betty is a great dancer." "Really? I didn't know ________."
5. ________ questions are quite difficult.

4. **우리말과 일치하도록 괄호 안의 단어를 알맞게 배열하시오.**

1. 그것은 좋은 질문이다. (that/ a good question/ is)

____

2. 이것이 네가 산거야? (what you bought/ this/ is/?)

____

3. 이 모델은 2006년도에 나왔다. (came out /this model/ in 2006)

____

4. 그 셔츠는 나에게 맞지 않는다. (doesn't/ fit me/ that shirt)

____

5. 이렇게 늦게 전화해서 미안해. (to call you/ I'm sorry/ this late)

____

6. 나는 네가 이렇게 일찍 올 줄 몰랐다. (you to come/ I didn't/ this early/ expect)

____

7. 나는 그렇게 빨리 못 달려. (that fast/ run/ I can't)

____

Writing Pattern Practice | 지시대명사

Pattern 1_ 지시대명사 this/these, that/those

이것은 내 모자다.(cap) ____________________

이것은 선글라스다. ____________________

이 사람은 내 처입니다. ____________________

저것은 내 컴퓨터야. ____________________

저것들은 뭐니? ____________________

쟤가 내 여자친구야. ____________________

Pattern 2_ 지시형용사 this/these, that/those

나는 이번 주말에 바쁠 거야. ____________________

이 모델은 2006년도에 나왔다.(come out) ____________________

이 가위가 매우 무겁다.(awfully) ____________________

저 시끄러운 소리는 뭐야?(loud) ____________________

그 셔츠는 나에게 맞지 않는다.(fit) ____________________

저 스커트들을 봐. ____________________

그 문제들은 꽤 어렵다.(quite) ____________________

Pattern 3_ 부사 this, that

네가 이렇게 일찍 오리라 예상하지 못했어. (I didn't expect you to~)

____

네게 이렇게 늦게 전화해서 미안해.(I'm sorry to~) ____________________

나는 그렇게 많이 못 먹어. ____________________

나는 그렇게 빨리 못 달려. ____________________

Sarah는 그렇게 예쁘지는 않아.(pretty) ____________________

그의 영어는 그렇게 훌륭하지 않아.(good) ____________________

Unit

33 재귀대명사

● Pattern 1. myself/yourself/herself/himself
2. yourselves/ourselves/themselves

Grammar in Practice

A: This is a great birthday party. Can I blow out the candles now?
B: Yeah, just don't forget to make a wish.
A: Sure. Thank you all.
B: Let's eat! Please help yourselves!

Grammar in Use

1. 재귀대명사

재귀대명사는 「인칭대명사의 소유격/목적격-self/selves」 형태로 '~자신'이라는 뜻으로 쓴다.

	단수	복수
1인칭	myself	ourselves
2인칭	yourself	yourselves
3인칭	himself/herself/itself	themselves

2. 「재귀」의 의미

재귀대명사를 사용하는 가장 흔한 경우로 문장 안에서 주어와 목적어가 같을 때 쓴다.
John cut **himself** shaving this morning. John은 오늘 아침 면도를 하다가 베었다.
We took a bath and dried **ourselves.** 우리는 목욕하고 몸을 말렸다.
Look at **yourself** in the mirror. 거울로 자신을 봐.

3. 「강조」의 의미

강조할 경우 '다른 사람/것'이 아니라 '바로 그 사람/것'이라는 뜻으로 재귀대명사를 문장 끝이나 강조하고자 하는 명사 뒤에 쓴다. 이때 재귀대명사는 생략 가능하다.
It's cheaper if you do it **yourself.** 네가 직접 하면 더 저렴해.
The shirt **itself** looks nice, but it's too expensive. 그 셔츠 자체는 멋있어 보이는데 너무 비싸.

4. 재귀대명사가 포함된 관용표현

by oneself 홀로 say(talk) to oneself 혼잣말하다
of itself(=by itself) 저절로 enjoy oneself 즐기다 help oneself 마음껏 먹다
make oneself at home 편히 있다 (=make oneself comfortable)
come to oneself 의식을 회복하다 be proud of oneself ~를 자랑스럽게 여기다

Unit Test

1. 재귀대명사를 사용하여 문장을 완성하시오.

1. I have a party tomorrow night. I'm going to the mall to get ____________ a dress.
2. You don't have to pay for me. I'll pay for ____________ .
3. The old lady seems weird. She sometimes talks to ____________ .
4. It's our fault. We should blame ____________ .
5. "Where did you buy that cake?" "I made it ____________ ."
6. We painted the house ____________ . It was cheaper.
7. Do you(너) want to eat some? Then help ____________ .
8. You(너희들) can sit here. Make ____________ at home.
9. Don't worry about me. I can take care of ____________ .
10. "How was your trip?" "We enjoyed ____________ very much."

2. 밑줄 친 재귀대명사가 생략가능하면 괄호 안에 ✓표 하시오.

1. His letters are all about <u>himself.</u> (   )
2. Look at <u>yourself</u> in the mirror. (   )
3. I'll see the manager <u>himself</u> if necessary. (   )
4. My baby fell and hurt <u>himself.</u> (   )
5. Jully had a great time. She enjoyed <u>herself.</u> (   )
6. That pot is too hot. Don't burn <u>yourself.</u> (   )
7. The book <u>itself</u> wasn' t very good. (   )
8. Susan <u>herself</u> didn't think that she could get the prize. (   )
9. My grandmother sometimes talks to <u>herself</u>. (   )
10. I <u>myself</u> did the laundry. (   )

3. 빈칸에 알맞은 재귀대명사를 넣어 대화를 완성하시오.

1. A: I want you to do my homework.
   B: No, I think you should do it ____________ .
2. A: Who repaired the car?
   B: I did it ____________ .
3. A: Who told you that Lisa was moving to San Francisco?
   B: Lisa ____________ told me.
4. A: Who did you go with?
   B: I went there by ____________ .

Writing Pattern Practice 재귀대명사

Pattern 1_ 재귀의 의미

myself/ yourself/ herself/ himself/ yourselves/ ourselves/ themselves

John은 오늘 아침 면도를 하다가 베었다.(shaving) ______________________

우리는 목욕하고 몸을 말렸다.(take a bath) ______________________

거울로 네 자신을 봐.(Look~) ______________________

우리는 우리 자신을 탓해야 해.(should blame) ______________________

Pattern 2_ 강조의 의미 – 생략가능

myself/ yourself/ herself/ himself/ yourselves/ ourselves/ themselves

네가 직접 하면 더 저렴해.(It's cheaper~) ______________________

그 셔츠 자체는 멋있어 보이는데 너무 비싸.(nice, too) ______________________

Pattern 3_ 재귀대명사가 포함된 관용표현

by oneself 홀로 say(talk) to oneself 혼잣말하다

of itself(=by itself) 저절로 enjoy oneself 즐기다 help oneself 마음껏 먹다

make oneself at home 편히 있다 (=make oneself comfortable)

come to oneself 의식을 회복하다 be proud of oneself ~를 자랑스럽게 여기다

Cindy는 멕시코에 혼자 갔다. ______________________

Linda는 가끔 혼잣말을 한다.(talk) ______________________

우리는 파티에서 즐거웠다.(enjoy) ______________________

마음껏 먹어.(yourself) ______________________

편안히 있어.(yourself at home) ______________________

너는 네 자신이 자랑스러움에 틀림없어.(must) ______________________

Unit

34 부정대명사

● Pattern you/we/they, one/ones, one/another/other each other/ one another, somebody(someone)/ anybody (anyone)/nobody(no one), all/none

Grammar in Practice

A: Hey, Jess. Are you seeing anyone these days?
B: No. Why?
A: I know someone who would get along with you perfectly.
He is caring, funny, and gorgeous.
B: OK. Set me up with him. I'm free this weekend.

Grammar in Use

1. 부정대명사
특정하게 정해지지 않은 막연한 대상을 가리키는 대명사를 부정대명사라고 한다.

2. you/we/they
You can't learn Spanish in a month. (you: 일반적인 사람) 스페인어를 한 달 만에 배울 수는 없다.
We dial 911 in an emergency. (we: 일반적인 사람) 비상시에는 911을 누른다.
They speak English and French in that state. (they: 말하는 사람과 듣는 사람을 제외한 제3의 집단인 경우, 또는 '사람들이 ~라고 말하다' 라고 말하는 경우)
그 주에서는 영어와 프랑스를 사용한다.
*you나 we 대신 one을 쓸 수 있지만 딱딱한 표현이다.

3. one/ones
I have three roses; a red **one** and two white **ones.** (one: a+명사, ones: one의 복수형) 나는 장미 세 송이가 있다. 빨간 장미 한 송이와 하얀 장미 두 송이다.
I need a pen. Do you have **one**? 나는 펜이 필요해. 하나 있니?
*one은 「a+명사」로 불특정한 명사를 가리키고, it은 「the+명사」로 특정한 명사를 가리킨다.
You can turn off the radio. I'm not listening to **it**. (it: the radio) 라디오를 꺼도 돼. 듣고 있지 않아.

4. one/another/other
● one~the other··· (둘 중에서) 하나는~ 나머지 하나는···
I have two caps. **One** is blue, and **the other** is white.
나는 모자가 두개 있다. 하나는 파란색이고 다른 하나는 하얀색이다.

●-one
△-the other

- one~another…the other– (셋 중에서) 하나는~ 다른 하나는… 나머지 하나는–

  She has three sons. **One** is five years old, **another** is eight, and **the other** is eleven. 그녀는 아들이 셋 있다. 하나는 5살이고 다른 하나는 8살이고 나머지 하나는 11살이다.

●–one
△–another
■–the other

- some~others… (여럿 중에서) 어떤 것들은~ 다른 어떤 것들은…

  People are having a party here. **Some** of them look happy, and **others** look bored. 사람들이 여기에서 파티를 하고 있다. 몇몇은 행복해 보이고 다른 몇몇은 지루해 보인다.

●●
●●–some ■■
△△△ ■■
△△–others

- some~the others… (정해진 여럿 중에서) 어떤 것들은~나머지 것들은…

  There are ten apples here. **Some** of them are green, and **the others** are red. 여기에 10개의 사과가 있다. 어떤 것들은 초록색이고 나머지 것들은 붉은 색이다.

●●
●●–some
△△△
△△–the others

5. each other/ one another

each other는 둘 사이에 '서로서로'이고 one another는 셋 이상 사이에 '서로서로'이다. 큰 구별 없이 쓰기도 한다.

How long have you and Sally known **each other?** 너와 Sally는 서로 얼마나 오래 알아 왔니?

6. somebody(someone)/ anybody(anyone)/ nobody(no one)

somebody와 anybody는 '누군가'의 뜻으로 긍정문은 some–을, '누구든지'라고 강조하거나 부정문과 의문문은 any–를 주로 쓴다. nobody는 '아무도~않다'라는 뜻이다. 모두 단수취급한다.

Someone is here to see you. 누군가 너를 보러 여기에 왔어.

The exam was very easy. **Anybody** could have passed. 시험은 매우 쉬웠다. 누구라도 합격할 수 있었을 것이다.

Has **anyone** seen Katie? 누구 Katie 본 사람 있어?

Nobody tells me anything. 아무도 내게 얘기해주지 않는다.

7. all/ none

All I want is money. 내가 원하는 것은 단지 돈이다.

Are you **all** ready? 여러분 모두 준비 됐어요?

*all의 단수취급: (총괄적으로) 모두, 만사, 일체

*all의 복수취급: (복수의 사람이나 물건을 합쳐서) 전부, 모두

None of us have a question. 우리 중에 아무도 질문이 없다.

*none은 주로 복수 취급하지만 none of 다음에 단수대명사나 셀 수 없는 명사가 오는 경우 단수취급한다.

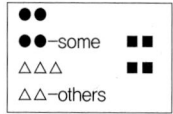

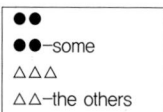

Unit Test

1. 둘 중 알맞은 것을 고르시오.

1. I need a pen. Do you have (one/ ones)?
2. I have three roses; a red one and two white (one/ ones).
3. You can turn off the TV. I'm not watching (one/ it).
4. I have two bags. One is brown, and (the other/ the others) is white.
5. There are ten apples here. Some of them are green, and (the others/ others) are red.
6. How long have you and Kate known (each other/ another)?
7. None of them (have/ has) a car.

2. somebody와 anybody 중 알맞은 것을 써 넣어 문장을 완성하시오.

1. I didn't tell ________________.
2. ________________ wants to see you at the door.
3. This job is very easy. ________________ could do it.
4. I don't have ________________ to hang out with.
5. Has ________________ seen my cell phone?
6. I'll introduce ________________ to you tonight.
7. I don't know ________________ here in Seoul.
8. Isn't there ________________ who can give me a hand?
9. There isn't ________________ at the station.
10. I looked out the window, but I couldn't see ________________.

3. 1번과 같이 빈칸에 알맞은 말을 보기에서 찾아 써 넣으시오.

보기	the other	the others	others

1.
●-one　　△-the other

2.
●●
●●-some　　■■
△△△　　■■
△△-(　　　)

3.
●-one
△-another
■-(　　　)

4.
●●
●●-some
△△△
△△-(　　　)

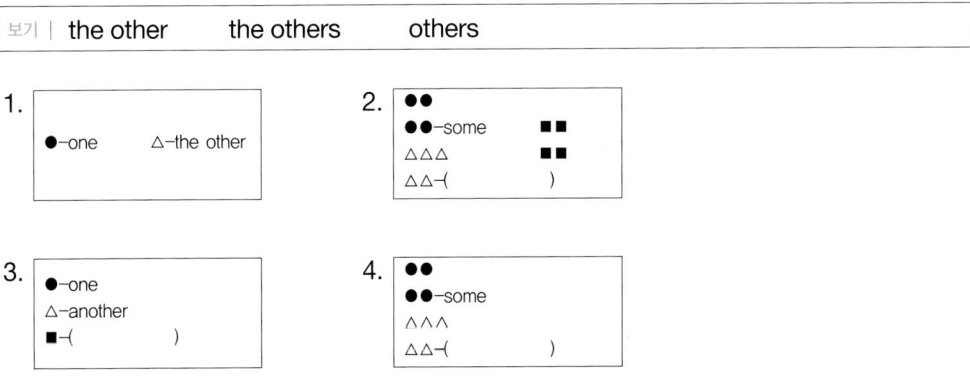

Writing Pattern Practice | 부정대명사

Pattern 1_ You/We ~ 일반적인 사람, They~ 제3의 집단

스페인어를 한 달 만에 배울 수는 없다.(You~) ____________________

비상시에는 911을 누른다.(We~, in an emergency) ____________________

그 주는 영어와 불어를 쓴다.(They~, speak) ____________________

Pattern 2_ one/ ones

I need a pen. 너 하나 있니? ____________________

제게 빨간 거로 두개 주세요.(ones) ____________________

Pattern 3_ one~the other… (둘 중에서) 하나는~ 나머지 하나는…
one~another…the other– (셋 중에서) 하나는~ 다른 하나는… 나머지 하나는–
some~others… (여럿 중에서) 어떤 것들은~ 다른 어떤 것들은…
some~the others… (정해진 여럿 중에서) 어떤 것들은~나머지 것들은…

하나는 파란색이고 나머지 하나는 하얀색이다. ____________________

하나는 다섯 살이고, 다른 하나는 여덟 살이고, 나머지 하나는 열한 살이다.

____

그들 중 몇몇은 행복해보이고 다른 몇몇은 지루해 보인다.(Some of them~)

____

그것들 중 어떤 것들은 초록색이고, 나머지 것들은 빨간색이다.(Some of them~)

____

Pattern 4_ each other/ one another

너와 Sally는 서로 얼마나 오래 알아왔니? ____________________

Pattern 5_ somebody(someone)/ anybody(anyone)/ nobody(no one)

누군가 너를 보러 여기에 왔어.(be here) ____________________

누구라도 합격할 수 있었을 것이다.(could have p.p) ____________________

누구 Katie 본 사람 있어? ____________________

아무도 내게 아무 것도 얘기해주지 않는다.(Nobody~) ____________________

Pattern 6_ all/ none

내가 원하는 것은 단지 돈이다.(All I want~) ____________________

여러분 모두 준비 됐어요? ____________________

우리 중에 아무도 질문이 없다. ____________________

REVIEW 1

1. 틀린 곳을 찾아 밑줄치고 고쳐 쓰시오.

1. This vase is made of a glass →
2. Janet never drinks a wine. →
3. Physics are my favorite subject. →
4. The news were surprising. →
5. One of my friends work for IBM. →
6. I'd like to have two piece of cake. →
7. There are a little things you have to know. →
8. The number of languages are used in the world. →
9. Ann isn't very popular. She has little friends. →
10. Both my grandparents lives in London. →

2. 둘 중 알맞은 것을 고르시오.

1. I didn't have (a/ X) breakfast.
2. Tennis is (a/ X) sport.
3. Who is (the/ X) girl over there with Ted?
4. (The/ X) sun came up.
5. Have you ever been to (the/ X) United States?
6. You are (the/ X) only one that I can count on.
7. Let's meet on (a/ X) Monday.
8. I usually go to work by (a/ X) bus.
9. I like listening to (the/ X) rain.
10. The Earth is (a/ X) planet.
11. Lisa is (a friend of mine/ a my friend).
12. Can I borrow (some books of yours/ some your books)?
13. I need a pencil. Do you have (one/ ones)?
14. I have two hats. One is red and (another/ the other) is white.
15. I looked out the window, but I couldn't see (somebody/ anybody).

3. 밑줄 친 부분을 어법에 맞게 고치시오.

1. I have a lot of homeworks today. →
2. Cindy left for Las Vegas on the September 20. →
3. Every student have an I.D. card. →
4. There was only a few pizza left. →
5. Jason goes everywhere by bus. He doesn't have car. →
6. I'm not ready yet. Wait minute. →
7. We eat a rice everyday. →
8. I'm going to buy a bread. →
9. These furnitures are mine. →
10. Do you have any luggages? →

4. **밑줄 친 부분 중 어법상 어색한 것을 고르시오.**

1. Ken left for a L.A. on December 30.
A B C D
2. I need to buy two pound of butter and a jar of jam.
A B C D
3. How many hour do you work?
A B C D
4. One of my friends are getting married.
A B C D
5. Tell the children to blow their nose.
A B C D
6. Alice and I am going to be late.
A B C D
7. People used to think Earth was flat.
A B C D
8. Lend me your pen. I haven't got pen.
A B C D
9. She lives in a big house over there.
A B C D
10. Write your name in a space at the bottom of the page.
A B C D

5. **다음 밑줄 친 부분을 해석하시오. 해석할 필요가 없으면 X표 하시오.**

1. What is that loud noise? (   )
2. These flowers smell nice. (   )
3. I didn't expect you to come this early. (   )
4. His English is not that good. (   )
5. This is my wife, Kimberly. (   )
6. That is my twin sister. (   )
7. It's freezing out there. (   )
8. How far is it to London? (   )
9. "How does it taste?" "It tastes terrific." (   )
10. It's Monday again. (   )

REVIEW 2

[1-6] 다음 빈칸에 가장 적절한 것을 고르시오.

1. I'd like to have two ________ of bread.

① piece
② pieces
③ jar
④ jars

2. Thank you so much. You've been ______ great help.

① the
② any
③ a
④ X

3. I have __________ money to spend.

① a few
② few
③ plenty of
④ a number of

4. ____________ still have to be solved.

① A number of problems
② The number of problems
③ A number of problem
④ The number of problem

5. Benny has ________ .

① few money
② little money
③ a few money
④ many money

6. Do you like ________ ?

① strong black coffee
② cat
③ French cheeses
④ big city

7. 다음 글을 읽고, 빈칸에 차례로 들어갈 알맞은 말을 고르시오.

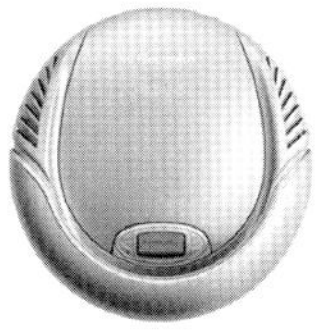

Nowadays there are _____ kinds of robots in lots of places. They have computers which control what they do. Different kinds of robots do different things. Factory robots make things, such as cars and fridges. The police also use a lot of robots to take apart bombs and stop explosions. __________ even go to other planets. The Pathfinder spaceship went to ______ planet Mars. It carried a little robot that looked like a toy truck, which moved around to study rocks. It worked very well. Robots are also used around us. Several vacuum cleaner companies have spent the last few years trying to introduce a household robot cleaner. So robot cleaners are being used in many houses now.

① many - Robots - a
② many - Robots - the
③ much - Robot - a
④ much - Robot - the

Chapter 4 | 수식어류

문장에서 수식어 역할을 하는 것은 크게 형용사와 부사이다. 형용사는 내용상 어떤 대상의 상태나 모양 등을 나타내는 말로 형용사의 문법적인 기능은 명사나 대명사 앞 또는 뒤에서 그 명사나 대명사를 수식하거나 동사의 보어역할을 한다. 부사는 문장에서 보조역할을 담당하면서 동사, 형용사, 다른 부사, 그리고 문장전체를 수식하는 기능을 한다. 부사를 종류별로 잘 살펴 그 역할과 사용되는 위치에 유의해야 하겠다.

Unit

35 형용사

● Pattern 1. 형용사 + 명사/대명사, 명사/대명사 + 형용사
2. 주어 + 동사 + 형용사, 주어 + 동사 + 목적어 + 형용사

Grammar in Practice

A: My brother bought a computer yesterday.
B: Can I come over and take a look?
A: I'll ask my brother. I didn't know you were interested in computers.

Grammar in Use

1. 형용사의 쓰임

● 형용사란 명사의 상태나 성질, 모양 등을 나타낸다.

A: What does he look like? 걔 인상이 어때?
B: He looks **nice, good-looking, tall** and **well-built.** 멋지고 얼굴도 잘 생겼고 키도 크고 그리고 몸도 좋던데.

● 형용사는 명사나 대명사를 앞이나 뒤에서 수식하며 주어나 목적어의 상태를 설명하기도 한다.
Susan lives in a **nice** house. Susan은 좋은 집에서 산다.(명사 앞에서 수식)
I want to eat something **new**. 나는 뭔가 새로운 것을 먹고 싶다.(명사 뒤에서 수식)
Sue seemed **upset** this morning. Sue는 오늘 아침 화난 듯했다.(주어 설명)
Let's paint the kitchen **yellow.** 부엌을 노란색으로 칠하자.(목적어 설명)

| MORE TIPS | 대부분의 형용사는 명사 앞과 동사 뒤에 모두 올 수 있지만 예외가 있다. afraid, alive, alike, aware, ashamed, asleep, alone 등과 같은 형용사는 "I'm afraid of being in the dark"와 같이 연결동사 뒤에 와서 서술적으로만 사용되는 반면 main, only, live, mere, elder, former, upper, drunken 등의 형용사는 "What is the main idea of this passage?"와 같이 명사 앞에 와서 그 명사를 꾸미는 기능만 한다.

2. 형용사의 어순

● 「주관적형용사(opinion) + 객관적형용사(description)」
주관적인 의견이 포함된 형용사가 객관적인 사실을 묘사하는 형용사보다 주로 앞에 위치한다.
My friend lives in a **beautiful new** house. 친구는 아름다운 새 집에 살고 있다.

● 「지시 + 수량 + 크기(size, length) + 신구 + 모양(shape, width) + 색깔 + 출신 + 재료」

an **old French** song
a **new white cotton** shirt
a **large round wooden** table
a **small round** table
a **tall skinny Korean** woman
a **big black plastic** bag

3. -ing나 -ed로 끝나는 형용사 〈예문 p 166 참조〉

-ing형태 형용사	-ed형태 형용사
boring 지겹게 하는	bored 지루한
tiring 지치게 하는	tired 피곤한
interesting 흥미롭게 하는	interested 흥미있는
exciting 신나게 하는	excited 신나는
satisfying 만족스럽게 하는	satisfied 만족스러운
depressing 우울하게 하는	depressed 우울한
disappointing 실망시키는	disappointed 실망한
shocking 충격을 주는	shocked 충격받은
surprising 놀라게 하는	surprised 놀란
amazing 놀라게 하는, 굉장한	amazed 놀란
embarrassing 당황하게 하는	embarrassed 당황스러운
terrifying 놀라게 하는, 무서운	terrified 무서워하는, 겁먹은
annoying 짜증나게 하는	annoyed 짜 증 나 는
disgusting 구역질나게 하는	disgusted 구역질나는, 싫증난
touching 감동하게 하는	touched 감동한

4. 명사 · 대명사 뒤에 놓이는 형용사

다음과 같은 경우는, 「명사/대명사 + 형용사」의 어순이 된다.

- '-thing, -body, -one'으로 끝나는 복합대명사를 수식하는 경우
  Please give me **something cold.** 차가운 것 좀 주세요.

- 형용사가 단독이 아니고 다른 어구를 동반하고 있을 때
  She gave me a glass **full of milk.** 그녀는 우유가 담긴 잔을 줬다.
  This is a letter **written in English.** 이 편지는 영어로 씌어져 있다.

5. 「the + 형용사」, 「the + 국민명」

「the + 형용사」는 '~사람들'이라는 뜻이고 「the + 국민명」은 '~나라 사람들'이라는 뜻으로 둘 다 복수취급한다.

- the young(젊은 사람들) the old(나이든 분들)
  the rich(부자들) the poor(가난한사람들)
  the sick(아픈 사람들) the blind(시각장애자들)
  the deaf(청각장애자들) the handicapped(장애자들)
  the disabled(신체장애자들) the homeless(집 없는 사람들)
  the unemployed(실직자들) the jobless(실직자들)
- the English(영국사람) the Dutch(네덜란드사람)
  the French(프랑스사람) the Spanish(스페인사람)

WRAP-UP | -ing나 -ed로 끝나는 형용사 예문

현재분사(~ing)와 과거분사(-ed)는 동사의 변형된 형태로 문장안에서 기능적으로 형용사 역할을 한다. 형용사로 자주 쓰이는 분사는 다음과 같다.

-ing 형태 형용사	-ed 형태 형용사
• boring 지겹게 하는 Janet' s job is so **boring.**	• bored 지루한 I' m **bored** with my job.
• tiring 지치게 하는 It has been a long and **tiring** day.	• tired 피곤한 I' m always **tired** when I get home from work.
• interesting 흥미롭게 하는 Did you meet anyone **interesting** at the party?	• interested 흥미있는 Are you **interested** in fishing?
• exciting 신나게 하는 The game was getting **exciting.**	• excited 신나는 I was really **excited** to see James.
• satisfying 만족스럽게 하는 It had been a busy, but **satisfying** day for Tom Hagen.	• satisfied 만족스러운 You should be **satisfied** with what you have.
• depressing 우울하게 하는 That was a **depressing** movie, wasn' t it?	• depressed 우울한 People eat more when they' re **depressed.**
• disappointing 실망시키는 The wine was excellent, but the food was **disappointing.**	• disappointed 실망한 I was **disappointed** that Kelly wasn't at the party.
• shocking 충격을 주는 The news was **shocking.**	• shocked 충격받은 I was **shocked** when I heard the news.
• surprising 놀라게 하는 It was quite **surprising** that he passed the exam.	• surprised 놀란 We were **surprised** that he passed the exam.
• amazing 놀라게 하는, 굉장한 She is an **amazing** golfer.	• amazed 몹시 놀란 He was **amazed** at the sight.
• embarrassing 당황하게 하는 What was the most **embarrassing** moment in your life?	• embarrassed 당황스러운 I was really **embarassed** when I knocked the cup of tea over my teacher.
• touching 감동하게 하는 It was a **touching** story.	• touched 감동한 I was **touched** when he gave me a present.
• disgusting 구역질나게 하는 Smoking is a **disgusting** habit.	• disgusted 구역질나는, 싫증 난 I am quite **disgusted** at his stupidity.
• annoying 짜증나게 하는 You must have found my attitude **annoying.**	• annoyed 짜증나는 Cindy was **annoyed** by his rude manner.
• terrifying 놀라게 하는, 무서운 If something is **terrifying,** it makes you very frightened.	• terrified 무서워하는, 겁먹은 He was **terrified** of heights.

Unit Test

1. **다음 형용사와 명사를 적당한 순서대로 다시 쓰시오.**

1. brown/ beautiful/ long/ hair →
2. an/ French/ old/ song →
3. a/ round/ small table →
4. a/ white/ new/ cotton/ shirt →
5. a/ plastic/ big/ black/ bag →
6. a/ tall/ Korean/ thin/ woman →
7. a/ round/ wooden/ large/ table →
8. a/ fat/ big/ black/ cat →
9. a/ sunny/ lovely/ day →
10. a/ narrow/ long/ street →

2. **둘 중 알맞은 것을 고르시오.**

1. My job is (tired/ tiring).
2. David is (bored/ boring) with his job.
3. I'm (satisfied/ satisfying) with my salary.
4. We were (disappointed/ disappointing) in the movie.
5. He was (terrified/ terrifying) of heights.
6. It was one of the most (amazed/ amazing) films I've ever seen.
7. People eat more when they're (depressed/ depressing).
8. I feel (embarrassed/ embarrassing) in front of a lot of people.
9. The news was (shocked/ shocking).
10. Smoking is a (disgusted/ disgusting) habit.

3. **우리말과 일치하도록 괄호 안의 단어를 알맞게 배열하시오.**

1. 뭔가 차가운 것을 줘요. (cold/ something/ please give me)

2. 나는 누군가 새로운 사람을 만나고 싶어요. (somebody/ I want to meet/ new)

3. 이것은 영어로 쓰여진 편지다. (a letter/ written in English/ this is)

4. 실직자들이 희망을 잃어가고 있다. (are/ the/ losing hope/ unemployed)

5. 부자라고 항상 행복한 것은 아니다. (always happy/ the/ are not/ rich)

Writing Pattern Practice | 형용사

Pattern 1_ 「주관적형용사(opinion) + 객관적형용사(description)」
「지시 + 수량 + 크기(size, length) + 신구 + 모양(shape, width) + 색깔 + 출신 + 재료」

아름다운 새 집 ________________________________

오래된 프랑스 노래 ________________________________

새로운 하얀 면 셔츠 ________________________________

큰 검정색 비닐 봉투 ________________________________

Pattern 2_ -ing나 -ed로 끝나는 형용사

그 남자는 따분하다. ________________________________

그 소식은 충격적이었다. ________________________________

피곤한 날이었다.(It has been~) ________________________________

너는 낚시에 관심 있니? ________________________________

나는 그 영화에 실망했었다.(the movie) ________________________________

나는 짜증났었다. ________________________________

나는 쉽게 당황한다.(get) ________________________________

Pattern 3_ 「명사, 대명사 + 형용사」

나는 뭔가 재미있는 것이 필요하다.(fun) ________________________________

나는 새로운 누군가를 만나기를 원한다.(somebody) ________________________________

그녀는 나에게 우유가 가득 찬 잔을 줬다.(full of) ________________________________

Pattern 4_ 「the + 형용사」, 「the + 국민명」

우리는 시각장애인들을 위해 돈을 모으고 있다. ________________________________

실직자들이 희망을 잃어가고 있다. ________________________________

영국사람들은 매우 오래된 전통을 가지고 있다. ________________________________

Unit

36 부사

● Pattern 부사 + 동사
부사 + 형용사
부사 + 부사/ 부사 + 문장

Grammar in Practice

A: Let's go dancing.
B: I really don't feel like it tonight.
A: Well, do you want to do something else?
B: No. I want to get to bed early tonight.

Grammar in Use

1. 부사의 쓰임

부사는 동사, 형용사, 다른 부사, 또는 문장 전체를 수식한다.

He **certainly** looks like a gentleman. 그는 정말 신사같아 보인다. (동사수식)
I felt **really** excited at the concert. 콘서트에서 정말 재미있었다. (형용사수식)
We see her **quite** often. 우리는 그녀를 꽤 자주 만난다. (부사수식)
Stupidly, I forgot my keys. 어리석게도 열쇠를 안 가져왔다. (문장전체수식)

2. 부사의 형태

● 부사는 주로 「형용사 + ly」

happy(행복한) → happily(행복하게)	easy(쉬운) → easily(쉽게)
gentle(부드러운) → gently(부드럽게)	extreme(극도의) → extremely(극도로, 매우)
quick(빠른) → quickly(빨리)	happy(행복한) → happily(행복하게)
terrible(끔찍한) → terribly(끔찍하게)	sudden(갑작스러운) → suddenly(갑자기)
careful(조심스러운) → carefully(조심스럽게)	serious(심각한) → seriously(심각하게)

It was an **extremely** fine day in May. 무척 맑은 5월의 어느 날이었다.
We have **suddenly** decided to sell the house. 우리는 집을 팔기로 갑자기 결정했다.

| MORE TIPS | 「명사+ly」, 「-ly」 또는 「날씨명사+y」 형태의 형용사도 있음을 유의한다.

friendly(정다운)	lovely(멋진)	curly(곱슬의)	ugly(못생긴, 추한)
silly(어리석은)	lonely(외로운)	likely(~할 것 같은)	cloudy(구름낀)
foggy(안개낀)	snowy(눈오는)	rainy(비오는)	sunny(화창한) 등

- She gave me a **friendly** smile. 그녀는 나에게 정답게 미소 지었다.
- What a **lovely** day! 정말 멋진 날이야!
- It is **likely** to rain. 비가 올 것 같다.
- It is **foggy** outside. 밖에 안개가 꼈다.

- 형용사와 부사의 형태가 같은 경우

early(이른–일찍)	fast(빠른–빠르게)	late(늦은–늦게)	high(높은–높게)
right(옳은–옳게)	near(가까운–가깝게)	wrong(틀린–틀리게)	straight(곧바른–곧바르게)

I'm not an **early** bird. (형용사) 나는 일찍 일어나는 사람이 아니다.
Get up as **early** as you can. (부사) 가능한 일찍 일어나라.

I'm **late** for school. (형용사) 나는 학교에 늦었다.
I hate arriving **late.** (부사) 나는 늦게 도착하는 것이 싫어.

Grace has long **straight** dark hair. (형용사) Grace의 머리는 길고 곧은 검은색이다.
Go **straight** for three blocks. (부사) 세 블럭을 곧장 가세요.

- 명사와 부사의 형태가 같은 경우

home(집–집에)	today(오늘–오늘)

I'm studying at **home.** (명사) 나는 집에서 공부하고 있다.
Come **home** early. (부사) 집에 일찍 와라.

Today is Sunday. (명사) 오늘은 일요일이다.
It's cloudy **today.** (부사) 오늘은 구름이 꼈다.

- 형용사에 –ly를 붙여 뜻이 달라지는 경우

hard(어려운) → hardly(거의~않다)	near(가까운) → nearly(거의)
late(늦은) → lately(최근에)	high(높은) → highly(매우)

Success and **hard** work go together. 성공에는 고생이 따르기 마련이다
I **hardly** know him. 나는 그를 거의 알지 못한다.

Am I **late**? 내가 늦었니?
I haven't seen Janet **lately.** 나는 최근에 Janet을 본 적이 없다.

Prices are too **high**. 물가가 너무 높다.
I **highly** recommend that you see that movie. 나는 그 영화를 보라고 적극 추천한다.

Unit Test

1. **다음 형용사를 괄호안의 뜻에 알맞게 부사로 바꿔 쓰시오.**

1. happy(행복한) →_______________(행복하게)
2. near(가까운) →_______________(가깝게)
3. easy(쉬운) →_______________(쉽게)
4. gentle(부드러운) →_______________(부드럽게)
5. straight(곧바른) →_______________(곧바르게)
6. extreme(극도의) →_______________(극도로)
7. high(높은) →_______________(높게)
8. terrible(끔찍한) →_______________(끔찍하게)
9. sudden(갑작스러운) →_______________(갑자기)
10. careful(조심스러운) →_______________(조심스럽게)
11. serious(심각한) →_______________(심각하게)
12. early(이른) →_______________(일찍)
13. fast(빠른) →_______________(빠르게)
14. late(늦은) →_______________(늦게)
15. quick(빠른) →_______________(빨리)
16. right(옳은) →_______________(옳게)

2. **다음 밑줄 친 부분을 해석하시오.**

1. She gave me a friendly smile.
2. What a lovely day!
3. It's likely to rain.
4. Success and hard work go together.
5. I hardly know him.
6. Am I late?
7. I haven't seen Janet lately.

3. **다음 밑줄 친 단어가 형용사일 경우 동그라미를, 부사일 경우 세모를 하시오.**

1. Her singing was lovely.
2. She danced happily into the room.
3. It's terribly cold.
4. The driver of the car was seriously injured.
5. The train was late.
6. I hardly ate anything.
7. I'm not an early bird.

Writing Pattern Practice | 부사

Pattern 1_ 형용사 + ly → 부사

그는 행복하게 미소 지었다. ______________________

나는 정말 미안하다.(terribly) ______________________

John은 조심스럽게 운전했다. ______________________

조용히 말해주세요.(Please speak~) ______________________

두 사람이 심각하게 부상당했다.(seriously, injured) ______________________

Tom은 나를 슬프게 쳐다봤다.(look at) ______________________

음식이 정말 좋았다.(The food~, extremely) ______________________

Pattern 2_ 형용사의 형태 = 부사의 형태

나는 일찍 일어나는 사람이 아니다.(an early bird) ______________________

가능한 일찍 일어나라. ______________________

내가 늦었나요?(현재) ______________________

나는 늦게 도착하는 것을 싫어한다.(hate arriving) ______________________

Grace는 곧은 머리를 가지고 있다. ______________________

세 블럭을 곧장 가세요. ______________________

Pattern 3_ 명사의 형태 = 부사의 형태

나는 집에 있다. ______________________

집에 일찍 와라. ______________________

오늘은 일요일이다. ______________________

오늘 구름이 꼈다.(~ today) ______________________

Pattern 4_ 형용사 + ly → 다른 뜻의 부사

그것은 정말 힘든 일이었다.(incredibly) ______________________

나는 그를 거의 알지 못한다. ______________________

늦지마. ______________________

나는 최근에 Janet은 본 적 없다.(I haven't~) ______________________

물가가 너무 높다.(too) ______________________

나는 그것을 적극적으로 추천할 수 있다.(highly recommend)

____

Unit

37 부사의 종류

● Pattern
1. 부사 + 문장
2. 주어+be동사/조동사+부사~, 주어+부사+일반동사~
3. 문장 + 부사

Grammar in Practice

A: How about going on a picnic?
B: Great. Where to?
A: Let's call Ted and ask him. He always knows the best places to go.
B: OK.

Grammar in Use

1. 부사의 위치에 따른 종류

● front position (문두에 위치하는 부사)

① 연결부사: then, next, however 등

I studied until midnight. **Then** I went to bed. 나는 자정까지 공부했다. 그리고 잠자리에 들었다.

② 코멘트부사: fortunately, stupidly 등

Fortunately, the insurance will cover it. 다행히 보험 처리가 될 거예요.

③ 몇몇 추측부사: maybe, perhaps 등

Maybe you're right. 아마 당신이 옳을 거예요.

● mid-position (문장 가운데 위치하는 부사 – be동사와 조동사 뒤, 일반동사 앞)

① 대부분의 추측부사 certainly, definitely, obviously, probably 등

He **probably** does not know the truth. 그는 아마 진실을 알지 못할 거다.
You are **obviously** not welcome here. 너는 여기에서 명백하게 환영받지 못한다.

② 빈도부사

0%						100%
never	hardly	rarely	sometimes	often	usually	always

You **always** forgot my birthday. 너는 항상 내 생일을 잊었었지.
I **usually** take a shower in the morning. 나는 보통 아침에 샤워를 한다.
My boss is **often** bad-tempered. 사장님은 자주 성질이 고약해진다.
I **sometimes** eat Chinese food. 나는 가끔 중국 음식을 먹는다.
My grandfather **rarely** goes out. 할아버지는 드물게 외출하신다.
I can **hardly** believe it. 거의 믿어지지 않는다.
I have **never** lost the weight I put on in my teens.
10대 때 찐 살이 전혀 빠지지 않았다.

③ 수식부사 completely, partly, kind of, sort of, almost, hardly 등

I have **completely** forgotten his name. 나는 그의 이름을 완전히 잊어버렸다.

I **kind of** expected it. 나는 어느 정도 예상했다.

④ 강조부사 just, neither, only, really, terribly 등

We're **only** going for three days. 우리는 단지 3일 동안만 갈 거야.

- end position (문장 뒤에 위치하는 부사)

① 장소부사 here, there, upstairs, downstairs, around, to bed, in London 등

Come and sit **here**. 와서 여기에 앉아.

There is someone **upstairs**. 누군가 위층에 있다.

*here와 there가 문두에 오는 경우는 'Here comes~', 'There goes~', 'Here/There is~' 와 같은 형태로 쓰는데 대명사가 주어로 오는 경우 그 대명사를 here나 there 바로 다음에 쓴다.

Here comes your bus. 여기 네 버스 온다.

Here it comes. 여기 오네.

② 시간부사 today, yesterday, every week, daily, weekly, monthly, in July 등

We play golf **every week**. 우리는 매주 골프를 친다.

| MORE TIPS | 부사의 위치는 주로 위와 같이 나누어 볼 수 있지만 무엇을 강조하느냐에 따라 그 위치는 달라지는 경우도 있음을 유의한다.

- **Today** I'm going to Japan. 오늘 나는 일본에 간다.
- **Usually** I get up early. 보통 나는 일찍 일어난다.

2. 주의해야할 부사

- too/ enough '너무' '충분히'

too는 형용사나 부사의 앞에 와서 '너무 ~한'의 뜻으로 쓴다. enough는 '충분히'라는 뜻으로 형용사나 부사의 뒤에 온다. 명사 앞에 오는 경우 형용사로 쓰이기도 한다.

He spoke **too** quickly to understand. 그는 알아듣기 너무 빨리 말했다.

I'm old **enough** to get married. 나는 결혼하기에 충분히 나이 먹었다.

If you don't have **enough** money, I can lend you some. 돈이 충분치 않으면 내가 좀 빌려줄 수 있어.(형용사)

- so/ such '매우'

so는 명사가 없는 문장에서 형용사나 부사를 강조한다. such는 명사가 있는 문장에서 형용사를 강조하면서 「such+a/an+형용사+명사」형태로 쓴다. 「such+a/an+명사」형태로 썼을 경우 such는 '그런~'이라는 뜻의 형용사로 쓰인 것임을 유의한다.

I was **so** sleepy that I fell asleep. 나는 너무 졸려서 잠들었다.

How do you speak **such** a good English? 어떻게 그렇게 영어를 잘 할 수 있니?

I've never seen **such** a mess. 그렇게 지저분한 것은 처음 봤다.(형용사)

| MORE TIPS | 정도를 강조할 때 쓰는 부사로 fairly/ quite/ rather/ pretty '꽤'가 있다.
(weaker) fairly 〈 quite 〈 rather≒pretty (stronger)

- I speak French **fairly** well. 나는 프랑스어를 꽤 잘한다.
- I **quite** enjoyed myself at the party. 파티에서 즐거웠어.
- I've had **rather** a long day. 꽤 (생각보다) 힘든 하루였다.
- Your English is **pretty** good. 너는 영어를 꽤 잘한다.

Unit Test

1. **괄호 안에 too나 enough 중 알맞은 것을 써 넣으시오.**

1. He spoke ____________ quickly to understand.
2. We're old ____________ to get married.
3. The coffee was ____________ hot to drink.
4. It's ____________ far to walk there.
5. I think he didn't study hard ____________.
6. This shirt is ____________tight to wear.
7. You don't have to go on a diet. You're skinny ____________.
8. This bag is ____________ heavy to carry.
9. I think you drink ____________ much.
10. You're old ____________ to know better.

2. **괄호 안에 so나 such 중 알맞은 것을 써 넣으시오.**

1. I got up ____________ early that I could see the sunrise.
2. How do you speak ____________ a good English?
3. You speak English ____________ fluently.
4. It's ____________ a beautiful house.
5. I didn't like the book. The story was ____________ stupid.
6. I didn't know it was ____________ a boring movie.
7. Tom and Mary are ____________ nice people.
8. I haven't seen you for ____________ a long time.
9. I was ____________ tired that I fell asleep in the middle of the movie.
10. We enjoyed our vacation. It was ____________ exciting.

3. **우리말과 일치하도록 괄호 안의 단어를 알맞게 배열하시오.**

1. 그는 아마 진실을 알지 못할 거다. (does not/ he probably/ know the truth)

____

2. 할아버지는 드물게 외출하신다. (rarely/ my grandfather/ goes out)

____

3. 나는 그것을 거의 못 믿겠다. (hardly/ I can/ believe it)

____

4. 나는 그것을 어느 정도 예상했다. (kind of/ I/ expected it)

____

5. 어떻게 그렇게 영어를 잘할 수 있니? (good/ a/ English/ how/ such/ do you speak/ ?)

____

Writing Pattern Practice | 부사의 종류

Pattern 1_ 「부사 + 주어 + 동사」

I studied until midnight. 그리고 나서 잠자리에 들었다. ______

어리석게도 내 열쇠를 안 가져왔다.(Stupidly, my keys) ______

아마 당신이 옳을 거예요.(Maybe~) ______

Pattern 2_ 「주어 + be동사/조동사 + 부사 ~」, 「주어 + 부사 + 일반동사 ~」

그는 아마 진실을 알지 못할 거다.(probably) ______

너는 내 생일을 항상 잊었었지. ______

나는 보통 아침에 샤워를 한다. ______

나는 그것을 거의 믿을 수 없다. ______

나는 그것을 어느 정도 예상했다.(kind of) ______

Pattern 3_ 「주어 + 동사 + 부사」

와서 여기에 앉아. ______

누군가 위층에 있다. ______

우리는 매주 골프를 친다. ______

Pattern 4_ 「too + 형용사/부사」

그것은 너무 비싸다. ______

그는 알아듣기에 너무 빠르게 말했다.(speak, to understand) ______

Pattern 5_ 「형용사/부사 + enough」

너는 충분히 말랐어.(skinny) ______

나는 결혼하기에 충분히 나이 먹었다.(to get married) ______

Pattern 6_ 「so + 형용사/부사」

그녀는 정말 열심히 일했다. ______

그 콘서트는 정말 지루했다. ______

Pattern 7_ 「such + a(n) + 형용사 + 명사」

그들은 정말 좋은 사람들이다.(nice) ______

그것은 정말 좋은 영화였다.(good) ______

우리는 정말 좋은 시간을 가졌다.(good) ______

Unit

38 원급비교

- Pattern as + 형용사/부사 + as
- Meaning ~만큼…하다

Grammar in Practice

A: I don't think you have to go on a diet. You look just fine.
B: What are you talking about? I weigh almost twice as much as you do.

Grammar in Use

1. 형용사/부사의 비교급과 최상급 만들기

규칙	보통 -er, -est	old—older—oldest, fast—faste—fastest
	-e로 끝나는 단어: -r, -st	nice—nicer—nicest, late—later—latest
	단모음+단자음: 마지막 자음 -er, -est	big—bigger—biggest, thin—thinner—thinnest
	자음+y: -y → -ier, -iest	easy—easier—easiest, busy—busier—busiest
	-ful, -ous, -ing, -ed 등으로 끝나는 2음절어 또는 3음절어: more, most+원급	careful—more/most careful boring—more/most boring tired—more/most tired
불규칙	good/well—better—best far—*farther/further—farthest/furthest many/much—more—most	bad—worse—worst older—*older/elder—oldest/eldest little—less—least

*farther/farthest는 거리(distance)의 의미를, further/furthest는 further education, further information 과 같은 심화(additional)의 의미를 가진다.

*elder/eldest는 brother, sister, son, daughter, grandson, granddaughter 등과 함께 '손위'의 의미로 쓴다. older/oldest를 같이 쓰기도 한다.

2. 원급을 이용한 비교급 표현

- 「as+형용사/부사+as」, 「not+as(so)+형용사/부사+as」 ~만큼…하다/~만큼…하지 않다

It's **as cold as** ice. 그것은 얼음만큼 차다.
Some of these fish can weigh **as much as** 50kg. 몇몇 물고기는 50kg만큼 나간다.
Is it **as good as** you expected? 그것은 네가 기대한 것만큼 좋니?
He's **not as(so) tall as** his father. 그는 그의 아버지만큼 크지 않다.

- 「the same + (명사+) as」 ~와 …같다

  Tom is **the same age as** Mary. Tom은 Mary와 같은 나이다.

- 「as + 형용사/부사 + as possible」 = 「as + 원급 + as + 주어 + can」 가능한 ~하게

  I'll get back to you **as soon as possible.**=I'll get back to you as soon as I can. 가능한 빨리 다시 연락 줄게.

- 「배수 + as + 형용사/부사 + as」 (배수)만큼~하다

  Gas is **twice as expensive as** it was a couple of years ago. 휘발유가 2~3년 전보다 두 배로 비싸다.

Unit Test

1. **다음 형용사나 부사의 비교급과 최상급을 쓰시오.**

old — __________ — __________
fast — __________ — __________
lucky — __________ — __________
embarrassing — __________ — __________
quietly — __________ — __________
good — __________ — __________
well — __________ — __________
bored — __________ — __________
bad — __________ — __________
little — __________ — __________
many/much — __________ — __________
carefully — __________ — __________
thin — __________ — __________
serious — __________ — __________
interesting — __________ — __________
lage — __________ — __________

2. **우리말과 일치하도록 괄호 안의 단어를 알맞게 배열하시오.**

1. 나는 너만큼 키가 크다. (as/ I'm/ as/ tall /you)

____

2. 나는 Cindy만큼 영어를 잘 말한다. (speak English/ well/ as/ I/ as/ Cindy does)

____

3. Tom은 Mary와 같은 나이다. (the same/ as Mary/ Tom is/ age)

____

4. 그는 그의 아버지만큼 크지 않다. (he's not/ as/ his father/ tall/ as)

____

5. 나는 가능한 많이 먹었다. (ate/ as/ I/ much/ as/ possible)

____

6. 그의 차는 내차보다 세배 비싸다. (three times/ expensive as/ his car is/ as/ my car)

____

Writing Pattern Practice | 원급비교

Pattern 1_ 「as + 형용사/부사 + as」 ~만큼…하다

그것은 얼음만큼 차다. ______________________

나는 그녀만큼 피아노를 잘 칠 수 있다. ______________________

그것은 네가 기대했던 만큼 좋니?(expected) ______________________

원하는 만큼 가져가.(Take~, want) ______________________

Pattern 2_ 「not + as(so) + 형용사/부사 + as」 ~만큼…하지 않다

그것은 예전만 못하다.(good, used to be) ______________________

그것은 보이는 것만큼 어렵지는 않다.(it looks) ______________________

그는 그의 아버지만큼 크지 않다. ______________________

Pattern 3_ 「the same + (명사+) as」 ~와 같은…다

Tom은 Mary와 같은 나이다.(the same age) ______________________

David의 봉급은 내 것과 같다.(salary) ______________________

Pattern 4_ 「as + 형용사/부사 + as possible」 = 「as + 원급 + as + 주어 + can」 가능한 ~하게

가능하면 빨리 내게 전화하세요.(soon) ______________________

= Call me as soon as you can.

가능한 많이 가져가.(take) ______________________

= Take as much as you can.

나는 가능한 일찍 일어났다. ______________________

= I got up as early as I could.

Pattern 5_ 「배수 + as + 형용사/부사 + as」 배수만큼~하다

휘발유가 2~3년 전보다 두 배로 비싸다.(Gas~, it was a couple of years ago)

____

그의 차는 내 것에 비해 세배로 오래되었다.(old) ______________________

Unit

39 비교급

- **Pattern** 비교급 + than ~
- **Meaning** ~보다 더 …하다

Grammar in Practice

A: How much is this?
B: It's $80.
A: Oh, it's more expensive than I expected. Is there anything cheaper?
B: How about this one? It's on sale.

Grammar in Use

1. 비교급

- 「비교급 + than ~」 ~보다 더 …하다

Mary is **taller than** her three sisters. Mary는 세 언니들 보다 더 크다.
She is older **than I am**. (than me: informal) 그 여자는 나보다 나이가 많아.
You played **better than** the others in the team. 너는 팀에서 다른 사람들보다 잘했어.

- 「less + 원급 + than ~」(= not as(so) + 원급 + as) ~보다 덜 …하다

Susan is **less outgoing than** her sister. Susan은 여동생보다 덜 외향적이다.
=Susan **isn't as outgoing as** her sister.

- 「very much/much/a lot/even/far/a little + 비교급」 훨씬 더/약간 더 ~하다

Russian is **a lot more difficult** than English. 러시아어는 영어보다 훨씬 더 어렵다.
Could you speak **a little more slowly**? 조금 더 천천히 말씀해 주실래요?

2. 비교급을 이용한 다양한 표현

- 「the + 비교급 + of~」 ~ 중 더 …한

I like Jane and Molly, but I think Molly is **the nicer of** the two. 난 Jane과 Molly가 좋지만 둘 중 Molly가 더 착한 것 같다.

- 「비교급 + and + 비교급」 점점 ~한

I'm getting **fatter and fatter**. 나는 점점 더 살이 찐다.
It's getting **colder and colder**. 점점 더 추워진다.
He's driving **more and more slowly**. 그는 점점 더 천천히 차를 몰고 있다.

- 「the + 비교급~, the + 비교급…」 ~할수록 …한

The more I study, **the more** I learn. 많이 공부할수록 많이 배운다.
"How do you like your coffee?" "**The stronger the better.**" 커피 어떻게 해줄까? 진할수록 더 좋지.

- 「Which/Who ~ 비교급?」 어느 것/누가 더 ~하니?

Which do you like **better**, rice or noodles? 어느 것이 더 좋아요, 쌀이요, 국수요?

Unit Test

1. **다음 괄호 안의 단어를 비교급으로 바꿔 빈칸을 채우시오.**

1. You should take a subway. It's ___________ (cheap).
2. I can't understand what you are saying. Can you speak a little___________ (slowly)?
3. I don't play tennis these days. I used to play ___________ (often).
4. I was feeling tired last night, so I went to bed a little ___________ (early) than usual.
5. I know Jessie ___________ (well) than anybody else does.
6. My back really hurts. It's ___________ (bad) than yesterday.
7. You looked a little upset yesterday, but you look ___________ (good) today.
8. We're in a hurry. Can you walk ___________ (fast)?
9. Ted is only 17 years old, but he looks ___________ (old) than he really is.
10. The movie wasn't very good. I expected it to be ___________ (interesting).

2. **괄호 안의 단어를 이용하여 보기와 같이 비교급 문장을 완성하시오.**

보기 | You look <u>much prettier</u>(much/ pretty) today.

1. The problem is _______________ (a lot/ complicated) than I thought.
2. You're driving too fast. Could you drive _______________ (a little/ slowly)?
3. Put on your coat. It's _______________ (much/ cold) than yesterday.
4. I enjoyed the concert. It was _______________ (far/ interesting) than I expected.
5. Your English has improved. It's _______________ (very much/ good) than before.

3. **다음 괄호 안에 알맞은 말을 써 넣으시오.**

1. 내가 두 개 중에 더 큰 거 줄게.
   I'll give you the (   ) one of the two.
2. 네 영어가 점점 더 나아진다.
   Your English is getting (   ) and better.
3. 점점 집을 사기가 어려워진다.
   It's getting (   ) and (   ) difficult to buy a house.
4. "What size bag do you want?" "클수록 더 좋아."
   The (   ) the (   ).
5. 어떤 게 더 비싸, the Hyatt or the Ritz-Carton?
   Which is (   )(   ), the Hyatt or the Ritz-Carlton?

Writing Pattern Practice | 비교급

Pattern 1_ 「비교급 + than ~」 ~보다 더 …하다

Mary는 그녀의 세 언니들 보다 더 키 크다. ______________________

네 영어는 나보다 서툴다.(worse) ______________________

Pattern 2_ 「less + 원급 + than ~」 (= not as(so) + 원급 + as) ~보다 덜 …하다

Susan은 그녀의 여동생보다 덜 외향적이다.(outgoing)

____

= Susan isn't as outgoing as her sister.

Pattern 3_ 「very much/ much/ a lot/ even/ far/ a little + 비교급」 훨씬 더/약간 더 ~하다

러시아어는 영어보다 훨씬 더 어렵다.(a lot) ______________________

조금 더 천천히 말씀해 주실래요?(Could~, speak) ______________________

Pattern 4_ 「the + 비교급 + of~」 ~ 중 더 …한

내가 두 개 중에 더 큰 거 너에게 줄게. ______________________

그가 둘 중 더 어리다. ______________________

Pattern 5_ 「비교급 + and + 비교급」 점점 ~한

나는 점점 더 살이 찌고 있다.(fat) ______________________

점점 추워지고 있다. ______________________

그는 점점 더 천천히 차를 몰고 있다. ______________________

Pattern 6_ 「the + 비교급~, the + 비교급…」 ~할수록 …한

나는 많이 공부할수록 많이 배운다. ______________________

진할수록 더 좋다.(strong) ______________________

Pattern 7_ 「Which/Who ~ 비교급?」 어느 것/누가 더 ~하니?

어느 것이 더 좋아요, 쌀이요, 국수요?(like better) ______________________

누가 더 키가 크니, 너야 네 여동생이야? ______________________

Unit

40 최상급

- **Pattern** the + 최상급
- **Meaning** 가장 ~한

Grammar in Practice

A: Hello? This is Joe, a friend of Michael. Can I speak to Katie?
B: This is she. You must be calling me regarding the blind date Michael was talking about.
A: That's right. I'm wondering what day would suit you best?
B: Well, I'm free this Saturday.

Grammar in Use

1. 최상급

- 최상급은 셋 이상을 비교하여 그 중 정도가 가장 높거나 낮음을 표현하는 말이다. 형용사의 최상급 앞에는 the를 붙인다.

  I'm **the happiest** man in the world. 나는 세상에서 가장 행복한 사람이다.
  Your English is **the best** of all. 네 영어가 모두 중 최고다.

| MORE TIPS | 구어체(informal)에서 the를 가끔 생략하고 말하는 경우가 있지만 수식하는 표현이 따라오는 경우 생략하지 않는다.
- Which of the boys is (the) tallest? 소년 중에서 누가 가장 키가 크니?
- This movie is (the) greatest. 그 영화는 최고다.
- This is the greatest movie I've ever seen. 이 영화는 내가 본 것 중 최고다.

- 부사의 최상급일 경우 the를 생략할 수 있다.

  What sport do you like **best**? 너는 어떤 스포츠를 가장 좋아하니?
  She runs **fastest** of them all. 그들 중 그녀가 가장 빨리 뛴다.

- 최상급은 보통 장소, 범위, 종류 등을 나타내기 위해 in~, of~, on~ 등의 표현과 함께 쓰는 경우가 많다.

  「최상급 + in + 단수명사」 예 in the team, in the world, in my family 등
  Your English is **the best in the class.** 우리 반에서 네 영어가 최고야.

  「최상급 + of + 복수명사」 예 of all, of four seasons, of all the movies 등
  Cindy sings **(the) best of us all.** 우리 모두 중에서 Cindy가 가장 노래를 잘한다.

  「최상급 + of + 기간명사」 예 of the year, of the week, of my life 등
  Yesterday was **the coldest day of the year.** 어제는 일 년 중 가장 추운 날이었다.
  It was **the happiest moment of my life.** 내 인생에서 가장 행복한 순간이었다.

- 최상급의 의미를 강조하는 표현이 있다. 「quite/ much/ nearly+최상급」 꽤/매우/거의/ 가장 ~한

  She's **quite the most beautiful** woman I've ever met. 그녀는 내가 만난 여자 중 정말 가장 아름다운 여자다.

| MORE TIPS | 동일한 사람/사물의 상태에 대해 비교할 경우 the를 붙이지 않는다.

- He's **nicest** when he's had a few drinks. 그는 술을 몇 잔 마셨을 때가 가장 좋다.
- Korea is **best** in fall. 한국은 가을에 최고다.

2. 최상급의 다양한 표현

- 「최상급 + 주어 + have/has + ever + 과거분사」 '해본 것 중에 가장 …하다'

  What's **the best book you've ever read**? 읽어본 것 중에 뭐가 최고의 책이니?

  It's **the best movie I've ever seen.** 내가 본 것 중 최고의 영화다.

- 「the + 서수 + 최상급」 '~번째로 …한'

  Minnesota is **the second coldest** state in the United States. 미네소타는 미국에서 두 번째로 추운 주다.

- 「one of + 최상급」 '가장 ~한 …것들 중 하나'

  Titanic is **one of the greatest** movies. 타이타닉은 가장 훌륭한 영화 중 하나다.

3. 원급/비교급을 이용한 최상급표현

He is **the most famous** actor in Korea. 그는 한국에서 가장 유명한 영화배우이다.

- 「No~ as(so) + 원급 + as」 '누구도 ~만큼 …하지 않은'

  No actor in Korea is **as famous as** him. 그 누구도 한국에서 그만큼 유명한 배우는 없다.

- 「No~ 비교급 + than」 '누구도 ~보다 …하지 않은'

  No actor in Korea is **more famous than** him. 그 누구도 한국에서 그보다 더 유명한 배우는 없다.

- 「비교급 + than any other + 단수명사」 '다른 어떤 ~보다도 더 …한'

  He is **more famous than any other actor** in Korea. 그는 한국에서 다른 어떤 배우보다 더 유명하다.

- 「비교급 + than all the (other) + 복수명사」 '다른 모든 ~보다도 더 …한'

  He is **more famous than all the other actors** in Korea. 그는 한국에서 다른 모든 배우들보다 더 유명하다.

Unit Test

1. **빈칸에 알맞은 최상급 형태와 전치사를 보기와 같이 써 넣으시오.**

보기	She's a very pretty girl. She's <u>the prettiest girl of</u> all.

1. It's a very long river. It's ______________________________ the world.
2. It's a very expensive hotel. It's ______________________________ Seoul.
3. Yesterday was a very hot day. It was ______________________________ the year.
4. Susie is a very smart student. She's ______________________________ the class.
5. It's a very cheap restaurant. It's ______________________________ this Town.

2. **우리말과 일치하도록 괄호 안의 단어를 알맞게 배열하시오.**

1. 나는 세상에서 가장 행복한 사람이다. (the happiest man/ I'm/ in the world)

____

2. 내가 본 영화 중 최고다. (I've ever / it's/ seen/ the best movie)

____

3. Cindy는 반에서 두 번째로 키 큰 학생이다. (the second/ in the class/ Cindy is/ tallest student)

____

4. 타이타닉은 가장 훌륭한 영화중 하나다. (one of/ *Titanic* is/ the greatest movies)

____

5. 그녀와 같이 예쁜 배우는 한국에 없다. (is/ as pretty as/ no actress in Korea/ her)

____

3. **다음 질문에 보기와 같이 각자 대답해 보시오.**

보기	What's the best movie you've ever seen? <u>*Mission* is the best movie I've ever seen.</u>

1. What's the most exciting movie you've ever seen?

____

2. What's the most boring movie you've ever seen?

____

3. Who is the eldest in your family?

____

4. What's the most delicious food you've ever tried?

____

Writing Pattern Practice | 최상급

Pattern 1_ 「the + 형용사의 최상급」 가장 ~한

나는 세상에서 가장 행복한 사람이다.(man) ____________________

네 영어가 모두 중 최고다. ____________________

Pattern 2_ 「(the) + 부사의 최상급」 가장 ~하게

너는 어떤 스포츠를 가장 좋아하니?(sport) ____________________

그녀가 그들 모두 중 가장 빨리 뛴다. ____________________

Pattern 3_ 「최상급 + in + 단수명사」, 「최상급 + of + 복수명사」, 「최상급 + of + 기간명사」 ~중에

반에서 네 영어가 최고야. ____________________

우리 모두 중에서 Cindy가 가장 노래를 잘한다. ____________________

어제는 일 년 중 가장 추운 날이었다. ____________________

내 인생에서 가장 행복한 순간이었다.(It~) ____________________

Pattern 4_ 「quite/ much/ nearly + 최상급」 꽤/매우/거의/ 가장 ~한

그녀는 내가 만난 여자 중 정말 가장 아름다운 여자다.(quite)

____

Pattern 5_ 「최상급문장 + 주어 + have/has + ever + 과거분사」

읽어본 것 중에 뭐가 최고의 책이니? ____________________

그것은 내가 본 영화 중 최고다. ____________________

Pattern 6_ 「the + 서수 + 최상급」 '~번째로 …한'

James는 반에서 세 번째로 키가 큰 소년이다. ____________________

미네소타는 미국에서 두 번째로 추운 주다. ____________________

Pattern 7_ 「one of + 최상급」 '가장 ~한 …들 중 하나'

Sears Tower는 시카고에서 가장 높은 건물들 중 하나다.

____

타이타닉은 가장 훌륭한 영화들 중 하나다.(great) ____________________

REVIEW 1

1. 틀린 곳을 찾아 밑줄치고 고쳐 쓰시오.

1. Janet's job is so bored. →
2. It has been a long and tired day. →
3. People eat more when they're depressing. →
4. Smoking is a disgusted habit. →
5. He was terrifying of heights. →
6. It's terrible cold outside. →
7. Grace has long straightly dark hair. →
8. The driver of the car was serious injured. →
9. She gave me a friend smile. →
10. It was an extreme fine day in May. →
11. Please be quietly. →
12. We couldn't go on a picnic because it was raining heavy.
→
13. The children are usually very lively but they're quietly now.
→
14. Every woman at the party was colorful dressed.
→
15. Max learned English incredible quickly. →

2. 둘 중 알맞은 것을 고르시오.

1. He spoke (too/ enough) fast to understand.
2. I'm old (too/ enough) to get married.
3. This dress is (too/ enough) big for me. I need a smaller one.
4. She wasn't experienced (too/ enough) to do the job.
5. The river wasn't clean (too/ enough) to swim in.
6. The coffee was (too/ enough) hot to drink.
7. I can't take a vacation. It costs (too/ enough) much.
8. The bag is (too/ enough) heavy for me.
9. You'd better take a taxi. It's (too/ enough) far from here.
10. You're skinny (too/ enough) to be a model.
11. I didn't like the movie. It was (so/ such) a boring story.
12. We had (so/ such) a great time at the party.
13. He always speaks (so/ such) fast.
14. The food at the hotel was (so/ such) terrific.
15. The book was (so/ such) interesting that I couldn't put it down.
16. I was (so/ such) sleepy that I dozed over the class.
17. How do you speak (so/ such) a good Korean?
18. I think Ann is (so/ such) a beautiful girl.
19. I haven't talked to her for (so/ such) a long time.
20. I like your parents. They are (so/ such) kind.

3. 밑줄 친 부분 중 어법상 어색한 것을 고르시오.

1. I thought the hotel would be <u>very</u>(A) <u>expensive,</u>(B) but it was <u>reasonable</u>(C) <u>cheap</u>(D).
2. I'm <u>exhausted</u>(A) because I've <u>been</u>(B) <u>working</u>(C) <u>hardly</u>(D).
3. I was <u>disappointing</u>(A) in <u>the movie</u>(B). <u>The story</u>(C) was <u>stupid</u>(D).
4. Why does your brother <u>look</u>(A) <u>so</u>(B) <u>depressing</u>(C) <u>today</u>(D)?
5. You <u>always</u>(A) <u>look</u>(B) <u>bored</u>(C). Is your job <u>bored</u>(D)?
6. Do you <u>get</u>(A) <u>embarrassing</u>(B) <u>easily</u>(C) in front of <u>a lot of</u>(D) people?
7. Nancy <u>drove</u>(A) <u>careful</u>(B) <u>along</u>(C) the <u>narrow</u>(D) road.
8. I was <u>so</u>(A) <u>shocked</u>(B) when I <u>heard</u>(C) the news. I could <u>hard</u>(D) speak.

4. 틀린 곳을 찾아 밑줄치고 고쳐 쓰시오.

1. My job is boring. I'd like to do something interestinger. → ______________
2. I was tired last night, so I went to bed more early than usual. → ______________
3. I can't walk that fast. Can you walk a little slowlier? → ______________
4. "How do you feel today? Do you feel better?" "No, I feel badder." → ______________
5. This bag is a lot expensiver than I thought. It's almost $1000. → ______________

[1-2] 다음 밑줄친 문장과 바꿔 쓸 수 있는 것을 고르시오.

1. <u>The department store was less crowded than usual.</u>

① The department store wasn't as crowded as usual.
② The department store was more crowded than usual.
③ The department store was as crowded as usual.
④ The department store was a lot more crowded than usual.

2. <u>This restaurant is the cheapest in town.</u>

① This restaurant is the most expensive in town.
② This restaurant is more expensive than any other restaurant in town.
③ This restaurant is cheaper than all the other restaurants in town.
④ No restaurant in town is more expensive than this restaurant.

3. **다음 도표는 '관광객 지출 경비'와 관련된 도표이다. 질문에 답하시오.**

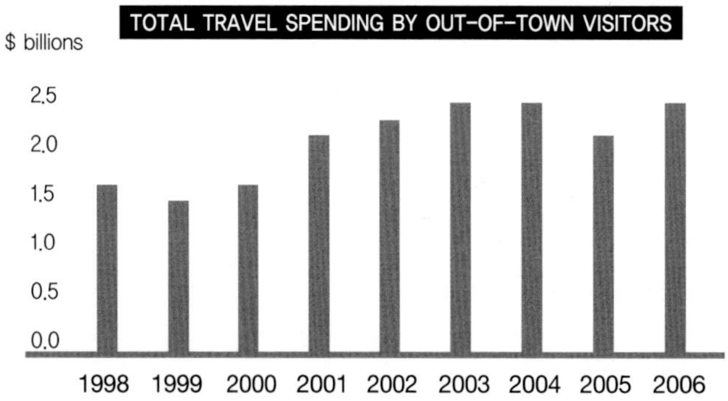

Q: Which year shows the least amount of spending by out-of-town visitors?

① 1998 ② 1999 ③ 2000 ④ 2005

4. **다음 글을 읽고, 빈칸에 차례로 들어갈 알맞은 말을 고르시오.**

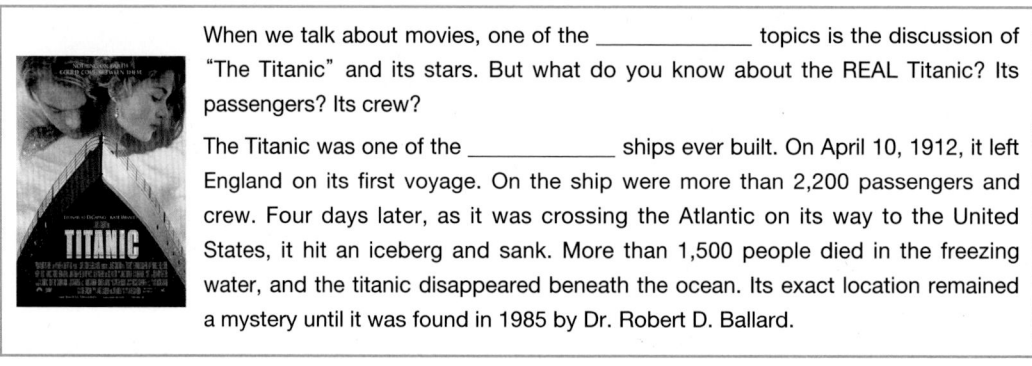

When we talk about movies, one of the ______________ topics is the discussion of "The Titanic" and its stars. But what do you know about the REAL Titanic? Its passengers? Its crew?

The Titanic was one of the _____________ ships ever built. On April 10, 1912, it left England on its first voyage. On the ship were more than 2,200 passengers and crew. Four days later, as it was crossing the Atlantic on its way to the United States, it hit an iceberg and sank. More than 1,500 people died in the freezing water, and the titanic disappeared beneath the ocean. Its exact location remained a mystery until it was found in 1985 by Dr. Robert D. Ballard.

① hottest - greatest ② hotter - greater ③ hottest - greater ④ hotter - greatest

5. **다음 글을 읽고, 빈칸에 차례로 들어갈 알맞은 말을 고르시오.**

From: Cindy Smith Date: 10 May To: Ted O'Harris

Subject: Can we reschedule? Sorry, this is on such _______ notice, but could we postpone our 1:00 tomorrow meeting until 2:00? Something _______ has come up, and I've got to work through lunch. I can meet you at 2:00, if that's convenient for you. Please let me know if this is a problem or if you prefer to reschedule for later in the week.

① short - urgent ② shortly - urgent ③ short - urgently ④ shortly- urgently

KEY GRAMMAR POINTS FOR ENGLISH LEARNERS

SMART English Grammar

for Speaking & Writing

1

머리에 쏙쏙 들어오는

정답 및 해설

MENTORS

SMART English Grammar

for Speaking & Writing

1권

정답 및 해설

Chapter 01 시제

Unit 1_ 현재시제

P.24

Dialogue

A: 있지, 새 아파트 구했어.
B: 정말? 어떤데?
A: 정말 좋아. 전망도 좋구.
B: 방은 몇 개야?
A: 방 세 개인데, 욕실, 부엌 그리고 거실이 있어.

Unit Test

1.
1 closes 2. drives 3. don't grow
4. speaks 5. teaches 6. doesn't drink
7. doesn't seem 8. wears
9. don't look 10. sets

2.
1. Does Sam start his new job next Monday?
2. Do you need money?
3. Does this shop open on Sundays?
4. Does snakes eat frogs?
5. Does his father drive a bus for a living?

3.
1. Where do you come from?
2. What does this word mean?
3. The Olympic games take place every four years.
4. Jackie has brown hair.
5. Do you walk your dog everyday?

Writing Pattern Practice

1.
I have brown hair and brown eyes.
Brush your teeth before you go to bed.
We usually go to church on Sundays.
Tom and Mary go to the same school.

2.
She gets angry a lot.
Jack comes from Seattle.
Cindy really hates cockroaches.
The first class begins at 8:00.
The flight to Seoul arrives at 8:00 today.

3.
Do you walk your dog every day?
Does Katie take a shower every day?
What do you do?
When does that store open?

4.
I don't drink beer.
They don't sell shoes at that store.
David doesn't eat out a lot.
We don't leave tonight.
Your shoes don't go well with your skirt.

Unit 2_ 과거시제

P.28

Dialogue

A: 어디에서 태어났어요?
B: 멕시코에서 태어났어요.
A: 언제 여기에 이사 왔어요?
B: 5년 전 고등학교 다닐 때 이사 왔어요.
A: 고등학교에서 영어 배웠어요?
B: 네, 그랬어요.

Unit Test

1.
1. I had lunch. 2. She got up.
3. Did you drive here? 4. Did it rain?
5. We didn't go out last night.
6. They didn't know much about her.

2.
1. wrote 2. sold 3. spent 4. invited
5. cost 6. put 7. fell 8. was
9. went 10. ate

3.
3. Did you have dinner?
4. What did you eat?
5. Did you have a good time?
6. Did you drive her home?
7. When did you go back home?

Writing Pattern Practice

1.
I got up early.
I bought these shoes two years ago.

Jack drank a lot last night.
The doorbell rang.
We went shopping yesterday.
We spent a lot of money.

2.
Did I wake you?
Did I bother you?
Did you brush your teeth?
Did you take a shower?
Did it rain?
Did they walk home?

3.
What did you do yesterday?
What did you eat for lunch?
When did it happen?
Why did you fight?
How did you know my phone number?
Who did you call?
Where did they meet?

4.
I didn't do anything wrong.
You didn't clean your room.
David didn't invite me.
It didn't rain.
They didn't drive here.

Unit 3_ 미래시제 1

P.31

Dialogue

A: 식당에 상 좀 차려줄래?
B: 네, 엄마. 오늘 밤에 손님 오세요?
A: 그래, 아빠 친구 분들이 저녁식사 하러 오신단다.

Unit Test

1.
1. I'm going to have a baby next month.
2. It's going to rain.
3. Are you going to see the movie tonight?
4. Is Tom going to leave for Japan?
5. We aren't going to have a meeting tomorrow morning.
6. They aren't going to get divorced.

2.
1. I'll help you clean the house.
2. He'll come on time.
3. Will you go to the party?
4. Will Kelly be here in a few minutes?
5. Jack won't stay in Seoul.
6. They won't lend you the money.

3.
1. will 2. will 3. am going to 4. will
5. am going to 6. will 7. are going to

Writing Pattern Practice

1.
I'll have some orange juice.
I'll go home now.
I'll eat spaghetti for lunch.
I'll miss you.
It'll be spring soon.
It'll be cold tomorrow.

2.
Will you come?
Will it be OK?
What will you do?
When will you go out?
Where will you spend the night?

3.
I won't tell a lie again.
Sally won't be late.
We won't be back.
It won't rain tomorrow.

4.
I'm going to be late.
I'm going to keep asking her out until she says 'yes.'
It's going to be windy.
We're going to buy a house next year.
We're going to crash.

5.
Are you going to get your hair cut?
Is she going to marry Mark?
Is it going to rain?
Is it going to be sunny?
What are you going to do?
When are you going to leave?
Where are they going to play soccer?

6.
I'm not going to ask her out.
Cindy is not going to go out this afternoon.
It's not going to snow.
We're not going to take a train.

Unit 4_ 미래시제 2

P.36

Dialogue

A: 수업 끝나고 영화 보러가자.
B: 미안하지만 집에 일찍 가봐야 해. 오후에 여동생을 돌봐야 하거든.

Unit Test

1.
1. I'm about to eat breakfast.
2. Jully is about to clean her room.
3. The singer is about to sing.
4. The movie is about to begin.
5. Tom and I are about to leave.

2.
1. I'm supposed to be at home by 11.
2. You're supposed to finish the report by noon.
3. Janet is supposed to meet Dr. Smith today.
4. David is supposed to do the laundry this afternoon.
5. Jack and I are supposed to leave tonight.

3.
1. The queen is to visit next month.
2. The APEC Ministerial meeting is to be held in Chile.
3. The technicians are to go on a strike sooner or later.

Writing Pattern Practice

1.
I'm about to call Jason.
The movie is about to begin.
My tooth is about to fall out.
We're about to eat dinner.
We were about to go out.

2.
You're supposed to do the laundry today.
I'm supposed to meet Dr. Walf this afternoon.
You were supposed to get here one hour ago.
What am I supposed to do?
How am I supposed to live without you?

3.
The President is to visit Malaysia.
Mr. Smith is soon to be promoted.

4.
Shiela could be fired sooner or later.
I might see a movie with my friends this weekend.
Jane might give you a ride there.

Unit 5_ 현재진행시제

P.39

Dialogue

A: 몸이 안 좋아요. 일찍 가봐야겠어요.
B: 1시간 전에는 아주 괜찮아 보였는데. 무슨 일이예요?
A: 감기 같은 것에 걸리는 것 같아요. 목이 따끔따끔하고 콧물이 나기 시작해요.
B: 그럼 집에 가서 쉬어야겠네요.

Unit Test

1.
1. I'm taking a shower.
2. My mother and I are doing the laundry.
3. I'm not talking about money.
4. You aren't listening to me.
5. Is Jack talking on the phone?
6. Is the sun shining?

2.
1. know　2. is having　3. Do you hate
4. Does David have　5. believe
6. is snowing　7. usually eat　8. smells
9. Does this belong　10. Do you understand

3.
1. Everybody is dozing.
2. My parents are living in Seattle these days.
3. You are always forgetting something.
4. Am I bothering you?
5. Are Jack and Mary leaving tonight?
6. We are having a great time here.

Writing Pattern Practice

1.
I'm vacuuming the floor.
I'm taking a computer class these days.
You're always forgetting something.
Janet is always complaining.
Jack and I are staying in New York.

2.
Am I bothering you?
Are you taking a shower?
Is Jack talking on the phone?
Is your sister playing the piano?
Is it raining?

3.
What am I doing?
Where are you drinking?
When is Jessy leaving?
Why are they fighting?
How are you doing?
Who are you talking about?

4.
I'm not studying English.
You aren't listening to me.
David isn't taking a nap.
We aren't talking about you.

Unit 6_ 과거진행시제

P.43

Dialogue

A: 저기 말야, Karen을 우연히 만났어.
B: 정말? 어디에서 만났는데?
A: 집에 걸어오다가 걔가 버스 기다리고 있는 걸 봤어.
B: 근처에 살아?
A: 응, 두 달 전에 이사 왔어.

Unit Test

1.
1 was raining 2. was having lunch
3. was cutting 4. was trying
5. was taking 6. were taking
7. was watching 8. was vacuuming
9. were sleeping 10. was waiting

2.
1. was reading 2. burned 3. happened

3.
1. was driving to work 2. was working hard
3. was having spaghetti for dinner
4. was watching a movie on TV

Writing Pattern Practice

1.
I was sleeping.
We were playing tennis.
Susan was writing a letter.
The sun was shining brightly.

2.
Were you working?
Were you driving fast?
Was Jack riding a bicycle?
Why were you crying there?
What were you doing at 9:00 last night?

3.
I wasn't driving fast.
I wasn't looking at you.
Tom wasn't working.
They weren't smiling.

4.
When I met Ted, he was waiting for the bus.
When the phone rang, Nicole was watching TV.

5.
While you were taking a shower, Kate called.
While I was cooking, I burned my finger.

Unit 7_ 미래진행시제

P.46

Dialogue

A: 10시에 가도 되나요?
B: 아니오, 그때는 회의가 있을 거예요.
A: 그럼, 12시는 어때요?
B: 좋아요. 회의가 그때까지는 끝날 거예요.

Unit Test

1.
1. will be having 2. will be seeing

3. will be having	4. will be playing
5. will be sitting	6. will be seeing
7. will be lying	8. will be working
9. will, be arriving	10. will, be leaving

2.

1. Will, be using	2. Will, be working
3. Will, be staying	4. Will, be going out
5. will, be staying	

3.

1. We will be having dinner at home.
2. He will be leaving work then.
3. David will be seeing her tomorrow.
4. Will you be staying at home tonight?
5. How long will you be using your computer?

Writing Pattern Practice

1.

I'll be working.
I'll be missing you.
I'll be standing here.
I'll be sitting here.
I'll be waiting for you here.
I'll be eating ice-cream here.
I'll be talking on the phone here.
I'll be lying on the sofa.
She'll be teaching English in Japan.
He'll be working for IBM.
This time tomorrow I'll be skiing.
This time next week I'll be traveling.
This time next year I'll be staying in Canada.

2.

Will you be using your car today?
Will you be working tomorrow?
Will you be staying at home tonight?
Will you be going out for dinner?
How long will you be staying here?

Unit 8_ 현재완료시제

P.49

Dialogue

A: 이게 누구야! Jane Johnson 아니야?
B: Mark! 어머, 진짜 오랜만이다. 그 동안 어떻게 지냈어?
A: 잘 지내지. 너는 잘 지내?
B: 글쎄, 늘상 그렇지 뭐.

Unit Test

1.

1. Have you ever driven a car?
2. Has she already had lunch?
3. Has Ben always lived in Seoul?
4. How long have they known each other?
5. Have you heard from Tom lately?

2.

1. been	2. gone	3. already
4. yet	5. yet	

3.

1. have bought → bought
2. Have you seen → Did you see
3. has started → started
4. hasn't gone → didn't go
5. 've seen → saw

4.

1. Have you traveled a lot?
2. My brother has never had a cell phone.
3. Has Tom just gone to work?
4. I haven't eaten anything since breakfast.
5. We haven't seen Janet since last month.

Writing Pattern Practice

1.

I've just got up.
I've forgotten his name.
I've just had a big dinner.
I've been to China twice.
It's rained for a couple of days.
Cindy has already left.
He's gone out.

2.

Have you seen her?
Have you been to Japan?
Has is stopped snowing yet?
Have they already gone out?

3.

Where have you been?
How have you been?
How long have you known each other?
How often has Jack tried skydiving?

How long has it rained?
How long have they lived in Seoul?

4.
I haven't seen her for a week.
I haven't slept well lately.
You haven't eaten anything all day.
It hasn't rained for two months.
They haven't sold their car yet.

Unit 9_ 현재완료진행시제

P.53

Dialogue

A: 힘든 하루였어. 정말 지쳤어.
B: 요즘 일을 너무 많이 맡아서 해왔어.
A: 알아.
B: 우선순위를 정해서 해. 너도 한계가 있지.

Unit Test

1.
1. have been swimming 2. have been playing
3. have been learning 4. has been raining
5. has been snowing 6. have been traveling
7. have been working 8. have been teaching
9. has been gardening 10. have been eating

2.
1. Jane been sleeping all day?
2. you been waiting for Terry?
3. has her baby been sleeping?
4. has it been raining?
5. has she been living in California?

3.
1. It has been raining all day.
2. I have been learning English since I was eight.
3. My grandma has been gardening all afternoon.
4. We have been living in New York for a year.
5. How long has it been raining?

Writing Pattern Practice

1.
It's been raining all day.
I've been waiting for you for an hour.
It's been snowing for a week.
We've been looking all over for you.
We've been playing badminton for two hours.
Henry has been working here for a long time.
You've been sleeping all day.
Mary and I have been playing tennis since then.
We've been learning Spanish for six months.
They've been traveling since last month.
I've been working hard this week.
I've been teaching English since I was twenty-five.
My grandma has been gardening all afternoon.

2.
Have you been waiting for him?
Has it been raining for a long time?
How long has it been raining?
How long have you been waiting for him?
How long have they been learning English?

Unit 10_ 과거완료시제와 그밖의 시제

P.56

Dialogue

A: 하와이 여행 어땠어?
B: 있잖아. 하와이 가본 게 처음이었잖아. 정말 재미있었어.

Unit Test

1.
1. came, had forgotten
2. had already started, arrived
3. had lent 4. had lost
5. had painted, decided

2.
1. (과거완료) It had rained for a week.
(과거완료진행) It had been raining for a week.
(미래완료) It'll have rained for a week.
(미래완료진행) It'll have been raining for a week.
2. (과거완료) I had lived in Italy for 10 years.
(과거완료진행) I had been living in Italy for 10 years.
(미래완료) I'll have lived in Italy for 10 years.
(미래완료진행) I'll have been living in Italy for 10 years.

3.

1. Father, because he had been repairing his car.
2. Ted, because he had been practicing his Taekwondo.
3. Kate, because she had been swimming in the pool.

Writing Pattern Practice

1.

Janet had already left.
they had known each other for 10 years.
the movie had already begun.
it had rained for three weeks.
Because I had left my umbrella there,

2.

because she had been working too hard.
We had been walking since sunrise,

3.

He'll have finished the roof by Friday.
We'll have been married for ten years on December 1st.
Will he have arrived by the time we get there?

4.

Next month I'll have been teaching for ten years.
Next year I'll have been working at this company for twenty years.

REVIEW 1

1.

1. <u>is living</u> (현재진행) 2. <u>lived</u> (과거) 3. <u>was living</u> (과거진행) 4. <u>has lived</u> (현재완료) 5. <u>has been living</u> (현재완료진행) 6. <u>had lived</u> (과거완료) 7. <u>had been living</u> (과거완료진행) 8. <u>will be living</u> (미래진행) 9. <u>will have lived</u> (미래완료) 10. <u>will have been living</u> (미래완료진행)

2.

1. F (knew → have known) 2. T 3. F (is belonging → belongs) 4. T 5. T 6. T 7. F (have had → had) 8. T 9. F (is wanting → wants) 10. T 11. T 12. F (Have you called → Did you call 13. T 14. T 15. F (has gone → went) 16. F (had not → have not) 17. T 18. F (has gone → had gone) 19. F (do you have → have you had) 20. T

해설

1. since(~이래로)는 완료형과 함께 쓴다.
3. belong은 상태동사로 진행형을 쓰지 않는다.
7. 과거의 정확한 시점을 나타내는 표현은 현재완료시제와 함께 쓸 수 없다.
9. want는 상태동사로 진행형을 쓸 수 없다.
12. 15. 과거의 정확한 시점을 나타내는 표현은 현재완료시제와 함께 쓸 수 없다.
16. 현재상태에 영향을 미치는 시제는 현재완료시제.
18. 과거에 Cindy가 파티 장소에 없었던 것은 그 전에 집에 갔기 때문이다. 그러므로 과거완료시제를 쓴다.
19. '얼마나 그것을 가지고 있었니?' 라는 뜻으로 현재완료시제를 쓴다.

3.

1. It's snowing. 2. travels 3. didn't know 4. arrived 5. have thought 6. have known 7. got married 8. saw 9. hurt his finger 10. Do you believe

4.

1. (과거) I started my new job.
   (현재완료) I have started my new job.
   (미래) I will start my new job.
   (미래진행) I will be starting my new job.
2. (현재진행) I am living in Boston.
   (현재완료진행) I have been living in Boston
   (미래진행) I will be living in Boston.
   (미래완료진행) I will have been living in Boston.
3. (현재진행) Susan is leaving for Seattle.
   (과거) Susan left for Seattle.
   (과거진행) Susan was leaving for Seattle.
   (과거완료) Susan had left for Seattle.
4. (현재완료) Jack has worked here for about a year.
   (현재완료진행) Jack has been working here for about a year.
   (미래완료) Jack will have worked here for about a year.
   (미래완료진행) Jack will have been working here for about a year.

REVIEW 2

1 ③ 2. ① 3. ① 4. ①
5. will be leaving

해석

Watson씨, 전 이 회사를 곧 떠날 것입니다. 이 회사를 정말 존경하고 여기서 일하는 동안 정말 즐거운 시간이었습니다. 하지만 최근 도저히 거절할 수 없는 좋은 일을 제안받았습니다. 후임자 찾는데 문제가 생기지 않도록 가능한 빨리 알려드리고 싶었습니다. 저는 3주 후에 떠납니다.

*replacement 교체, 후임자

6. ②

해석

Christopher Columbus에 대해 들어본 적 있는가? 1492년에는 세상에 아메리카가 존재한다는 것을 아무도 몰랐었다. 대부분 사람들은 세상이 평평하다고 생각했었다. "서쪽으로 가면 세상 끝에서 떨어질 거야."라고 사람들이 말했다. 하지만 Christopher Columbus는 세상이 평평하다고 생각하지 않았다. 어느날 Columbus는 몇몇 항해사들과 아시아에 가기 위해 서쪽으로 항해했다. 그리고 어느날 그들은 눈앞에 육지를 발견했다. 하지만 아시아는 아니었다. 그것은 아메리카이었다. 그들은 아시아에 가는 대신 아메리카에 도착한 것이었다. 이렇게 해서 Columbus는 아메리카를 발견했다.

*flat 평평한

Chapter 02 동사류

Unit 11_ 동작동사와 상태동사

P.64

Dialogue

A: 집에 가? 내가 차로 데려다 줄까?
B: 고마워, 그렇지만 너한테 부담주기 싫은데.
A: 괜찮아. 어차피 너 네 집 지나는 길인데 뭐.
B: 정말 고마워.

Unit Test

1.
eat, write, walk

2.
notice, own, like, prefer, hate

3.
1. am looking 2. tastes 3. smells 4. are having
5. has

4.
1. is belonging → belongs
2. is wanting → wants
3. have → am having 4. have → are having
5. Are you knowing → Do you know

5.
1. You are eating too much.
2. Which one do you prefer?
3. Jason owns two houses.

Writing Pattern Practice

1.
I exercise in the park.
I take a shower.
I eat(=have) breakfast.
I drive to work.
I take a break after lunch.
I go to a computer class after work.
He goes to school.
He studies.
He eats(=has) lunch with his friends.
He plays soccer after school.
He goes home.

2.
I'm exercising in the park.
I'm taking a shower.
I'm eating(=having) breakfast.
I'm driving to work.
I'm taking a break after lunch.
I'm going to a computer class after work.
He's going to school.
He's studying.
He's eating(=having) lunch with his friends.
He's playing soccer after school.
He's going home.

3.
I believe in God.
I have a boyfriend.
Do you know his phone number?
Which one do you prefer?
This watch costs at least $1000.
Something smells terrible.

Unit 12_ 사역동사

P.68

Dialogue

A: 아빠, John이랑 데이트해도 돼요?
B: 그렇게 해라. 괜찮은 젊은이 같더라.
A: John하고 오늘 저녁 파티에 갈 건데요. 집에 늦게 올지도 몰라요.
B: 그래, 이번만 봐줄게. 그래도 10시 전엔 들어와야 한다.

Unit Test

1.

1. confess 2. give 3. look 4. pick up
5. to give up

2.

1. to read → read 2. to plant → plant
3. looked → look 4. to look → look
5. helped → help 6. answer → to answer
7. to call → call 8. go → to go
9. starting → to start
10. to change → change

3.

1. Have him come in.
2. You make us smile all the time.
3. That dress makes you look thinner.
4. Let me stay here.
5. Let me think about it for a while.

Writing Pattern Practice

1.

You always make me feel happy.
He made me go.
That dress makes you look thinner.
Did I make you feel embarrassed?
Did I make you feel tired?

2.

I had Tom clean the house.
Have him come in.
I had my sister do my homework.

3.

I couldn't get Jane to change her mind.
I got him to wash the dishes.
I got Mary to help us.

4.

Let me introduce myself.
Let me help you.
Let me stay here.
I let him use my car.

5.

I got my picture taken.
I had my hair cut.
I had my ears pierced.

Unit 13_ 감각, 지각동사

P.71

Dialogue

A: 정말 예쁜 드레스야!
B: 나한테 잘 어울려 보여?
A: 응, 네 신발과도 잘 어울려.
B: 별로 비싸지 않았어.
A: 정말? 진짜 비싸 보이는데.

Unit Test

1.

1. happy 2. good 3. pretty 4. good
5. like a good idea

2.

1. to dance → dance/ dancing
2. cheated → cheat/ cheating
3. walked → walk/ walking
4. to play → play/ playing
5. touching → touched

3.

1. You look like your sister.
2. Something smells.
3. This bread tastes like(of) garlic.
4. It sounds like a good idea.
5. You sound like my mother.
6. I saw you running to school.
7. Did you see John doze over the class?
8. I like watching you dance.
9. I felt her crying.
10. I heard the doorbell ring.

Writing Pattern Practice

1.
You look great.
You look just like your mother.

2.
I feel fine.
Her fur coat felt so soft.

3.
Does it taste good?
It tastes terrific.

4.
This soup smells funny.
Something smells.
That dog smells.

5.
You sound unhappy.
Your idea sounds great.
You sound like my mother.

6.
I saw you walk(walking) down the street.
Did you see me dance(dancing)?
I like watching you eat(eating).

7.
I heard you yell(yelling) at her.
Did you hear them fight(fighting)?
I felt someone move(moving) in the kitchen.
I suddenly felt an insect crawl(crawling) up my leg.

Unit 14_ 변화동사

P.75

Dialogue

A: 밤새 어떤 남자가 계속 전화하고 끊고 그랬어.
B: 어머. 전화에 발신자표시 없었어?
A: 발신자제한이라고 쓰여져 있더라구. 미치겠어.
B: 경찰에 신고하지 그래?

Unit Test

1.
1. turns 2. became 3. get to
4. got 5. went

2.
1. got 2. come 3. kept
4. become 5. turn

3.
1. He wants to become a professor.
2. The leaves are turning red.
3. It was getting hot.
4. Your dream will come true.
5. I got married two months ago.
6. Everything will come right in the end.
7. Keep going straight for three blocks.

Writing Pattern Practice

1.
It was becoming dark.
What do I have to do to become a pilot?

2.
My mother went white with anger.
Everything went black and I passed out.

3.
Your dream will come true.
Everything will come right in the end.

4.
The weather grew colder.
It's growing dark.

5.
The leaves are turning red.
Tadpoles turn into frogs.

6.
Stay awake.
Debbie stayed single.
Mary kept quiet.
They remained silent.
Keep running.

7.
It was getting cold.
Jack and Mary got married in 2002.
We got to know the truth.

Unit 15_ 능력의 조동사

P.79

Dialogue

A: 딸꾹질이나. 멈출 수가 없어.
B: 숨을 가능한 오래 참아봐.
A: 해봤는데 효과 없었어. 계속 다시 하게 돼.
B: 그럼 물 좀 마셔봐. 괜찮아질 거야.

Unit Test

1.
1. be able to　　2. be able to
3. am not be able to　　4. be able to
5. are not able to

2.
1. can't　2. can　3. can't　4. couldn't
5. couldn't　6. couldn't　7. be able to
8. be able to　9. be able to　10. be able to

3.
1. Can you speak any foreign languages?
2. I wasn't able to afford a BMW.
3. Can you hear me?
4. How can I use this copy machine?
5. he could smell gas.

Writing Pattern Practice

1.
I can drive.
I can speak English well.
I can see you tomorrow morning.
Mr. Parker can see you at 12:00.
I can't see you on Friday.

2.
I'll be able to get there on time.
She'll be able to walk in a few weeks.
I want to be able to get this report done by tonight.
Jane is able to speak a few foreign languages.
I haven't been able to sleep well recently.

3.
I could read when I was four.
I could ride a bicycle when I was five.
Jane played badminton well, but she couldn't beat me.
He couldn't find the ticket office.

4.
I wasn't able to call you last night.
We were able to persuade him.
A fire broke out in that building, but everybody was able to escape.

Unit 16_ 허가의 조동사

P.82

Dialogue

A: Bill. 오늘 좀 일찍 가 봐도 될까요?
B: 그렇게 해. 내일 회의자료 정리 모두 확실하게 해두고.
A: 이미 했어요. 책상위에 올려놓았어요.
B: 좋아. 그럼 내일 보지.

Unit Test

1. Can I pay you tomorrow?
2. Can I have something to drink?
3. Could I take a day off?
4. Could I take it back to you tomorrow?
5. May I take a coffee break?
6. May I borrow your book?
7. Can we see that movie?
8. Can students use this library?
9. Could we smoke in this building?
10. You can give it back to me tomorrow.
11. You can use my car if you want.
12. You may go inside and wait.

Writing Pattern Practice

1.
You can(=may) park here.
You can(=may) give it back to me tomorrow.
You can(=may) use my phone.
You can(=may) take my bike.
You can(=may) watch a video.

2.
Can I take this book home?
Can I ask you a question?
Could I use your phone?
Could I sit here?
May I help you with those bags?
May I help you?

3.
You cannot(can't) go in.
You cannot(can't) use this phone.
You may not smoke here.

4.
You're allowed to smoke here.
You're allowed to use that computer.
You're not allowed to drink.
You're not allowed to go in.

Unit 17_ 추측/가능성의 조동사

P.85

Dialogue

A: Ann, 여기는 뭐가 맛있어?
B: 파스타와 피자.
A: 피자 두개랑 파스타 두개. 아, 그리고 샐러드 시키자.
B: John, 너무 많이 시키는 것 같아. 남은 것 싸가지고 가야할 것 같아.

Unit Test

1.
1. Bob might be in his office.
2. She might know where Jane is.
3. It might be David.
4. She might be working.
5. He might take a shower.

2.
1. You must be tired.
2. You must be joking.
3. Your watch must be expensive.
4. Jane must be out.
5. That restaurant must be very good.

3.
1. This watch might not be cheap.
2. She might not be working.
3. He might not want to see me.
4. Elizabeth might not know the truth.
5. Bob might not be busy working.

4.
1. You can't be serious.
2. This restaurant can't be good.
3. He can't be hungry.
4. There can't be misunderstanding between us.
5. Those shoes can't be expensive.

Writing Pattern Practice

1.
That story could be true.
David could be at the library.

2.
It might rain in the afternoon.
Your parents may understand what you did.

3.
Leo should be at work at this hour.
Jessie should get here soon.

4.
You've got to be kidding.
He's got to be a doctor.

5.
Susie must have a problem.
Your sister must weigh over 60kg.
They must be playing soccer.

6.
They might(=may) not know you're in Busan.
Cindy might(=may) not be there.

7.
She must not(mustn't) be at home.
They must not(mustn't) be your shoes.

8.
She can't be sick.
He can't be working now.

Unit 18_ 충고/경고의 조동사

P.89

Dialogue

A: John, 괜찮니? 좀 창백해 보인다.
B: 그렇게 보여? 감기 기운이 있어.
A: 퇴근 후에 병원에 가는 게 어때?
B: 아무래도 그래야겠어.

Unit Test

1.
1. shouldn't 2. should

3. shouldn't 4. should
5. should

2.
1. had better 2. had better not
3. had better 4. had better
5. had better not

3.
1. How long should I wait?
2. Where should I put my bike?
3. What should I do on the weekend?
4. When should I return this book?
5. How should I cook a crab?

Writing Pattern Practice

1.
I should take this medicine once a day.
You really should quit smoking.
You should apologize.
You should apply for this job.
You should go to bed.
I think you should drive more carefully.

2.
People ought to drive carefully.
You ought to wear boots.
We ought to keep that in mind.

3.
You'd better turn that music down before your mother gets angry.
You'd better bundle up.
You'd better be quiet.

4.
You shouldn't be late for the meeting.
People shouldn't eat too much.
I don't think they should get married.

5.
You'd better not be late.
You'd better not stay up all night.
You'd better not bother him.

Unit 19_ 의무의 조동사

P.93

Dialogue

A: 너 토요일에 시간 있어?
B: 응, 아무 일도 없어. 왜 그러는데?
A: 놀이동산 갈래? 나 무료입장권이 두 장 생겼거든.
B: 재미는 있을 것 같은데, 난 못 가. 놀이기구 타는 거 싫어하거든.

Unit Test

1.
1. Do I have to go to the hospital?
2. Dose Jack have to work late?
3. Must we get to the store before 8?
4. Has she got to visit her aunt?
5. Did they have to stay up all night?

2.
1. We don't have to hurry up.
2. Kimberly doesn't have to get up early tomorrow morning.
3. You don't have to get a visa to go to the United States.

3.
1. have to 2. had to 3. have to 4. has to
5. had to

4.
1. doesn't have to 2. mustn't
3. don't have to 4. mustn't
5. doesn't have to

Writing Pattern Practice

1.
I have to work late.
Ann really has to cut down on sweets.
Do I have to clean all the rooms?

2.
I've got to go home right now.
He's got to see the dentist.
Have you got to leave this early?

3.
I really must go home.
Must you wear that tie?

4.
I don't have to wear a tie at work.
We don't have to water the garden.

5.
You must not make a U-turn here.
You must not bother your father while he's working.

6.
Next year I'll have to get a job.
You'll have to meet Jack this afternoon.

7.
Edward had to stay up late last night.
Did you have to work yesterday?

Unit 20_ 부탁/제안의 조동사

P.97

Dialogue

A: 저희 사진 좀 찍어 주실래요?
B: 물론이죠. 어떻게 작동하는 거죠?
A: 카메라 위에 있는 버튼만 누르시면 되요.
B: 알겠어요. 그럼 찍습니다. 치즈!

Unit Test

1.
1. Can you pass the salt?
2. Could you pick me up?
3. Will you give me a ride to the airport?
4. Would you explain it to me again?
5. Would you mind opening the window?

2.
1. Let's go to see a movie.
2. Why don't we take a coffee break?
3. How about going on a picnic?

3.
1. Why don't you 2. Why don't you
3. Why don't we 4. Why don't you
5. Why don't we

Writing Pattern Practice

1.
Can you give me a hand?
Can you do me a favor?

2.
Will you be quiet, please?
Will you open the door?

3.
Could you help me with this bag?
Could you lend me some money?

4.
Would you watch the children?
Would you pass me the salt?

5.
Would you mind taking our picture?
Would you mind opening the window?

6.
Let's go for a walk.
Let's rent a movie.

7.
Why don't we go out for dinner?
Why don't we drink some orange juice?

8.
How about seeing a movie tonight?
How about going shopping?

Unit 21_ 과거습관/필요의 조동사

P.100

Dialogue

A: 나는 차를 몰고 출근했었지만 지금은 버스를 타고 다녀.
B: 잘됐네. 네 건강을 위해서는 그게 더 좋아.

Unit Test

1.
1. I used to exercise every morning.
2. I used to like opera.
3. I used to smoke a lot.
4. She used to work for Samsung
5. They used to love each other.

2.
1. used to 2. used to 3. used to
4. used to, would 5. used to

3.

1. Do you need help?
2. She doesn't need to keep awake.
3. He needs to say that again.

Writing Pattern Practice

1.

I used to smoke a lot.
You used to be very skinny.
You didn't use to like him.
I didn't use to eat sweets.
There used to be a bank here.
There used to be a tall building here.

2.

I would exercise in the park.
I would go jogging with my sister.

3.

I need go now.
He need go now.
Need I go now?
I need not(needn't) go now.
He need not(needn't) go now.
Need he go now?

4.

I need to pay now.
He needs to pay now.
Do I need to pay now?
Does he need to pay now?
I don't need to pay now.
He doesn't need to pay now.

Unit 22_ 조동사 + have + 과거분사

P.103

Dialogue

A: Sue한테 무슨 일이지? 한 시간 전에 여기에 왔어야하는데.
B: 핸드폰으로 전화해봤어?
A: 물론이지, 열 번 이상은 해봤지만 꺼져 있었어.
B: 무슨 일이 있거나 잃어버렸겠지.

Unit Test

1.

1. You should have had lunch.
2. I should have brought my umbrella.
3. He should have come on time.

2.

1. You might have left your cell phone in the car.
2. He might have forgotten our appointment.
3. Jenny might have been in a bad mood.

3.

1. I must have dropped my keys in my office.
2. The movie must have been boring.
3. She must have been out of her mind.

Writing Pattern Practice

1.

I should have studied hard.
I should have brought my umbrella.
You should have come.
You should have gone to bed earlier.

2.

I could have made a lot of money.
You could have helped me.
She could have got the job.
They could have come here on time.

3.

I might have left my keys in my office.
James might have missed the bus.
She might have been at home.
They might have left work.

4.

Tina must have forgotten our appointment.
It must have been love.
There must have been a lot of people in the park.
She must have got up late.

REVIEW I

1.

1. F (am believing → believe) 2. T
3. F (are you preferring → do you prefer) 4. T
5. F (is costing → costs)
6. F (Are you understanding → Do you understand)
7. T 8. T 9. T
10. F (is belonging → belongs)
11. F (is smelling → smells) 12. T

13. F ('m supposing → suppose)
14. F (are you wanting → do you want)   15. T

2.

1. smile	2. feel	3. pick up
4. call	5. to answer	6. to change
7. go	8. happen	9. cut
10. pierced	11. repaired	12. taken
13. look	14. smell of	15. felt
16. tastes	17. smell	18. sounds like
19. walk	20. crawl	

해설

1.2. '~한테…하도록 만들다' 라는 뜻으로 「make+목적어+동사원형」 형태로 쓴다.
3.4. '~한테…하도록 시키다' 라는 뜻으로 「have+목적어+동사원형」 형태로 쓴다.
5.6. '~한테…하도록 시키다' 라는 뜻으로 「get+목적어+to부정사」 형태로 쓴다.
7.8. '~한테…하도록 허락하다' 라는 뜻으로 「let+목적어+동사원형」 형태로 쓴다.
9.10.11.12. '~를…되도록 하다' (목적어와 목적보어가 수동관계)라는 뜻으로 「have/get+목적어+과거분사」 형태로 쓴다.
13. '~해 보인다' 라는 뜻으로 「look+형용사」 형태로 쓴다.
14. '~ 냄새가 난다' 라는 뜻으로 「smell of(llike)+명사」 형태로 쓴다.
15. '~한 느낌이 난다' 라는 뜻으로 「feel+형용사」 형태로 쓴다.
16. '~한 맛이 난다' 라는 뜻으로 「taste+형용사」 형태로 쓴다.
17. '~한 냄새가 난다' 라는 뜻으로 「smell+형용사」 형태로 쓴다.
18. '~한 소리가 난다' 또는 '~하게 들린다' 라는 뜻으로 「sound like+명사」 형태로 쓴다.
19. '~가…하는 것을 보다' 라는 뜻으로 「see+목적어+동사/동사-ing」 형태로 쓴다.
20. '~가…하는 것을 느끼다' 라는 뜻으로 「feel+목적어+동사/동사-ing」 형태로 쓴다.

REVIEW 2

1. ④   2. ④   3. ②   4. ②   5. ④
6. ①   7. ②   8. ②   9. ④   10. ③
11. ③

해석

전문 사진 작가가 되는 법을 배우세요!

여러분이 찍은 사진이 잡지에 실리는 꿈을 꿔 보신 적이 있나요? 그렇다면 이제 여러분의 꿈이 실현될 수 있습니다!

저희는 여러분이 집에서 편안하게 여가 시간을 이용해 전문 사진 작가가 될 수 있도록 알려드립니다.

이 강좌에서 다루게 되는 과목을 간단히 소개하자면:
카메라, 렌즈, 필름, 조명, 구도
필름/슬라이드 현상 및 인화
모델 사진 작업
사진 현상소 창업

* 초보에서 고급 과정까지 집에서 가르칩니다!
* 모든 강의, 비디오 테이프, 오디오 테이프 포함!
* 성공 보장!

강좌에 관한 자세한 사항은 저희 웹사이트 www.photoinstitute.org를 방문하세요.

12. ①

해석

오늘날 미국인들은 1세기 전보다 더 적게 잠을 잔다. 1900년에 미국인들은 하루 평균 8.5시간을 잤다. 최근의 한 여론 조사에 따르면 오늘날 수면 시간은 6.5시간으로 줄었다고 한다. 일부 회사들은 근무 시간에 낮잠을 잘 수 있도록 허용하는 방침을 시행했으며, 심지어 직원들을 위해 수면실을 제공하는 회사도 생겨났다. NSC의 연구원들에 따르면 15분 간의 낮잠은 그 다음 서너 시간에 필요한 에너지를 재충전하는 데 충분하다고 한다. "낮잠을 자는 게 인간의 기본적인 생물학적 요구라고 말하는 건 정당하다고 생각해요."라고 NSC의 연구 소장인 Sue Serby 박사는 말한다. "15분 간의 낮잠이 근로자의 생산성을 향상시키고 전반적인 건강을 증진시키는 데 중요한 역할을 할 수 있다는 사실을 회사들이 계속 인식하기를 희망합니다. 우리 모두는 낮잠을 장려해야 합니다."라고 Serby 박사는 말했다.

13. ④

해석

이사 가느라고 흰색 대형 냉장고 팝니다! 기숙사 방, 침실, 지하실에서 쓰기 딱 좋습니다. 1년 6개월밖에 사용하지 않아서 새 것이나 다름 없습니다. 170달러에 샀지만 60달러에 팔아요. 사실 분은 전화나 이메일 주세요.

Chapter

03 명사류

Unit 23_ 셀 수 있는 명사

P.112

Dialogue

A: 너는 좋아하는 간식이 뭐니?
B: 고기와 야채와 꿀을 넣은 샌드위치야.
A: 어떻게 만드는데?
B: 음, 먼저 고기와 야채를 빵 한 쪽에 얹어. 그리고 꿀을 그 위에 뿌린 다음 위에 남은 쪽 빵을 올려 놔. 그러면 돼.

Unit Test

1.

1. months	2. buses	3. pianos
4. photos	5. potatoes	6. tomatoes
7. centuries	8. ladies	9. lives
10. leaves	11. proofs	12. teeth
13. feet	14. women	15. mice
16. fish	17. deer	18. sheep
19. children	20. oxen	

2.

1. has	2. flies	3. times
4. is	5. is	6. is
7. was	8. is	9. are
10. nail-scissors	11. wear	12. have

3.

1. a chicken	2. chicken	3. beers
4. Beer	5. Time	6. times
7. wine	8. wines	9. glass
10. a glass		

Writing Pattern Practice

1.
I drink coffee a lot.
I'll have a coffee.
Do you want chicken or beef?
There's a chicken in the garden.
Jane never drinks wine.
France produces some wonderful wines.

2.
Mathematics is my favorite subject.
Ten miles is a long way to walk.
The news was shocking.
The United states is smaller than Canada.
One of my friends works for IBM.

3.
My jeans are too tight.
Where are my glasses?

4.
The police are questioning a man.
Most people are interested in movies.

5.
How are your family?
The average family has 3.5 members.

Unit 24_ 셀 수 없는 명사

P.117

Dialogue

A: 엄마, 뭐가 타는 것 같아요.
오븐에서 연기가 나요.
B: 어머! 조심해서 꺼.

Unit Test

1.

1. Mozart	2. fruit	3. sugar
4. Kelly	5. a big	6. a nice
7. time	8. doesn' t	9. advice
10. Her hair is		

2.
1. slice → slices 2. coffees → coffee
3. spoonful → spoonfuls 4. glass → glasses
5. waters → water

3.
1. I don't usually have a big lunch.
2. Have a good time.
3. You've been a great help.
4. You need a good sleep.
5. My parents wanted me to have a good education.

Writing Pattern Practice

1.
December 25th is Christmas.

Tom and Mary met in Paris.
Kate left for Africa.

2.
Grapes and apples are fruit.
Chairs and tables are furniture.
Letters and postcards are mail.

3.
Jack drank two bottles of beer.
Give me a piece of paper.
A loaf of bread and a glass of milk is my breakfast.

4.
Experience teaches.
I appreciate your kindness.
It was bad luck.

5.
I don't usually have a big lunch.
Have a good time.
You've been a great help.
You need a good sleep.

Unit 25_ 수량을 나타내는 표현

P.121

Dialogue

A: 어디에 가?
B: 밴드 연습가.
A: 밴드에서 연주하는지 몰랐어.
B: 이 삼주 전에 시작 했어.

Unit Test

1.
1. few 2. few 3. little 4. little 5. little
6. a few 7. a few 8. A few 9. many
10. many 11. much 12. many 13. much

2.
1. little → a little 2. ○ 3. few → a few
4. a number of → plenty of/ a great deal of
5. ○

3.
1. much time 2. many people
3. much money 4. much sugar
5. many trourists

Writing Pattern Practice

1.
There were few people in the park.
There are a few things you have to know.
Can you stay a couple of days longer?
Several students didn't come to class.
Are there many opera houses in Korea?
A number of people disagree.

2.
Cactuses need little water.
I need a little time.
I didn't eat much breakfast.
We need a great deal of time to finish the project.

3.
Sorry, I have no time.
He has no brothers.
Mary has some interesting ideas.
Could I have some coffee?
Do you know any good jokes?
I don't need any help.
You have a lot of work to do.
There are plenty of nice restaurants in this city.

Unit 26_ 그 밖의 수량표현

P.125

Dialogue

A: 오늘밤 공연 티켓 지금도 구할 수 있을까요?
B: 이층 앞좌석은 아직 가능합니다.
A: 다른 좌석은 없어요?
B: 죄송하지만 없어요.

Unit Test

1.
1. X 2. X 3. of 4. of 5. X 6. X
7. X 8. X 9. X 10. of

2.
1. live 2. phones 3. stories
4. minute 5. another 6. All
7. one 8. Most 9. student
10. friends

3.
1. Another year has gone.
2. Where are the other people?
3. I ate all the food.
4. The students listened to his every word.
5. Most people like to eat fruit.

Writing Pattern Practice

1.
Both (of) my parents live in Seoul.

2.
You can use either of the phones.

3.
Neither of my brothers came here.

4.
Show me another one.

5.
I have no other appointments.

6.
I went home every other week.

7.
All of the cars are used ones.

8.
Every room is being used.

9.
Half of my friends are single.

10.
Brush your teeth after each meal.

11.
Most people like shopping.

Unit 27_ 부정관사

P.129

Dialogue
(호텔에서)

A: 이틀 밤 묵을 수 있는 독방 있습니까?
B: 작은 스위트밖에는 없는데요.
A: 얼마입니까?
B: 아침 식사 포함해서 하룻밤 120달러입니다.

Unit Test

1.
<u>an</u> umbrella
<u>a</u> one-way conversation
<u>an</u> hour　　<u>an</u> honest boy
<u>an</u> MP　　<u>an</u> SOS
<u>a</u> useful book　　<u>a</u> university
<u>an</u> interesting book

2.

1. an	2. a	3. a	4. an	5. X, a	6. a
7. an	8. a	9. a	10. a	11. X	12. an

3.
1. A fox is a cunning animal.
2. An elephant can swim very well.
3. A doctor must like people.
4. An island is surrounded by water.
5. A flower smells good.

Writing Pattern Practice

1.
We live in an old house.
Let's see a movie.
I have a sister.

2.
A fox is a very cunning animal.
Crocodiles can swim well.
A dog is a faithful animal.

3.
I travel once a year.
I see a movie a couple of times a month.
Heather works eight hours a day, five days a week.

4.
Mark is a mechanic.
A glider is a plane with no engine.
Tennis is a sport.
She's an English teacher.

5.
I had a big lunch.
We had a wonderful time.
It's an extremely hot day.

Unit 28_ 정관사

P.132

Dialogue

(버스에서)
A: 이 버스 하이야트호텔 가요?
B: 아니오. 은행에서 내려서 83번을 타야할 거예요.
A: 얼마나 걸려요?
B: 30분 정도요.

Unit Test

1.
1. the 2. the 3. a 4. a, the 5. the
6. The 7. the 8. a 9. the 10. a

2.
3. I like listening to ✓ rain.
2. Alaska is ✓ largest state in the United States.
3. ✓ Earth is a planet.
4. I'm fed up with doing ✓ same things everyday.
5. Does this bus go to ✓ Hyatt.
6. He hit me on ✓ head.
7. Do you want to live in ✓ county?
8. You're ✓ only person that I trust.
9. Look at ✓ woman wearing sunglasses.
10. Have you ever been to ✓ Philippines?

3.
1. My grandma is the oldest in my family.
2. Ken and I went to the same high school.
3. She kicked him on the knee.

Writing Pattern Practice

1.
Could you open the window?
Ann is in the kitchen.
Did you enjoy the party?

2.
She showed us the car today.
The boy is nine years old.

3.
Who is the girl over there with Terry?
The man in black is my boss.

4.
People used to think that the Earth was flat.
I haven't seen the sun for days.

5.
My grandma is the oldest in my family.
Ken and I went to the same high school.

6.
She kicked him on the knee.
He hit me on the head.

7.
I like listening to the rain.
British people talk about the weather a lot.

8.
the Pacific
the Indian
the Alps
the L.A. Times
the Empire State Building
the Titanic
the United States of America
the Netherlands

Unit 29_ 관사의 생략

P.136

Dialogue

(예약하기)
A: 21일 일요일 달라스 행이요.
B: 잠깐만요, 비행편이 있나 알아볼게요.
A: 일등석으로 부탁합니다.
B: 네. 저녁 8시 반에 떠나는 직행 비행기편이 있네요.

Unit Test

1.
Africa Tokyo Main Street
January Portugal

2.
1. X 2. the, the 3. X 4. X 5. the
6. X 7. X 8. the 9. the 10. X 11. the
12. X 13. the 14. X 15. X 16. X, X
17. X, X 18. X 19. X 20. X 21. The, X
22. X 23. the 24. X, X 25. the

Writing Pattern Practice

1.
School starts at 9:00.
She's in prison.
You should be in bed.

2.
I've just had lunch.
Let's meet on Monday.
It snows a lot in January.
What do you usually do at Christmas?

3.
I usually go to school by bus.
We went to Busan by train.
It takes an hour on foot.

4.
The couple were walking arm in arm.
They eat with knife and fork.

5.
Uncle Tom visited us.
I'm supposed to meet Doctor Johnson today.
Who is Professor Kim?

6.
What's on TV?
In fact, we don't have enough money.
The bakery is on fire.

Unit 30_ 인칭대명사와 it

P.141

Dialogue

A: Cindy, 내 여동생 Mary를 소개할게.
B: 만나서 반가워요.
C: 만나서 반가워요. 지금까지 미네소타 어때요?
B: 매우 춥고, 고향이 좀 그립네요.
C: 처음에는 그렇게 느끼기 마련일 거예요. 새로운 장소에 익숙해지는 건 항상 시간이 걸리죠.

Unit Test

1
2. G 3. B 4. D 5. E 6. F 7. A

2.
1. I → me 2. we → us
3. I and my mother → My mother and I
4. he → him
5. me and Jane → Jane and me

3.
1. Look at us
2. Jack and I are close friends.
3. Everybody except him can come.
4. It's worth visiting Paris.
5. It's no use trying to explain.

Writing Pattern Practice

1.
I miss her.
Tell me what to do.
Look at us.
It's me.

2.
Jack and I are close friends.
That's a matter for Peter and me.

3.
I can speak English better than her.
Everybody except him can come.

4.
It's nine thirty.
It's freezing out there.
It's Monday again.
It's January 1st.
It's ten miles to the nearest bank.
How is it going?

5.
It's nice to talk to you.
We found it strange that she was absent for two weeks.

6.
It's worth visiting Italy.
It's no use crying over spilt milk.

Unit 31 소유격과 소유대명사

P.145

Dialogue

A: 네 전화 울리는 거야?
B: 내 거 아닌데. 내 휴대폰은 진동으로 돼 있어.

A: 여긴 도서관이잖아.
B: 응 맞아. 도서관에서 전화기 안 꺼 놓는 사람들 정말 싫어.

Unit Test

1.

1. the beginning of the movie
2. my parents' car
3. yesterday's newspaper
4. the roof of this house
5. your boyfriend's name

2.

1. OK 2. OK 3. hours's → hours'
4. The hair of Jean → Jean's hair
5. OK 6. the son of Karen → Karen's son
7. OK 8. OK 9. a my friend → a friend of mine 혹은 'a' 생략 10. OK

3.

1. Which is yours? 2. Are those his?
3. Those are Karen's 4. This is Cindy's
5. This is my sister's

Writing Pattern Practice

1.
This is my sister.
May I ask your phone number?

2.
Laura is a friend of mine.
Can I borrow some books of yours?

3.
Emily is Ted's sister.
Where is the manager's office?
This is my parents' car.
This is my sisters' room.
These are children's backpacks.
Do you have today's newspaper?
We need at least seven hours' sleep a night.

4.
Do you know the name of this street?
Tell me the title of this song.

5.
That's mine.
Which is yours?
Those are Karen's.

Unit 32_ 지시대명사

P.149

Dialogue

A: 이 처방전대로 조제해 주세요.
B: 즉시 해 드리죠.
A: 그리고 햇빛에 탄데 바를 만한 것 좀 주세요.
B: 이걸 써 보세요. 새로 나온 제품입니다.

Unit Test

1.

1 — c 2 — a 3 — b

2.

1. these 2. this 3. this 4. This
5. These

3.

1. that 2. those 3. That 4. that
5. Those

4.

1. That is a good question.
2. Is this what you bought?
3. This model came out in 2006.
4. That shirt doesn't fit me.
5. I'm sorry to call you this late.
6. I didn't expect you to come this early.
7. I can't run that fast.

Writing Pattern Practice

1.
This is my cap.
These are sunglasses.
This is my wife.
That is my computer.
What are those?
That is my girlfriend.

2.
I'll be busy this weekend.
This model came out in 2006.
These scissors are awfully heavy.
What is that loud noise?
That shirt doesn't fit me.

Look at those skirts.
Those questions are quite difficult.

3.
I didn't expect you to come this early.
I'm sorry to call you this late.
I can't eat that much.
I can't run that fast.
Sarah isn't that pretty.
His English isn't that good.

Unit 33_ 재귀대명사

P.152

Dialogue

A: 정말 멋진 생일 파티야. 지금 촛불 꺼도 되지?
B: 응, 소원 비는 거 잊지 마.
A: 그럼. 모두 고마워.
B: 먹자. 많이들 먹어.

Unit Test

1.
1 myself 2. myself 3. herself
4. ourselves 5. myself 6. ourselves
7. yourself 8. yourselves 9. myself
10. ourselves

2.
3. ✓ 7. ✓ 8. ✓ 10. ✓

3.
1. yourself 2. myself 3. herself 4. myself

Writing Pattern Practice

1.
John cut himself shaving this morning.
We took a bath and dried ourselves.
Look at yourself in the mirror.
We should blame ourselves.

2.
It's cheaper if you do it yourself.
The shirt itself looks nice, but it's too expensive.

3.
Cindy went to Mexico by herself.
Linda sometimes talks to herself.
We enjoyed ourselves at the party.
Help yourself.
Make yourself at home.
You must be proud of yourself.

Unit 34_ 부정대명사

P.155

Dialogue

A: 안녕, Jess. 요즘 누구 만나니?
B: 아니. 왜?
A: 너랑 딱 맞을 사람 아는데. 상냥하고 재미있고 멋진 사람이야.
B: 좋아. 만나게 해줘. 이번 주말에 시간 있어.

Unit Test

1.
1. one 2. ones 3. it 4. the other
5. the others 6. each other 7. have

2.
1. anybody 2. Somebody 3. Anybody
4. anybody 5. anybody 6. somebody
7. anybody 8. anybody 9. anybody
10. anybody

3.
2. others 3. the other 4. the others

Writing Pattern Practice

1.
You can't learn Spanish in a month.
We dial 911 in an emergency.
They speak English and French in that state.

2.
Do you have one?
Give me two red ones.

3.
One is blue, and the other is white.
One is five years old, another is eight, and the other is eleven.
Some of them look happy, and others look bored.
Some of them are green, and the others are red.

4.
How long have you and Sally known each other?

5.
Someone(Somebody) is here to see you.
Anyone(Anybody) could have passed.
Has anyone(anybody) seen Katie?
Nobody tells me anything.

6.
All I want is money.
Are you all ready?
None of us have a question.

REVIEW 1

1.
1 a glass → glass 2. a wine → wine
3. are → is 4. were → was
5. work → works 6. piece → pieces
7. a little → a few
8. The number of → A number of
9. little → few 10. lives → live

해설
1. glass(유리)는 셀 수 없는 명사이다.
2. wine(와인)은 셀 수 없는 명사이다.
3. -s로 끝나는 과목명은 단수취급한다.
4. news는 단수취급한다.
5.「one of+복수명사」는 단수취급한다.
6. 셀 수 없는 명사를 셀 경우 2개 이상일 때 단위명사에 -s를 붙인다.
7. things는 셀 수 있는 명사이므로 a little 대신 a few를 써야한다.
8. 문맥상 the number of(~의 수) 대신 a number of(수많은)를 써야한다.
9. friends는 셀 수 있는 명사이므로 little 대신 few를 써야한다.
10.「both+명사」는 복수취급한다.

2.
1. X 2. a 3. the 4. The 5. the
6. the 7. X 8. X 9. the 10. a
11. a friend of mine 12. some books of yours
13. one 14. the other 15. anybody

해설
1. 식사명 앞에는 관사를 쓰지 않는다.
2. 명사의 종류를 나타내는 경우 부정관사 a를 쓴다.
3. 수식어구가 있어 한정을 받는 경우 정관사 the를 쓴다.
4. 세상에서 유일한 것을 말하는 경우 정관사 the를 쓴다.
5. 복수국가명 앞에 정관사 the를 쓴다.
6. 수식어구가 있어 한정을 받는 경우 정관사 the를 쓴다.
7. 요일명 앞에 관사를 쓰지 않는다.
8. 교통수단을 나타내는 경우 관사를 쓰지 않는다.
9. 사람들의 일상에 친숙한 주변 환경을 말하는 경우 정관사 the를 쓴다.
10. 명사의 종류를 나타내는 경우 부정관사 a를 쓴다.
11. a/an 등이 명사 앞에 올 경우 소유격을 같이 쓰지 않고「a/an+명사+of+소유대명사」형태로 쓴다.
12. some 등이 명사 앞에 올 경우 소유격을 같이 쓰지 않고「some+명사+of+소유대명사」또는「some+of+소유격+명사」형태로 쓴다.
13. 불특정한 단수명사를 가리키므로 one을 쓴다.
14. 둘 중 나머지 하나는 the other을 쓴다.
15. 부정문에서는 보통 somebody대신 anybody를 쓴다.

3.
1 homeworks → homework
2. on the September 20. → on September 20.
3. have → has 4. a few → a little
5. car → a car
6. minute → a minute.
7. a rice → rice
8. a bread → a loaf of bread
9. These furnitures are → This furniture is
10. luggages → luggage

4.
1. B (a L.A. → L.A.) 2. A (pound → pounds)
3. B (hour → hours) 4. D (are → is)
5. D (nose → noses) 6. A (am → are)
7. C (Earth → the Earth) 8. D (pen → a pen)
9. B (a → the)
10. B (a space → the space)

5.
1. 저 2. 이(복수) 3. 이렇게 4. 그렇게
5. 이 사람은 6. 저 사람은 7. X 8. X
9. 그것은 10. X

REVIEW 2

1. ② 2. ③ 3. ③ 4. ① 5. ② 6. ①
7. ②

해석

현대에는 많은 종류의 로봇이 여러 곳에서 사용되어진다. 로봇들은 자체 행동을 제어하는 컴퓨터가 내장되어 있다. 다양한 종류의 로봇이 다양한 역할을 한다. 공장 로봇은 자동차나 냉장고와 같은 제품을 만든다. 경찰 역시 로봇을 폭탄을 제거하고 폭발을 막거나 하는 데 두루 사용한다. 로봇은 다른 행성에 가기도 한다. Pathfinder 우주선은 화성에 갔었다. 장난감 트럭을 닮은 소형 로봇을 싣고 갔는데 이 로봇은 이리저리 돌아다니면서 암석들을 연구하였다. 로봇은 우리 주변에서도 사용되어진다. 몇몇 로봇청소기 회사는 지난 몇 년 동안 가정용 로봇청소기를 홍보하기 위해 노력해왔다. 그러므로 현재 많은 가정에서 로봇청소기를 사용하고 있다.

*explosion 폭발

Chapter 04 | 수식어류

Unit 35_ 형용사

P.164

Dialogue

A: 내 남동생이 어제 컴퓨터를 샀어.
B: 가서 볼 수 있을까?
A: 남동생에게 물어볼게. 네가 컴퓨터에 관심이 있는지 몰랐어.

Unit Test

1.

1. beautiful long brown hair
2. an old French song
3. a small round table
4. a new white cotton shirt
5. a big black plastic bag
6. a tall thin Korean woman
7. a large round wooden table
8. a big fat black cat
9. a lovely sunny day
10. a long narrow street

2.

1. tiring	2. bored	3. satisfied
4. disappointed	5. terrified	6. amazing
7. depressed	8. embarrassed	9. shocking
10. disgusting		

3.

1. Please give me something cold.
2. I want to meet somebody new.
3. This is a letter written in English.
4. The unemployed are losing hope.
5. The rich are not always happy.

Writing Pattern Practice

1.

a beautiful new house
an old French song
a new white cotton shirt
a big black plastic bag

2.

The man is boring.
The news was shocking.
It has been a tiring day.
Are you interested in fishing?
I was disappointed in the movie.
I was annoyed.
I get embarrassed easily.

3.

I need something fun.
I want to meet somebody new.
She gave me a glass full of milk.

4.

We're collecting money for the blind.
The unemployed are losing hope.
The English have a very old tradition.

Unit 36_ 부사

P.169

Dialogue

A: 춤추러 가자.
B: 오늘밤은 별로 그럴 기분 아니야.
A: 그럼, 뭐 다른 거 하고 싶어?
B: 아니. 오늘밤은 일찍 자고 싶어.

Unit Test

1.

1. happily	2. near	3. easily
4. gently	5. straight	6. extremely
7. high	8. terribly	9. suddenly

10. carefully 11. seriously 12. early
13. fast 14. late 15. quickly
16. right

2.
1. 친근한 2. 아름다운 3. ~할 것 같은
4. 힘든 5. 거의 ~않다 6. 늦은 7. 최근에

3.
1. ○ 2. △ 3. △ 4. △ 5. ○ 6. △
7. ○

Writing Pattern Practice

1.
He smiled happily.
I'm terribly sorry.
John drove carefully.
Please speak quietly.
Two people were seriously injured.
Tom looked at me sadly.
The food was extremely good.

2.
I'm not an early bird.
Get up as early as you can.
Am I late?
I hate arriving late.
Grace has straight hair.
Go straight for three blocks.

3.
I'm at home.
Come home early.
Today is Sunday.
It's cloudy today.

4.
It was incredibly hard work.
I hardly know him.
Don't be late.
I haven't seen Janet lately.
Prices are too high.
I can highly recommend it.

Unit 37_ 부사의 종류

P.173

Dialogue

A: 피크닉 가는 게 어때?
B: 좋아. 어디로?
A: Ted한테 전화해서 물어보자. 그는 항상 놀러가기 좋은 곳을 알고 있잖아.
B: 알았어.

Unit Test

1.
1. too 2. enough 3. too 4. too
5. enough 6. too 7. enough 8. too
9. too 10. enough

2.
1. so 2. such 3. so 4. such 5. so
6. such 7. such 8. such 9. so 10. so

3.
1. He probably doesn't know the truth.
2. My grandfather rarely goes out.
3. I can hardly believe it.
4. I kind of expected it.
5. How do you speak such a good English?

Writing Pattern Practice

1.
Then I went to bed.
Stupidly I forgot my keys.
Maybe you're right.

2.
He probably doesn't know the truth.
You always forgot my birthday.
I usually take a shower in the morning.
I can hardly believe it.
I kind of expected it.

3.
Come and sit here.
There is someone upstairs.
We play golf every week.

4.
It's too expensive.
He spoke too quickly to understand.

5.
You're skinny enough.
I'm old enough to get married.

6.
She worked so hard.

The concert was so boring.

7.
They are such nice people.
It was such a good movie.
We had such a good time.

Unit 38_ 원급비교

P.177

Dialogue

A: 너 다이어트 안 해도 될 것 같아. 딱 보기 좋아.
B: 무슨 얘기 하는 거야? 너보다 몸무게가 거의 두배 나 나가는데.

Unit Test

1.
older/ elder - oldest/ eldest, faster - fastest,
luckier - luckiest,
more embarrassing - most embarrassing,
more quietly - most quietly,
better - best, better - best,
more bored - most bored,
worse - worst, less- least,
more - most,
more carefully - most carefully,
thinner - thinnest,
more serious - most serious,
more interesting - most interesting,
larger - largest

2.
1. I'm as tall as you.
2. I speak English as well as Cindy does.
3. Tom is the same age as Mary.
4. He's not as tall as his father.
5. I ate as much as possible.
6. His car is three times as expensive as my car.

Writing Pattern Practice

1.
It's as cold as ice.
I can play the piano as well as her.
Is it as good as you expected?
Take as much as you want.

2.
It's not as(so) good as it used to be.
It's not as(so) difficult as it looks.
He's not as(so) tall as his father.

3.
Tom is the same age as Mary.
David's salary is the same as mine.

4.
Call me as soon as possible.
Take as much as possible.
I got up as early as possible.

5.
Gas is twice as expensive as it was a couple of years ago.
His car is three times as old as mine.

Unit 39_ 비교급

P.181

Dialogue

A: 이거 얼마예요?
B: 80달러예요.
A: 예상했던 것 보다 비싸네요. 더 싼 것은 없나요?
B: 이건 어때요? 세일 중이거든요.

Unit Test

1.
1. cheaper 2. more slowly
3. more often/ oftener 4. earlier
5. better 6. worse
7. better 8. faster
9. older 10. more interesting

2.
1. a lot more complicated
2. a little more slowly
3. much colder
4. far more interesting
5. very much better

3.
1. bigger 2. better 3. more, more
4. bigger, better 5. more, expensive

Writing Pattern Practice

1.
Mary is taller than her three sisters.
Your English is worse than mine.

2.
Susan is less outgoing than her sister.

3.
Russian is a lot more difficult than English.
Could you speak a little more slowly?

4.
I'll give you the bigger (one) of the two.
He is the younger of the two.

5.
I'm getting fatter and fatter.
It's getting colder and colder.
He's driving more and more slowly.

6.
The more I study, the more I learn.
The stronger the better.

7.
Which do you like better, rice or noodles?
Who is taller, you or your sister?

Unit 40_ 최상급

P.184

Dialogue

A: 여보세요? 전 Michael 친구인 Joe예요, Katie 있습니까?
B: 전데요. Michael이 말하던 소개팅 때문에 전화하셨군요.
A: 맞아요. 약속 날짜로 언제가 가장 적당하신지 물어보려구요.
B: 글쎄요, 이번 토요일이 좋아요.

Unit Test

1.
1. the longest river in
2. the most expensive hotel in
3. the hottest day of
4. the smartest student in
5. the cheapest restaurant in

2.
1. I'm the happiest man in the world.
2. It's the best movie I've ever seen.
3. Cindy is the second tallest student in the class.
4. *Titanic* is one of the greatest movies.
5. No actress in Korea is as pretty as her.

Writing Pattern Practice

1.
I'm the happiest man in the world.
Your English is the best of all.

2.
What sport do you like (the) best?
She runs (the) fastest of them all.

3.
Your English is the best in the class.
Cindy sings (the) best of us all.
Yesterday was the coldest day of the year.
It was the happiest moment of my life.

4.
She's quite the most beautiful woman I've ever met.

5.
What's the best book you've ever read?
It's the best movie I've ever seen.

6.
James is the third tallest boy in the class.
Minnesota is the second coldest state in the United States.

7.
Sears Tower is one of the tallest buildings in Chicago.
Titanic is one of the greatest movies.

REVIEW I

1.
1. <u>bored</u> → boring
2. <u>tired</u> → tiring
3. <u>depressing</u> → depressed
4. <u>disgusted</u> → disgusting
5. <u>terrifying</u> → terrified
6. <u>terrible</u> → terribly

7. straightly → straight
8. serious → seriously
9. friend → friendly
10. extreme → extremely
11. quietly→ quiet
12. heavy→ heavily
13. quietly→ quiet
14. colorful→ colorfully
15. incredible→ incredibly

해설

1. bored: 지루한, boring: 지루하게 하는
2. tired: 피곤한, tiring: 피곤하게 하는
3. depressed: 우울한, depressing: 우울하게 하는
4. disgusted: 구역질나는, disgusting: 구역질나게 하는
5. terrified: 무서워하는, terrifying: 무섭게 하는
6. terrible: 끔찍한, terribly: 끔찍하게
7. straight: 곧바른, 곧바르게
8. serious: 심각한, seriously: 심각하게
9. friendly: 친근한
10. extreme: 극도의, extremely: 극도로
11. quiet: 조용한, quietly: 조용하게
12. heavy: 무거운/심한, heavily: 몹시/심하게
13. quiet: 조용한, quietly: 조용하게
14. colorful: 화려한, colorfully: 화려하게
15. incredible: 놀라운, incredibly: 놀랍게

2.

1. too 2. enough 3. too 4. enough
5. enough 6. too 7. too 8. too
9. too 10. enough 11. such 12. such
13. so 14. so 15. so 16. so 17. such
18. such 19. such 20. so

3.

1. C (reasonable →reasonably)
2. D (hardly → hard)
3. A (disappointing → disappointed)
4. C (depressing → depressed)
5. D (bored → boring)
6. B (embarrassing → embarrassed)
7. B (careful → carefully)
8. D (hard → hardly)

4.

1. interestinger → more interesting
2. more early → earlier
3. slowlier → more slowly
4. badder → worse
5. expensiver → more expensive

REVIEW 2

1. ① 2. ③
3. ②

해석

관광객의 지출액이 가장 낮았던 해는 언제인가?

4. ①

해석

우리가 영화에 대해 이야기 할 때 가장 인기 있는 주제 중에 하나는 타이타닉과 그 배우들이다. 하지만 진짜 타이타닉에 대해 당신은 얼마나 알고 있는가? 승객들? 승무원들? 타이타닉은 이제껏 지어졌던 배 중 가장 거대한 배 중 하나였다. 1912년 4월 10일, 타이타닉은 첫 항해로 영국을 떠났다. 배 위에는 2200명이 넘는 승객과 승무원이 있었다. 4일 뒤, 대서양을 가로지르며 미국으로 가는 도중에, 타이타닉은 빙하 한 덩이에 부딪히고 가라앉았다. 1500명이 넘는 사람이 얼음 물에서 죽었고, 타이타닉은 대양 아래로 사라졌다. 그것의 정확한 위치는 1985년 로버트 발라드 박사에 의해 발견될 때까지 미스테리로 남아있었다.

*iceberg 빙산

5. ①

해석

발신: Cindy Smith 날짜: 5월 10일 수신: Ted O' Harris
제목: 회의 일정을 변경할 수 있을까요? 너무 촉박하게 연락해서 미안하지만 내일 1시 회의를 2시로 미룰 수 있을까요? 급한 일이 생겨서 점심 시간에도 일을 해야 하거든요. 괜찮다면 2시에는 만날 수 있어요. 이렇게 하면 문제가 있는지 아니면 이번 주 다른 날로 회의 일정을 다시 잡기를 원하는지 알려 주세요.

*urgent 긴급한

MEMO

MEMO

KEY GRAMMAR POINTS FOR ENGLISH LEARNERS

SMART English Grammar

for Speaking & Writing

1